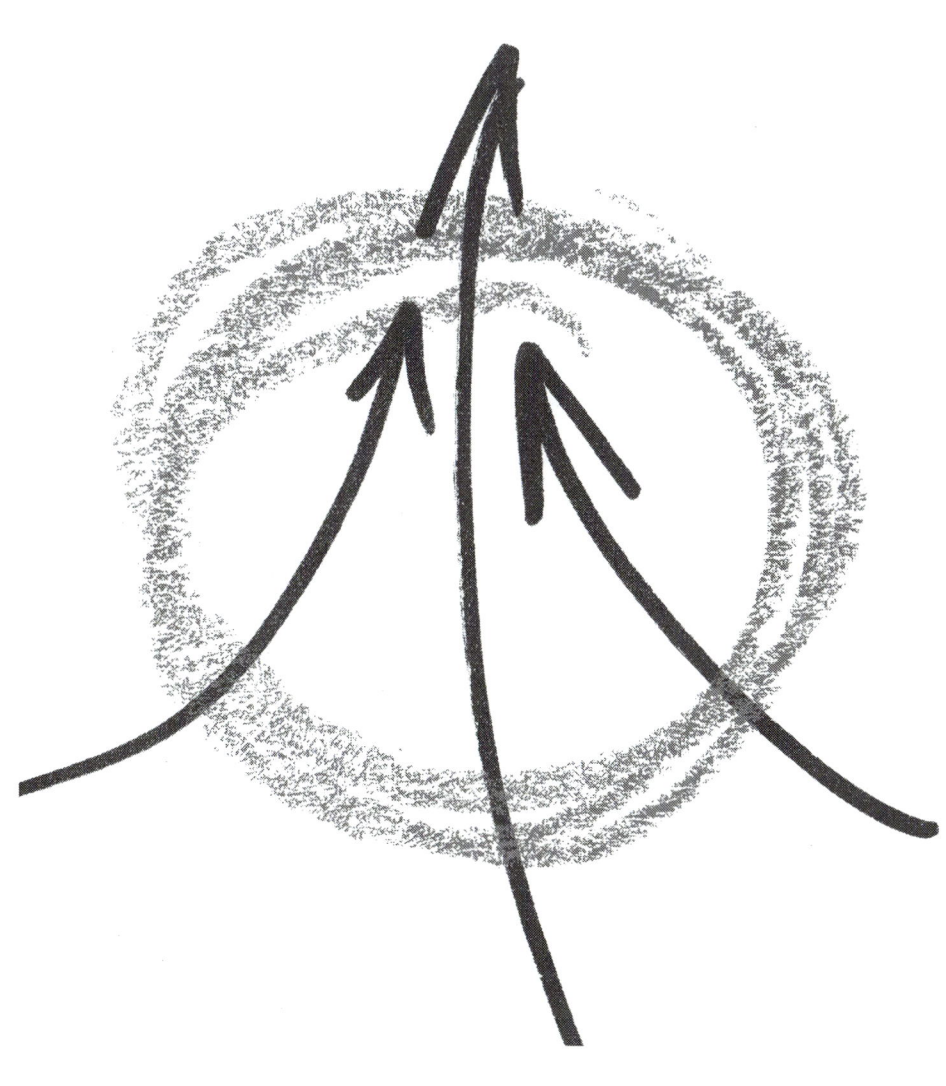

Drawn Together Through Visual Practice: An Anthology Edited by
Brandy Agerbeck, Kelvy Bird, Sam Bradd & Jennifer Shepherd

Copyright © 2016 by Visual Practice Publishing
Cover by: Brandy Agerbeck

All rights reserved. No part of this book may be reproduced in any form by any electronic or mechanical means including photocopying, recording, or information storage and retrieval without permission in writing from the publisher.

ISBN-13: 978-0692726006
ISBN-10: 0692726004

www.visualpracticebook.com

Printed in U.S.A.

Drawn Together Through
Visual Practice

An Anthology Edited by
Brandy Agerbeck, Kelvy Bird, Sam Bradd, & Jennifer Shepherd

This anthology contains exciting and varied contributions to the growing literature on visual language and its power to "draw us" together. The authors offer a wide range of experience, powerful illustrations and the core message that visual language enables us to learn, think, and grow in new ways – especially when considering the complex relationships that words alone can't illuminate. Drawn Together through Visual Practice reflects the power of this field to help transform organizations and communities in life-affirming ways.
– Juanita Brown PhD, Co-Founder, The World Cafe

After 45 years of drawing on the wall it is extraordinary to see this field bloom in such rich and contributive ways. The authors are the cambium layer—advancing and shaping it with practice and questions—providing inspiration for all of us who are living into this emergent, hopeful, phenomenon.
– David Sibbet, The Grove Consultants International

The field of visual practice has long been nurtured by the quiet presence of artists devoted to listening and serving the groups with whom they work. It is high time that they turned and faced the room and shared the depth of artisanal practice and craft that underscores their devotion to the work. This collection is a stunning revelation of the heart of this practice. Whatever your role in group work, you will be made better by listening to these voices and stories of experience, sensitivity and careful attention.
– Chris Corrigan, Art of Hosting and Harvest Moon Consulting

A first-rate look at the new world of visual practice. I know from personal experience that capturing content and discussion in real time imagery can help create communal understanding and memory. The images give participants a shared visual vocabulary that help capture complex ideas and enable the move to new discoveries and innovations. The book is a delightful dive into understanding the background and development of this new teaching/art form. Enjoy.
– Deborah Ancona, Seley Distinguished Professor of Management, Faculty Director of the MIT Leadership Center, MIT Sloan School of Management

I've seen visual practice map ideas, refresh memories, and provoke insights in many meetings involving dozens of professionals from business, government, and education. So it's a special delight to discover this collection representing the art, craft, and inspiration of visual practice from multiple perspectives.
– David N. Perkins, Carl H. Pforzheimer, Jr., Research Professor of Teaching and Learning, Harvard Graduate School of Education

Graphic facilitation is a powerful way for a group to come to know themselves and the work they want to do together. It is no wonder that it so quickly became a part of any good meeting, conference, or problem solving session! Drawn Together is a valuable book, timely and well thought through. It should be read and employed by all wanting to improve and accelerate the rate of change and innovation within an organization, executive team or community. The more diversity in the room, the more powerful visual imagery becomes.
– Gail Taylor, Co-Founder of MG Taylor, Inc., Founder of Tomorrow Makers, Inc.

At last! A compendium of stories, helpful approaches and mind sets that reflects the diversity, the richness of scope and the broad impact of the growing field of visual practice/visual language. Our visual practice not only encompasses 'making the invisible visible' and 'making the visible visual' through many artistic means, but also, it incorporates all the human elements of working together, listening, and inclusion that our world is crying for. The potential is unlimited. This is a must read for people who are looking for ways to make substantial change and impact in our world as a group or as an individual and who are looking for paths to go 'from my way to our way'.
– Susan Kelly, Visual Practitioner

Drawn Together offers me tools to reflect and improve on developing campaigns for Lush, and encourages personal reflection on my process. A tremendous job bringing together a picture of the evolving work and sharing best practices.
– Carleen Pickard, Ethical Campaigns Specialist, Lush Handmade Cosmetics, North America

Contents

The Visual Now: An introduction 1

Making Room for Making: In praise of imperfect drawings and the humans who make them
BRANDY AGERBECK 5

Drawing-to-Learn: A general studies course for first-year college students
DR. LAURENCE MUSGROVE 15

In Front of the Wall
ALFREDO CARLO 31

Visual Improvisation: How improvising influences my sketchnoting
EVA-LOTTA LAMM 39

Solo-Practitioner Partnerships: A conversation between Lisa Arora and Robert Mittman 53

Sensemaking through Arts-Infused, Person-Centered Planning Processes
AARON JOHANNES 63

Dancineering, Researchals, Bodystorming, and Informances: Movement-based approaches to sensemaking and transmediation through contemporary dance
CHRISTOPHER KNOWLTON 75

Stories and Storytelling
ANTHONY WEEKS 85

The Secret to Long-Term Impact in Your Engagements
MARY ALICE ARTHUR 97

Using Perspectives to Build a Practice
BRYAN COFFMAN 111

Cultivating Cultural Safety: The visual practitioner's role in motivating positive action
SAM BRADD 121

The Use of Imagery in Conflict Engagement
AFTAB ERFAN 133

Steady, to Scale
KELVY BIRD 143

A Learning Journey: Connecting self to planet
STINA BROWN 155

Sharing a *Dia* Experience
CLAUDIA MADRAZO 165

Embodied Mark-Making: The Big Brush experience
BARBARA BASH 173

Discovering Wisdom Within and Between: How storyboards, portraits, and visual explanations can help us learn to solve the puzzles of our time
JENNIFER SHEPHERD 185

Sensemaking, Potential Space, and Art Therapy with Organizations: Moving beyond language
MICHELLE WINKEL 197

Kinesthetic Modeling: Re-learning how to grope in the dark
JOHN WARD 205

Becoming a Visual Change Practitioner
NEVADA LANE 217

Four Mindsets of a Visual Ecology in the Workplace: Re-visioning language through visual thinking
MISHA MERCER 225

Rigorous Design of Visual Tools that Deepen Conversations and Spark New Insights
CHRISTINE MARTELL 241

Imagery That Travels Well: Making yourself understood across cultures with the help of visual language
PETER STOYKO 251

The Thermal Lift of Visualization: How to empower people in visual thinking, learning, and co-creation
MARTIN HAUSSMANN, INTERVIEWED BY BRANDY AGERBECK 271

Bridging on the Rise
JAYCE PEI YU LEE, INTERVIEWED BY KELVY BIRD 285

When We Cannot See the Future, Where Do We Begin?
BOB STILGER 295

Reflection and Visual Practice
JENNIFER SHEPHERD AND SAM BRADD 303

DRAWN TOGETHER THROUGH VISUAL PRACTICE

The Visual Now

An introduction

We find ourselves in an age of unprecedented complexity, with increased globalization and access to information, while boundaries all around us dissolve. Visual practice helps make sense of this changing landscape by shifting our relationship to self, other, and society. Drawings give shape to our ideas, provide sharing of methodology, and reframe what is possible.

Visual practice makes the fleeting and ephemeral nature of spoken conversation concrete. Drawings can take infinite form: brushstrokes expressing gesture, metaphors that offer common ground, maps to guide a system, and devices for reconciliation. Individuals and groups alike make these meaningful marks. Communities of thousands can access key content through the aid of images. We see our thoughts from new perspectives through visual interpretation, and we relate with fresh eyes to ourselves and others.

Visuals draw us together. They allow us to consider where we have been, who we are, and who we want to be in the future. We mark these transitions through the acts and artifacts of drawing.

Visual practice is a rich and diverse field. This anthology connects ideas and practitioners at a moment when our practice is dramatically expanding. Let's pause and survey the field to date: What work is being done? What questions currently guide us? Which theories inform us? Who do we serve, and what is the impact of our craft? What do we learn from our individual experience? And how do we contribute back to the greater field? **Now is the moment to embrace visual thinking, practice, and facilitation as a defining technology of our time.**

This anthology brings 27 voices together to paint a broad picture of our evolving work and the audiences we serve.

Our imagery generates meaning and shared understanding. It opens possibility, fosters discovery, and facilitates change. For example, educators share an art-based inquiry for children and a curriculum for first-year college students. Improvisation shows up in sketchnoting and through dance. A filmmaker describes how storytelling strengthens listening. Mark-makers trace early use of graffiti and calligraphy as seeds for their current work. Climate justice, personal planning for people with disabilities, conflict resolution, and cross-cultural communication all employ visuals for societal transformation.

We also explore the development of new tools and methodologies, such as photo cards and visual dictionaries, sharing the invention and process behind products geared to facilitate.

Skilled non-visual facilitators share insights on forming strong partnerships for seamless collaborations. Articles on harvesting and organizational development convey integrated, holistic applications of visuals within change initiatives. Kinesthetic modeling and art therapy demonstrate practices which move beyond verbal language. And a research-based review names the mindsets needed to re-envision our ways of working.

As editors, we also bring our diverse experiences to this picture. Brandy Agerbeck's article "Making Room for Making" shares best practices as we lead others to draw together. In "Steady, to Scale," Kelvy Bird turns our attention to the role of "containers" in how we hold ourselves and the spaces we support. In Jennifer Shepherd's "Discovering Wisdom Within and Between," we examine how storyboards, portraits, and visual explanations can help us tap into our existing inner wisdom to solve the problems of our time. Building on his experience working cross-culturally with Indigenous communities, Sam Bradd shares tools and observations for building cultural safety. And in the final chapter, Jennifer and Sam collaborate on a series of questions to guide practitioners in reflective inquiry.

How we were drawn towards this anthology

Visual practitioners frequently travel from event to event, and it's no surprise that the genesis of this book logged many air miles, too. It started in July 2013 when Sam (Vancouver, Canada) and Jennifer (Ottawa, Canada) shared a cab to the airport after an International Forum of Visual Practitioners (IFVP) conference in New York City. The ride provided just enough time to discover mutual interests in adult education theory, and within six months the two had hosted an international, online conversation series.

Powerful questions are contagious and lead to more questions. Attending EuViz in Berlin the following summer, Sam and Brandy (Chicago, USA) wished aloud that more colleagues would share their experiences and expertise in writing. Then at the 2015 IFVP conference in Austin, Sam invited Brandy and Kelvy (Cambridge, USA) to further dive into this exploration. Through these connected conversations, an anthology was born.

From four home cities we sought geographic diversity and reached out to visual practitioners around the world. Though we know no single book is ever complete, we hope this volume shares some perspectives with which you already resonate and opens alternative lenses.

We also hope these pages inspire new drawings, new methods, new connections, new conversations, and new writings on our practice. As editors, contributors, and readers alike, we all take part in shaping our visual future. More than ever, visual practice has a power to shift what we see, how we think, the stories we tell, and what becomes possible for us to create in the world.

The editors,
Brandy Agerbeck, Kelvy Bird, Sam Bradd, Jennifer Shepherd

DRAWN TOGETHER THROUGH VISUAL PRACTICE

Making Room for Making
In praise of imperfect drawings and the humans who make them

Brandy Agerbeck

During a breakout session at a business's strategy meeting, I saw a group of four colleagues huddled around a flip chart. They were all deep in discussion, writing and drawing with a yellow marker at the top of the paper, where the curve of the previous page cast a shadow on what they were making. As an outsider, the graphic facilitator for the day, my eye is always on making sure the group's work will be tangible and visible when I stand at the front and map their plenary discussions. I was concerned that the small scale and yellow ink they drew in wouldn't be visible when their team reported to the whole group. I offered them a darker marker to draw with.

One of them politely declined. "No, we're whispering."

In nearly 20 years of working professionally as a graphic facilitator, and four decades drawing personally and studying art both low-brow and high, here was one of my all-time favorite moments of drawing. This group had a perfect ease with their materials and their task. They were creating the visual equivalent of hushed tones, allowing them to work out their thinking in private together.

It is in these messy drawings that work really happens, clarity is found, discoveries are made, and we understand each other and our work in new ways. And yet, most people will say they can't draw. Therefore, they don't draw. **How do we cultivate the spaces that allow individuals and groups to make the drawings that help them make meaning for themselves?** Let's look at this from five angles.

1. Drawn towards

RELEVANCE OF VISUAL PRACTICE

With access to more media than ever—including YouTube, the world's second-largest search engine—our culture is unstoppably visual. I am 42 and I think about how in my lifetime, video games have gone from the lines and dots of *Pong* to fully immersive experiences. When I was in sixth grade, we were the last family to own a VCR; now I use a $300 camera to shoot videos in my home that reach a global audience. Production barriers fall away as every smartphone has a camera and we find that human connection overrides problems of lighting or audio quality. Our sophistication as viewers and makers gets ever stronger through experience, whether we have the language to talk about it or not.

With this teeming access comes information overload. We now expect ourselves to keep up with more media than we can reasonably handle. At best, one shifts from ordinary consumer, to curator, to critic, and learns to filter and sort all these inputs. At worst, one feels chronically overwhelmed and overstimulated.

The world itself, not just its reflection in accumulating media, is getting more and more complex. A common model I hear about more and more while mapping meetings is VUCA, a 1990s American military term that stands for Volatile, Uncertain, Complex, and Ambiguous. These conditions are now the state of things and the old methods of navigation and making sense no longer serve us.

We muddle through with old tools and methods that don't support us. Linear thinking can't accommodate the interdependencies and spatial organization needed to understand this complexity. Text-based mediums can't convey the nuance that a video can. Meetings are derided as time-wasters as the ephemeral nature of a conversation is lost in memory.

Increasing an individual's or a group's capacity to think and work visually, spatially, and kinesthetically is the key to navigating the complexity in which we now live. Visual practices and methodologies are crucial tools that enable us to learn and grow in this shifting world. They are what transform us from a passive consumer, to a discerning consumer, to an active producer.

2. Drawn in

ATTRACTION AND DELIGHTS OF VISUAL PRACTICE

For those of us living within established visual practices, it is easy to forget their novelty. There's something magical about seeing a graphic facilitator turn your live conversation into a large-scale drawing. There's something new and fun about picking up a colorful marker and making a mark, or bending a pipe-cleaner into a new shape. These hands-on activities are a pleasant disruption to business meetings as usual.

Using materials from our childhood taps into a strong sense memory. The joy a grown-up feels popping open a tub of Play-Doh and sniffing it, transported to youth; the smell of sharpening a pencil, or the scent of a Mr. Sketch marker; these evoke positive, playful feelings.

These physical materials also harken back to the time in our lives when we sensed the world through our whole selves, before we turned into thinking machines carried on top of a body. Tactile materials tune us back in to inputs of touch and smell—maybe even taste, if you catch someone eating the paste.

I lead interactive keynotes on the powers of drawing as a thinking tool. We discuss concrete tips, then the whole group splits into smaller groups to use their fresh, new drawing skills to tackle real issues at work. On one occasion, a big, tall man came up to me, arms crossed, shoulders pulled up by his ears. "This is so great," he said, "I feel like a kid again." His body language didn't match the excitement in his words—he was still adjusting to this new, old way of working. In the same group, a company president sat back, watching me with suspicion at the start of my talk. Intrigued, he slowly leaning forward over the course of the first hour. When we shifted into work, he pulled the paper off the table, onto the floor, ready to draw like a grade-schooler on his hands and knees.

Although manipulating physical materials is often neglected in many adult business and educational contexts, it gives one a sense of being in control of one's environment. Look at the zooming popularity of coloring books and Zentangles. These are simple, repetitive actions that give one a calming sense of being creatively capable—being fully present in a practice and in-the-zone. When people are set up to use visual materials and succeed with them, they can gain a sense of autonomy and accomplishment.

Developing visual practice gives a sense not just of capacity, but of command. When one gets past the initial "shiny toy" phase of drawing, and through hands-on practice discovers its adaptability and usefulness, one taps into deeper work.

3. Drawn out

BENEFITS AND VALUE OF VISUAL PRACTICE

In my second book, *The Idea Shapers: The power of putting your thinking in your own hands*, I describe four inherent properties of drawing that make it a powerful thinking tool. First, it is **simple**. Drawing only requires something to draw with and something to draw on. In our increasingly digital culture, there's a lovely reliability in using your four digits and your thumb, available any time there's paper and pen within reach.

The antidote to feeling overwhelmed can be as simple as getting your ideas out of your head and onto a piece of paper. Once you place your internal thoughts and feelings into a drawing, you've made them tangible and visible, and you can see them from a new perspective. This **tangibility** gives you distance and separation from the problem you are trying to solve. Especially useful in groups, the drawing becomes an object to which participants can respond, rather than attacking each other.

The **spatial** nature of the blank page is the third powerful property of drawing. Writing defaults our thinking to lined paper—words lined up into sentences, paragraphs, pages. Drawing allows our thinking to move in 360 degrees on a blank paper's surface. This flexibility in form allows for complexity. In a drawing you can sketch out all of the pieces of an issue at once, not just one at a time as in linear writing.

The fourth and final quality of drawing is its **physicality**. When you make a physical drawing you make choices: placement, proximity, scale, shape, line, color, shading. It is through making each of these visual and spatial choices that we make meaning for ourselves.

4. Drawn away

THE FEAR OF, AND REPULSION FROM, VISUAL PRACTICE

There is power and joy in drawing, as we have seen in the first three sections. Yet we face resistance when we ask ourselves and others to embrace these visual tools.

The two biggest barriers to drawing are the fear of failure and the focus on a perfect product. The fear of failure most often takes the form of the Inner Critic who berates us, telling us we're not qualified to even try. The critic questions one's identity—"You're not an artist"—confusing an action anyone can partake in (drawing) with a narrowly defined role (artist). There are Outer Critics too, who may or may not realize how fragile our willingness to draw can be. An offhand remark or a comparison can shut someone down instantly.

The focus on a perfect product comes from our product-focused culture. We're embarrassed to show our working sketch. Sharing something imperfect feels like showing someone your underwear drawer. This lack of transparency leads to the impossible expectation to create something fully formed—product without process; delivery without discovery. Our product-reliant and consumerist culture makes us expect a product to do this work for us, a push-button solution—Give me the drawing program to do this for me, or a template to fill in. The tackling of complexity needs a *tabula rasa* to draw upon. There are no quick fixes to tough problems.

The word *drawing* is both a noun and a verb. Most fear around drawing is when we think of it as a product and expect to be judged on whether that product is good or bad, beautiful or ugly. This fear cuts us off from the beauty of drawing as a process, where messy, fast drawings can bring clarity. The only judgment of these drawings is whether they get us a step closer to our task at hand.

5. Draw together

CREATING SPACE FOR, AND HABITS OF, VISUAL PRACTICE

Our goal is to help ourselves and others feel a sense of agency and autonomy; to feel empowered to use visual tools to tackle complex problems, find clarity, and take action. Here are my best practices for creating safe, yet challenging environments in which individuals and groups reclaim the power of paper and pen.

DISARM THE DISCOMFORT

There is great vulnerability in being in a learning phase, especially in a group setting, and even more so in a work setting. Feeling uneasy leads people to look for the escape hatch—making excuses not to participate, dismissing it as "just kindergarten," saying "that's not *my* job," or giving up as soon as an instruction is unclear or a pen has gone dry. Acknowledge the discomfort, while keeping people engaged.

When I lead an exercise in synesthesia—specifically, large-scale abstract drawings inspired by instrumental music—I begin by saying, "We're going to try something new and pretty odd. And if you hate it, the good news is it'll be over in ten minutes." This lets participants know that feeling uncomfortable is normal. And a fixed timeframe helps them ride out their discomfort.

BE MINDFUL OF MATERIALS AND EXAMPLES

Set people up for success. Give them the right tools for the job. For example, if you expect a group to discuss a wall of sticky notes they have written and drawn, give them sticky notes large enough to do their work and markers thick enough to be legible at a distance. When someone chooses to use their own ballpoint pen to draw, I'll gently say, "Please use these markers so we can see your contributions."

Using childhood materials, like Play-Doh, pipe-cleaners, and crayons, can bring joy and a sense of play to productive meeting. If someone denigrates the tools as too juvenile, simply say, "Yep, we're going back to the sandbox to look at this from a different perspective."

Don't be precious about materials. The fancier the supplies, the more pressure people feel to use them correctly. Make a blank sheet of paper less scary by simply tearing it in two. Now you've made a familiar format (portrait, letter-sized) unfamiliar and more forgiving (landscape, smaller, torn edge). Make sure there's an ample supply. A person can't get in a generative frame of mind if they feel like you're rationing Post-It notes.

If you want to share an example of what you're looking for, make it comparable with the relative drawing skills of your group. Putting your best drawer to the task and making the example immaculate or fancy makes the model feel unattainable.

CREATE DIALOG AROUND DRAWINGS

The reflection and conversations around process-focused drawing are as powerful as the drawing itself. I like to begin by asking, "How did that feel?" This opening can help diffuse nervousness and also reveal enjoyment. It tunes us in to our gut reaction.

Next, make observations. I ask, "What do you notice? What do you observe?" As professionals and adults, we are rewarded by making smart inferences. When possible, give yourself this space to use your senses before you come to intellectual conclusions. "I see a lot of people used red." "Wow, we all created a lot of Post-It notes in a short amount of time." Discoveries and nuance can be made when we stay in an observational space before we make meaning.

Tease out descriptions. Often people respond with "I like this" or "I don't like that." I follow up with broad questions such as "What appeals to you? Tell me more," or "What turns you off? Is it confusing?" Often this leads to specific observations that invite conversation.

Let language be imperfect. One's response may not be eloquent. There's a beauty in the grasping. It is unfair to expect laypeople to be visually articulate. They are often quite savvy, but not well-spoken. Respect their wording, and listen with an ear towards understanding.

Acknowledge all contributions and look for connections and patterns. This task favors the synthesis thinker, and outsiders can see themes more easily. Invite this meaning-making by asking, "What themes are you seeing? Where are the overlaps?"

AVOID EXPERT-ITIS

Respect the work happening in the room and each person's role and level of experience. You may be an expert in visual tools, but the participants are the experts in their content. Respect their drawings and never draw on their drawings or take over. Be careful not to lapse into artspeak or design jargon.

In my early days as a graphic facilitator, I was "farmed out" to help breakout groups in session. Often I was just drawing something specific and pretty, which let the participants lapse into being focused on product. Occasionally, I was able to really help a group develop a model. At worst, I arrived and they expected to me to do their work for them. Now I stand firm that I am there as a resource to teach them, ask questions, or help them think through their ideas, but that they think and draw for themselves. I don't want my expertise to impede others developing their own.

Model the behavior you want to see. One of my most frustrating moments was when I was partnered with a facilitator who declined drawing themselves, saying, "Oh, I don't do that. That's Brandy's job." Sadly, they gave every single participant permission to opt out.

WATCH WHAT YOU REWARD

Sure, clear penmanship and good spelling make a flipchart easier to read, but those qualities aren't critical to meaning-making. People can suss out bad handwriting or misspelled words. If you single these qualities

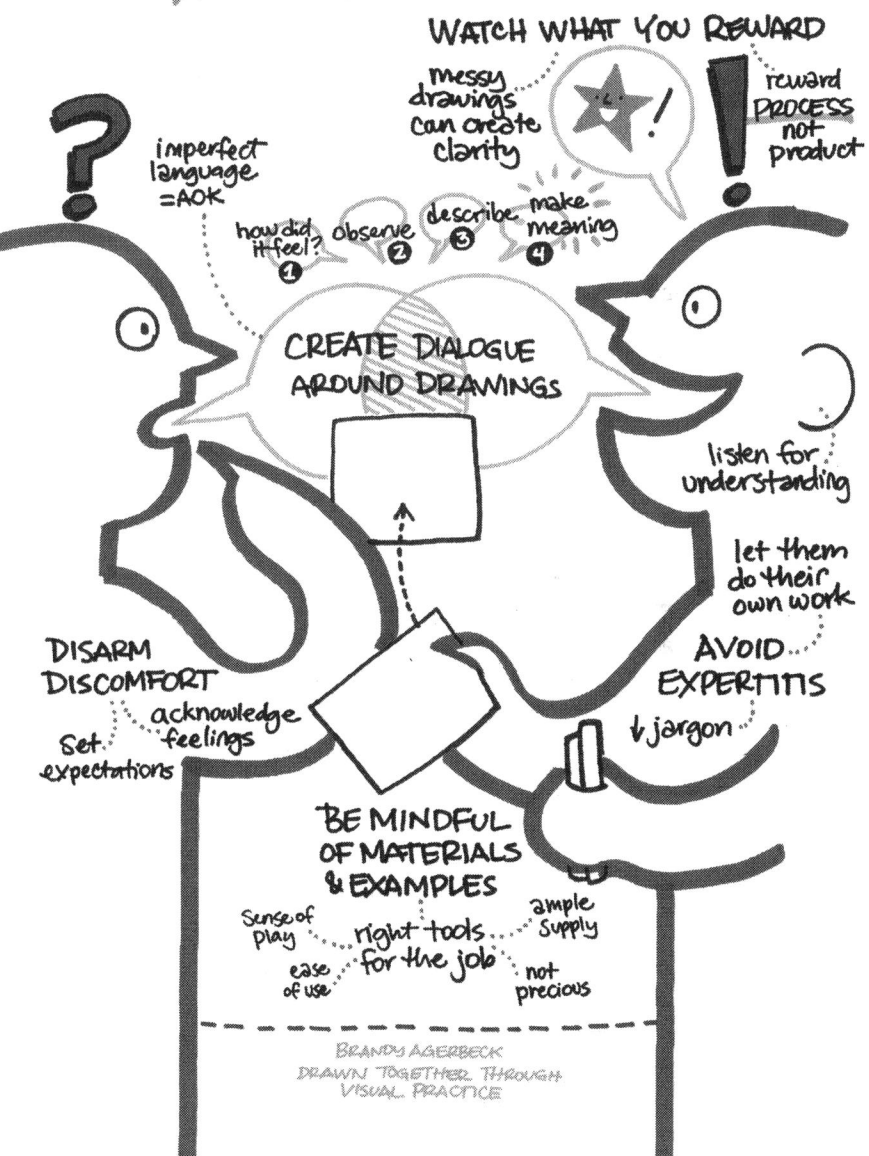

out to give someone a verbal gold star, you are distracting people from the process by praising the style of the product. This also puts people on the defensive about their own spelling or handwriting—skills few adults feel masterful about.

Recognize the state of iteration the drawing is at. It may be messy. Messy may be exactly where it needs to be in that point of the process. Messy drawings can easily be changed and refined later, if need be.

Always reward people for high-quality process. Compliment them for the work they are accomplishing. The product, the object of the drawing, is the artifact of the process. The longer and more deeply you can keep the focus on drawing as a verb, the more action, accountability, and agency people will take for themselves.

—

As of this writing in 2016, we are an increasingly visual and complex culture that is muddling through with old, linear, ephemeral methods that rely mostly on written and spoken text. The transition from fearful visual consumer to fearless visualizer takes care and guidance. You and I are the leaders in making room for making, in guiding people to reclaim drawing as a thinking tool and to make meaning through our wonderfully messy drawings. Through small acts—like the right markers for the task at hand, or saying a few encouraging words that help peers gain capacity and confidence—we create big changes towards a culture of visual mavens ready to think critically, communicate clearly, and tackle our most complex problems with paper and pen.

BRANDY AGERBECK writes, speaks and teaches on drawing as your best thinking tool. Her first book, *The Graphic Facilitator's Guide: How to use your listening, thinking and drawing skills to make meaning*, describes the nuance and responsibility of being the one person in the room dedicated to drawing a group's conversation. Her latest book, which teaches everyone visual thinking concepts to work through their thoughts and emotions, is *The Idea Shapers: The power of putting your thinking into your own hands*. Details and resources at Loosetooth.com.

Drawing-to-Learn

A general studies course for first-year college students

Dr. Laurence Musgrove

Introduction: Three languages

Creating lines and shapes through drawing is a transaction between the mind, eye, heart, body, and world. Similar transactions include reading and writing, which depend primarily on letters, and mathematics, which employs mainly numbers and letters. These three language systems are increasingly separated in school and developed in isolation. As a mode of learning and expression, drawing is traditionally relegated to the primary grades and eventually replaced by the more "mature" modes of learning and expression, writing and math. Consequently, visual thinking, learning, and expression are seen by educators and the public at large as more primal, basic, and immature methods for learning and communicating. Musical and movement practices suffer from the same undervaluation. Limiting language development to the narrow confines of textual and numerical practices impedes human engagement and progress. To explore ways in which drawing might actually enhance learning in school, I recently created an introductory college course on drawing-to-learn across the curriculum.

Personal and professional context

My interest in drawing as a teaching and learning tool has evolved out of my use of drawing in a wide range of writing and literature courses. I regularly have students sketch responses to prompts in order to focus their thinking, or I have them provide me with images that depict their relationships with reading or writing. I have used student drawings in my research into reading metaphors, and I have taught courses on graphic narratives wherein students have drawn comics to represent their research. In preparation for each class, I draw the day's lesson plan on a note card with simple icons, and then re-draw this visual agenda on the whiteboard at the beginning of each class.

Sample visual agenda note cards

My interest is also demonstrated in my scholarly and creative work. I wrote a book, *Handmade Thinking*, on how students can use drawing to improve their reading engagement. My daughter Myra Musgrove and I co-authored an academic article in comic format for the *Journal of the Assembly for Expanded Perspectives on Learning*, titled "Drawing is Learning: To Understand and To Be Understood."

I also co-authored with my daughter Myra a comic poem, "My Song," which appeared in *INK BRICK*, a new comic poetry journal. All of these occasions have helped me see the value of visual thinking and presentation in teaching, learning, academic research, and my creative work.

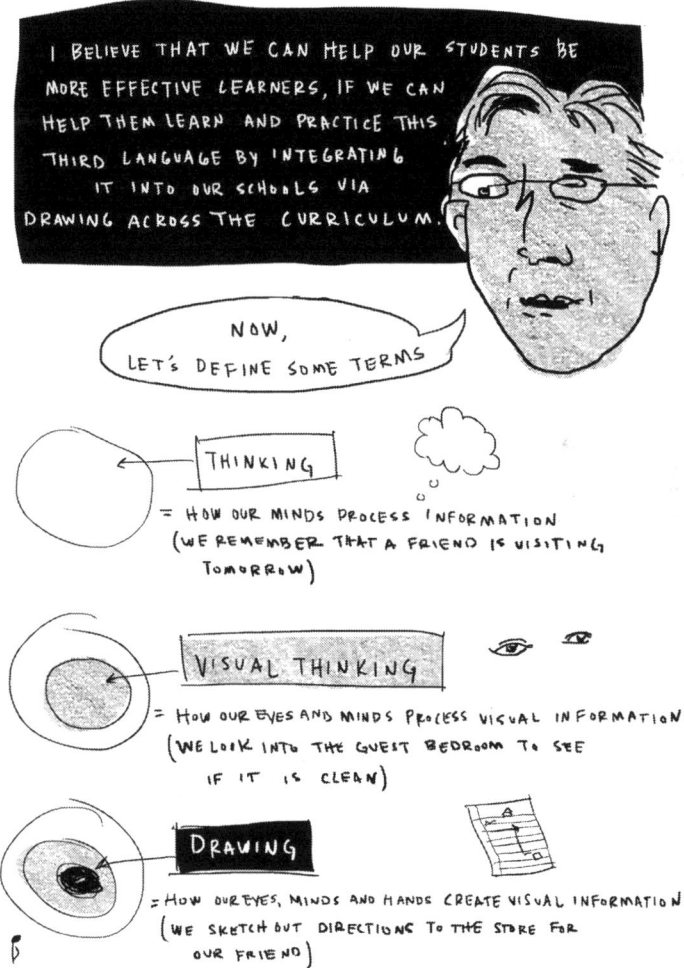

Sample page from JAEPL article

Course design

In the summer of 2015, my faculty colleagues and I received an invitation from the Freshman College at Angelo State University to develop sections of a general studies course for first-year students. This course would be a one-credit-hour course, meeting two times a week for an hour, and running for the first eight weeks of the fall term. Each section of the course would focus on a faculty member's area of interest. Each section would also include two written summaries of academic resources, an online introduction to information literacy, and general exposure to campus resources.

Because of my interest in "drawing-to-learn," I developed the following description for my section of this Freshman Seminar:

> This course provides you with an introduction to using drawing as a tool for thinking, learning, and communication in college. You will learn the values of visual thinking, doodling, common visual formats for problem-solving, and note-taking via simple drawing to easily capture recorded or live lectures. Advanced drawing ability is not a prerequisite for this course. You will learn sufficiently basic skills in order to complete coursework successfully.

A significant portion of the class time would be spent learning basic drawing skills, developing a visual vocabulary, and practicing six drawing-to-learn strategies. I also decided that I would use the special instructional support funds dedicated to sections of this course to buy each of my 25 students the drawing supplies they would bring to each class meeting: a set of 12 colored pencils, a blank Moleskine notebook, and a Blackwing Palomino Pencil.

Student grades would be based upon regular attendance and the following four assignments:

1. Two Summary Assignments. Students completed these assignments by (a) reading two articles on drawing-to-learn, (b) drawing handmade responses, and (c) writing a brief summary of each article.
2. Information Literacy Assignment. Students completed this online assignment by viewing a number of videos created

by our library staff and by completing corresponding assignments.
3. Sketchnote Response Assignment. Students completed this assignment by creating a sketchnote response to an approved university event, such as a public lecture.
4. Illustrated Speaking Assignment. Students completed this assignment by presenting a two- to three-minute speech on a topic or story they knew well while simultaneously illustrating their talk on the classroom whiteboard.

Successful completion of three of these assignments was dependent upon fairly intense, yet low-stakes practices designed to help students gain confidence in drawing, develop a vocabulary of images, and learn the six drawing-to-learn strategies.

Each class day was designed to include drawing attendance, learning some basic skill or developing an image vocabulary, and practicing a drawing-to-learn strategy. At the beginning of every class, I distributed small index cards and asked students to write their names and the day's date on one side, and then to draw on the reverse side an image, such as a self-portrait, a favorite thing or person, or a weather event. This strategy for keeping attendance and creating an initial sense of presence and comfort in the class comes from Lynda Barry's *Syllabus*, a scrapbook/graphic narrative reflection on her attempt to establish a course at University of Wisconsin-Madison that uses writing and drawing

For this attendance card, I asked students to draw a portrait of themselves at six years old

by hand to promote present mindfulness. In this book, she includes a copy of her illustrated syllabus for the course, wherein she describes how her students will begin each class recording their attendance by writing and drawing on an index card. In my drawing-to-learn class, students turned this card in at the end of class, and at the end of the course, I returned their cards to them so that they might see the progression of their drawing skill and comfort.

For the first two weeks, I taught basic drawing skills I learned from studying online video lessons from Dave Gray, Austin Kleon, and Doug Neill. Much of this work was helping students gain introductory confidence in drawing simple images. Along the way, they came to understand that the kind of image vocabulary I was asking them to develop had to be simple enough to be drawn quickly so they could capture and present learning as efficiently as possible. During this early period, I also showed students a number of TED Talk videos on creativity, visual thinking, note-taking, doodling, and drawing, such as those by Sunni Brown, Clive Thompson, Rachel Smith, and Brandy Agerbeck. These simple lessons and videos provided the visual and philosophical groundwork for moving students to the next series of daily mini-lessons on 12 categories of images that could be deployed in drawing-to-learn:

1. Letters and Numbers
2. Shapes and Lines
3. Containers
4. Faces
5. People
6. Objects
7. Animals
8. Nature
9. Page Layouts
10. Transportation
11. Buildings
12. Maps

Six drawing-to-learn strategies

Beyond learning these image vocabularies, I also taught six drawing-to-learn strategies that I thought would be most helpful to students across the curriculum. Each strategy was related to a specific purpose:

1. Drawing-to-Calm: Coloring
2. Drawing-to-Listen: Doodling
3. Drawing-to-Record-Learning: Sketchnoting
4. Drawing-to-Create-Learning: Handmade Thinking
5. Drawing-to-See: Representing
6. Drawing-to-Present-Learning: Illustrated Speaking

Coloring has recently experienced a rebirth as an effective practice in achieving a calm state of mind. According to a recent *Wall Street Journal* article by Hagerty and Trachtenberg, "[e]ight of the top 20 selling books on Amazon currently are coloring books designed for adults." Many of my students have difficulty slowing down, focusing their attention, and exhibiting the necessary concentration their studies require. Drawing-to-calm through coloring offers the opportunity to develop these habits of mind. In preparation for this lesson, I downloaded several mandala image files from the web, made copies of each, and distributed them to my students so that they had several options of mandalas to choose from. Then for 15 or 20 minutes, we colored in class. We repeated this practice over the course of three class meetings. The purpose was not to create beautifully colored mandalas. The end of drawing-to-calm is to create habits of quiet concentration and a unified sense of embodied mindfulness.

Students practicing drawing-to-calm with mandalas

Doodling can provide students the opportunity to focus their listening and learning. I take my definition of doodling from Sunni Brown's book *The Doodle Revolution:* "making spontaneous marks (with your mind and

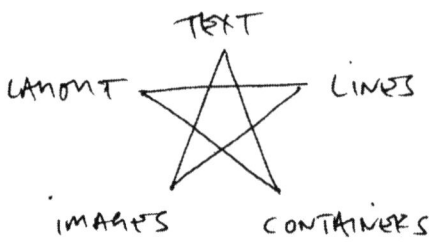

I drew this image on the whiteboard to depict the five common sketchnote ingredients

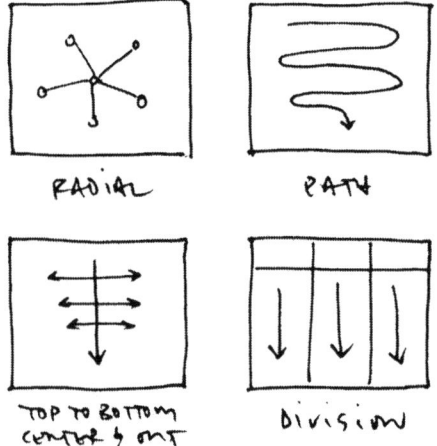

I drew these images on the whiteboard to depict the four common sketchnote layouts

body) to help yourself think." In this lesson, I asked students to doodle in their composition notebooks as they listened to TED Talk lectures. After the video clips were completed, I asked them to recount what they had learned from the lectures, such as the main idea, the overall structure of the lecture, and what they took to be the most important thing they had learned or remembered. We also repeated this practice over a number of class meetings to gain confidence in doodling or drawing-to-listen.

College students are expected to know quite a bit about what it means to be a college student and how best to learn in school, but many of those expectations are based upon uninformed assumptions. One of those false assumptions is that students know how to take notes in class. Drawing on the work of Mike Rohde, I introduced students to the five common ingredients and four common layouts for capturing learning from lectures or reading assignments via **sketchnoting**. The five common ingredients are text, lines, containers, images, and layout.

The four common layouts I found most helpful for my students included the radial, path, division, and top-to-bottom/center-and-out layouts.

We practiced sketchnoting in class while listening to a number of TED Talks, and then students attended a selected public lecture on campus and captured that lecture via a sketchnote.

A fourth drawing-to-learn strategy, drawing-to-create-learning or **handmade thinking**, is a practice I developed after encountering Dan Roam's *The Back of the Napkin*. In this fine book on the power of drawing to

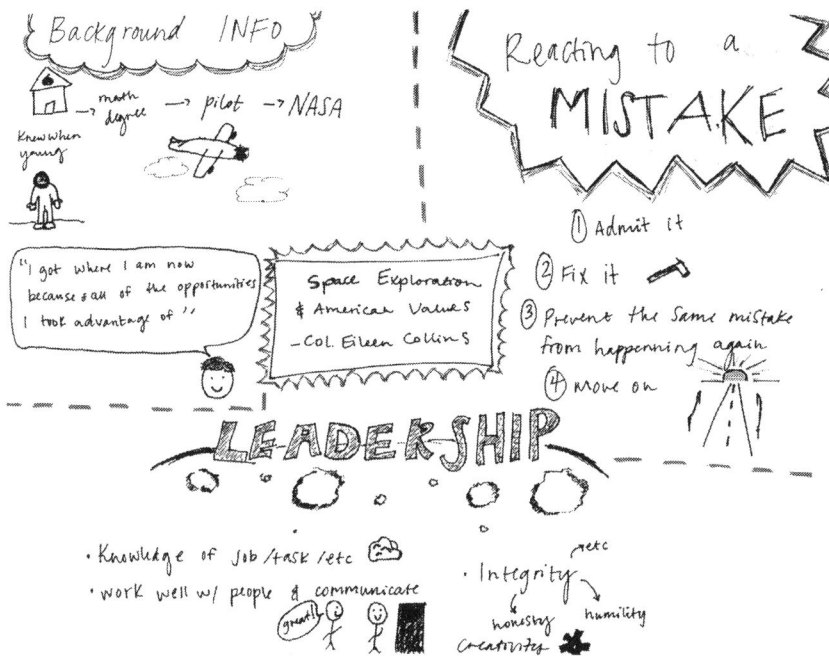

A student's sketchnote in response to a public lecture by visiting speaker Colonel Eileen Collins

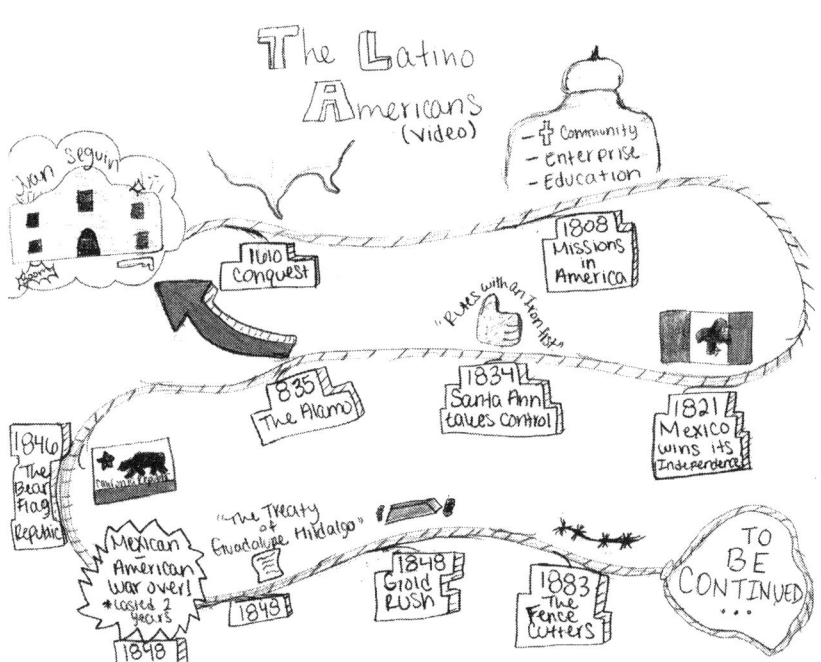

A student's sketchnote in response to a video presentation on early Latinos in the US

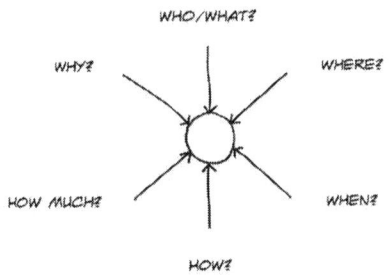

My image to demonstrate the power of six basic questions to interrogate a problem and define possible solutions

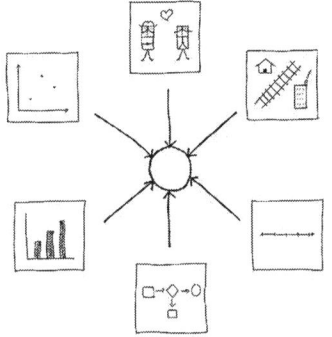

My image to show how simple pictures can also represent the power of six basic questions to interrogate a problem and define possible solutions

solve problems and present solutions, Roam argues that there are six basic visual formats for investigating problems, each relating to the six common questions: who or what, where, when, how, how much, and why.

The corresponding visual formats are the portrait, the map, the timeline, the process chart, the bar graph, and the multivariable chart.

I thought that these formats would be excellent ways for students to capture their responses to reading assignments, but I thought it would be helpful to offer students more options than these six. Thus, I created a series of 21 visual formats for students to use when drawing their responses, including portrait, map, comic, comparison/contrast, Venn diagram, seesaw, scales, tree, web, organization, genealogy, bar graph, pie chart, multivariable graph, timeline, before and after, equation, process chart, Freytag's plot pyramid, positive/negative plot, and layers.

For this practice, I assigned students a number of brief articles to read in class, and then had them draw their responses using one of these formats. Then, they incorporated a handmade response into their two reading summary assignments as part of the drafting process for those summaries. For more on this drawing-to-read strategy, see my book *Handmade Thinking*.

Using drawing-to-see, **representing** was the next strategy I briefly introduced. For this lesson, I asked students to draw a picture of me and try to include as much detail as possible. After they completed and shared their drawings with each other, I asked them to identify those physical attributes they were able to see more clearly through drawing.

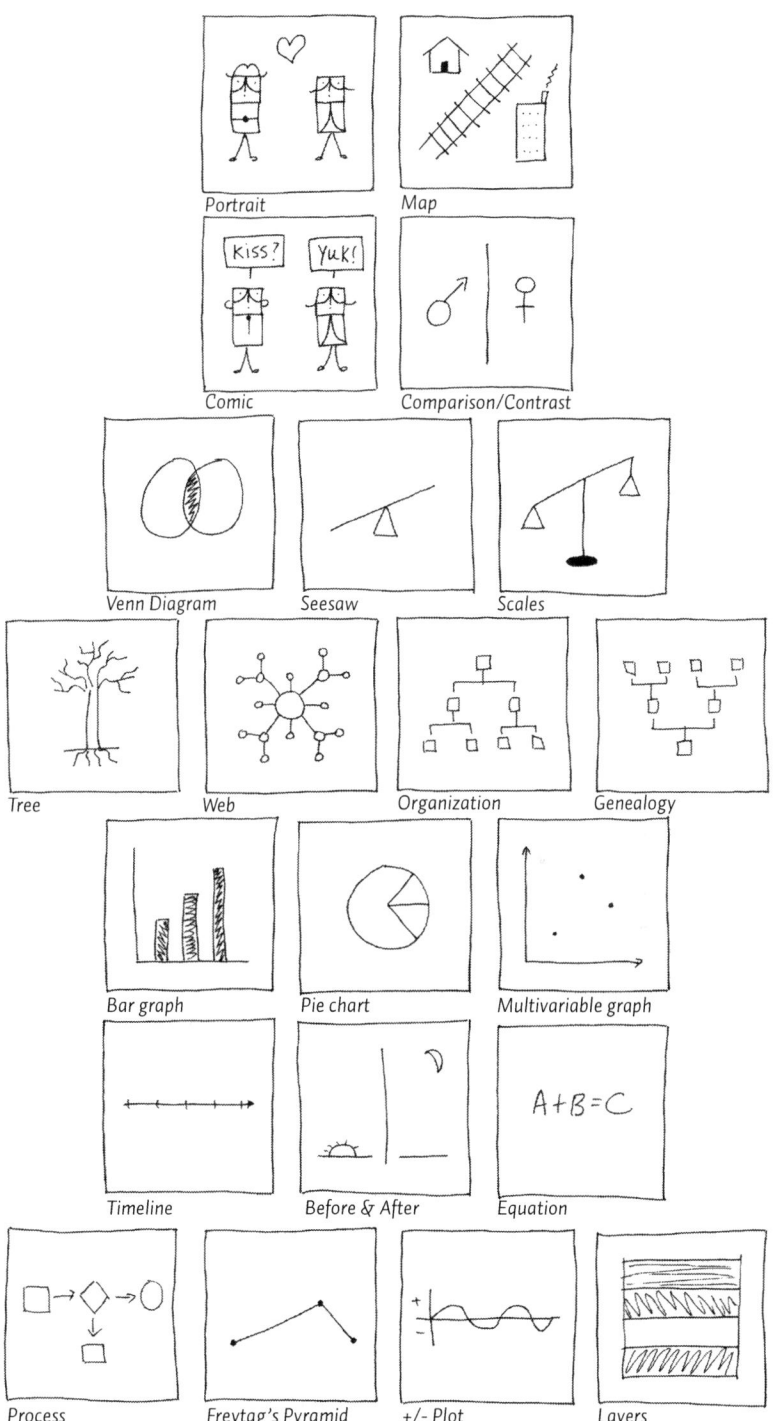

Twenty-one formats for handmade thinking

I also displayed a painting by John Singer Sargent titled "The Daughters of Edward Darley Boit" and asked them to sketch the painting as a way of looking closely at the relationships between form and content. After a period of drawing as a means of close inspection, a number of students noted the clear connection between the shapes of the tall vases in the scene and the shapes of the girls' dresses, suggesting that both represented delicate and fragile objects of beauty.

The final drawing-to-learn strategy was drawing-to-present-learning or **illustrated speaking**. Given all that students had learned and practiced up to this point, I felt they were adequately prepared to present a live drawing in class that illustrated a brief two- or three-minute speech. Prior to this assignment, I presented for the class an illustrated review of the six drawing-to-learn strategies in a radial layout format on the board. I also brought several extra erasable markers to class and gave students free time to practice writing and drawing on the whiteboard so they would get a feel for what it's like to stand and draw with a marker. Also in preparation for the assignment, I gave each student an index card. On one side, I asked them to write out the outline of their speech, and on the other side, I asked them to sketch the images they would draw as they spoke. They used these cards as reminders as they delivered their presentations and handed them in to me after the speech was completed. These brief speeches were given on the last four days of the course, and most of the students explained some process they knew well and could easily draw, such as how to shoot a free throw, how to procrastinate instead of studying, how to be an effective grocery store cashier, and how to fold a T-shirt.

Student feedback

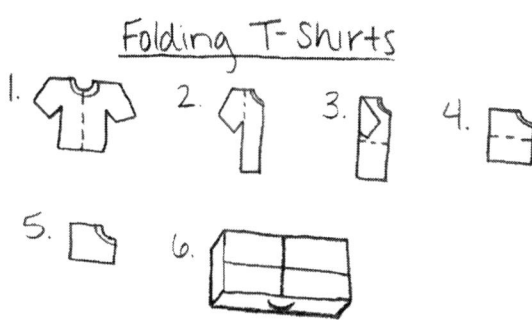

A student's note card for the illustrated speaking presentation

On the last day of class, I asked students to provide me with feedback on the course via a simple one-page comic in which they drew a self-portrait and included a speech bubble with their comments. I prompted them to let me know what they liked best, what they thought could be improved, and what they might remove from the course.

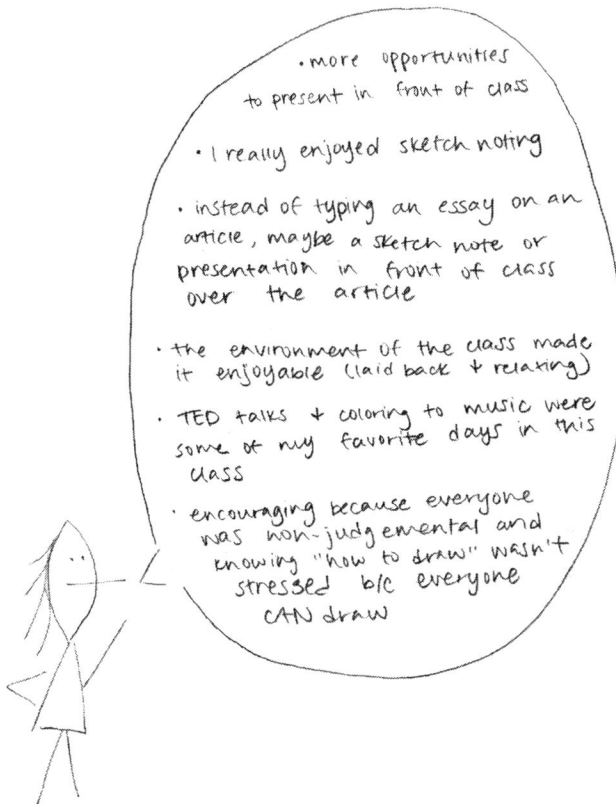

An example of a student's comic-format course evaluation

In general, these comments reflected students' desire for more opportunities to practice sketchnoting, draw presentations, and share their work in class. Several students said they liked best the drawing-to-calm strategy, and others mentioned they enjoyed the mini-lessons on 12 categories of images. Two students said they would have preferred only one summary assignment, and one student said there were too many videos. Another student wanted to learn how to sketchnote PowerPoint lectures, and a few mentioned they were already using sketchnotes in other classes.

I also emailed students during the subsequent semester and asked them if they might provide me feedback on the degree to which they were incorporating these strategies into their other courses. One student responded as follows via email:

> Hi Dr. Musgrove,
>
> Thank you for providing me with the opportunity to voice my feedback on the general studies course Drawing to Learn.
>
> This course has helped me in my other classes on campus by allowing me to take quicker, more concise, and more effective notes. When I use the skills I learned in Drawing to Learn, ideas seem to flow and connect better than they used to. Also, I am now able to pre-write for essays more successfully than before, allowing the writing process to require less time and less revision overall.
>
> In life, this course has allowed me to pay closer attention when listening to a speaker give a presentation and has allowed me to be more inclined to express myself in various forms besides writing.
>
> I hope this feedback can be helpful to you in some way.
>
> Thank you so much for offering this course; I enjoyed it very much. (Dunlap 2016)

I find this response helpful because it points to four learning objectives I can emphasize when I teach the course again:

1. Students will learn time-saving strategies for taking notes and planning projects.
2. Students will learn to more effectively understand and relate ideas.
3. Students will learn to listen more effectively to lectures and speakers.
4. Students will learn to express themselves in forms other than writing.

Changes to future courses

Based on these responses and on my own evaluation of the course, I believe that when I teach the course again, I will reduce the drawing-to-learn strategies from six to four, and as a consequence, restructure the assignments. I remember feeling most rushed in the course when we were practicing drawing-to-create-learning (handmade thinking) and drawing-to-see (representing). Removing those strategies from the course will allow more time for sketchnoting and illustrated speaking, which are more immediately useful to first-year students who often take large lecture sections and are required to give presentations in introductory public speaking courses. I will also adjust the summary assignments to utilize sketchnoting rather than handmade thinking, and provide students more time to share their work and to practice drawing-to-present. And of course, I will reinforce the four learning goals mentioned above.

As I continue to reflect upon this course, I'm grateful for the opportunity to follow this path of inquiry blazed by many explorers in the field of drawing-to-learn who have argued for its value in problem-solving and communication. Overall, I have found that my students have appreciated the joy and power drawing-to-learn offers. I'm also grateful for the chance to explore what an introductory course on what that joy and power might look like.

LAURENCE MUSGROVE is professor of English at Angelo State University in San Angelo, Texas, where he teaches creative writing, literature, visual thinking, and comics. He is the author of *Handmade Thinking*, offering students ways to depict their responses to literature visually. His recent collection of poetry, *Local Bird*, is from Lamar University Literary Press. His poems have appeared in *Southern Indiana Review*, *Buddhist Poetry Review*, *Inside Higher Ed*, and elsewhere. He blogs at www.theillustratedprofessor.com and cartoons at texosophy.com.

References

Agerbeck, B., *The Graphic Facilitator's Guide*, Chicago, Loosetooth.com Library, 2012.

Barry, L., *Syllabus: Notes from an Accidental Professor*, Montreal, Drawn & Quarterly, 2014.

Brown, S., *The Doodle Revolution*, New York, Portfolio/Penguin, 2014.

Dunlap, K. (2016). *Drawing to Learn—Following Up*.

Hagerty J. and J. Trachtenberg, "Adult Coloring Books Test Grown-Ups' Ability to Stay Inside the Lines," *Wall Street Journal*, 27 December 2015. www.wsj.com/articles/to-relax-grown-ups-try-to-stay-inside-the-lines-1451250613, (accessed 10 January 2016).

McCloud, S., *Understanding Comics*, New York, Harper, 1993.

Musgrove, L., *Handmade Thinking: A Picture Book on Reading and Drawing*, San Angelo, CreateSpace, 2011.

Musgrove, L. and M. Musgrove, "Drawing is Learning: To Understand and To Be Understood," *Journal of the Assembly for Expanded Perspectives on Learning*, vol. 20, 2014-2015, pp. 91-102.

Musgrove, L. and M. Musgrove, "My Song," *INKBRICK*, no. 3, 2015, pp. 16-19.

Roam, D., *The Back of the Napkin*, New York, Portfolio/Penguin, 2009.

Rohde, M., *The Sketchnote Handbook*, San Francisco, Peachpit/Pearson, 2013.

In Front of the Wall

Alfredo Carlo

At the age of three I used to draw on paper. At 16, I started painting in the streets and on trains. At the age of 24, I expanded this passion to draw on walls during business workshops and meetings.

I always enjoyed taking a pencil and a piece of paper to sketch, not caring what I drew, just liking the act of drawing. I guess all kids share this kind of joy and then, at some point while growing up, tend to lose the freedom to be whatever they want. Most of the time drawing is the first practice to go.

I almost completely quit drawing during high school, thinking there were more important things to do and take care of (really?). I didn't draw very much at all until falling in love with graffiti marking. I remember suddenly seeing this phenomenon appear in my city of Rome, around corners and on trains. I really liked the spontaneity of it and the colorful pictures—not to mention the fact these drawings were illegal! For a 16-year-old, what more could you ask for?

I then started painting in the streets and on trains, first copying and learning from others and, at the same time, practicing alone in my bedroom or with friends. The sense of community-building and belonging, combined with the pleasure of developing the quality of what I was doing, are feelings I carry with me to this day.

I remember spending afternoons taking time to sketch a piece I would paint on a train. Then, when encountering that steel at night, I would make the piece exactly the same, as quickly as possible. It was a great feeling to get it done and admire it the next morning, get the photos developed (that's right, there were no digital photos at the time—I still have all the negatives!), and share them with friends, and often family.

While getting better at graffiti, I learned that the best part was not reproducing at night what I was sketching in the afternoon, but instead the process of always painting something fresh, based on my constant practice. This was called "wild style," literally going wild with a style—just creating in the moment, sensing into it, and listening for an inner spark. That was a great feeling to experience, because I could love the results or hate them; the style brought a connection with the practice, and was really the only way to get better. Of course, it was also the best way to be quick and not get caught by the cops!

> The only way to get comfortable with what we do is practice; the practice of repeating something, especially if it makes us feel uncomfortable, is what builds our best strengths and differentiates us from everybody else.

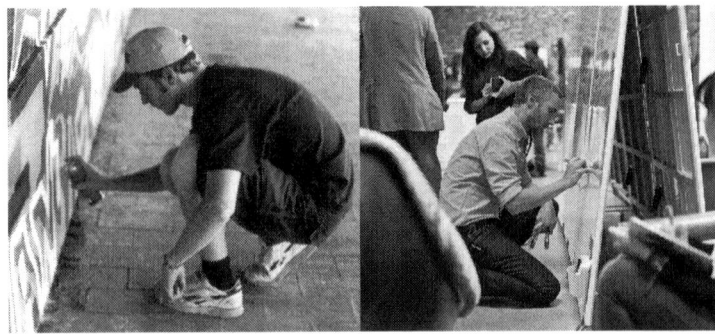

Practice: Then and now

I mention this story because I see a very strong connection between what my practice was then, and what it is today.

- It was a time when I saw a lot of talented people around me and was inspired by them. I was challenged to find my own style, my own way, and often I hit my head against the "white page," trying to really understand what I was doing and why, and to explain it to almost all of the people around me.
- It was a time of exploration, in unknown and fascinating territories, filled with exciting moments of trying new colors and new spray cans.
- It was a time for testing my capacity—what I was able to do and not do, prompting me to learn and expand what I was wanting to discover.

Challenge: Accept and embrace the new and different

Exploration: See what is out there, what I don't yet know

Testing: See the reaction (my own and others') to what I do

Trying: Do, fail, fail better

It's the same today in my practice as a visual designer, where I **embrace challenges, exploration, testing, and trying.**

Shift to scribing

When I transitioned to scribing, I had already given up graffiti; it was too dangerous and time-consuming at a point when I was investing in a new professional life and looking for new opportunities.

Scribing captured my attention for two main reasons: the real-time factor, and the freedom of expression. While drawing a conversation or visualizing a process, I would exercise my approach to graffiti: listening and paying attention, capturing what the creative side of my brain could process, and using the space at my disposal to map out content and ideas. The connection between the two practices, which I was only able to rationalize after a few years, is today so immediate and makes complete sense.

Another thing, slightly more subtle, is the relationship with the audience. In graffiti you do what you do to express yourself, but the ultimate goal is for the work to be seen and appreciated by as many people as possible. This has a strong connection with what I do today and why I do it; I enjoy creating "stuff" for others to make their lives easier and better. Visualization and, I believe, well-done graffiti both accomplish that.

I find that the wall—meant as any surface we work on vertically—is a great link between my first love (graffiti) and my recent one (graphic facilitation). We learn to draw and write on a horizontal surface, and therefore we think every surface should be like that. The moment of going from a horizontal orientation to a vertical one is often the hardest transition for people. It is, in fact, unusual for our normal habits.

For me, the verticality is the part I most enjoy. Having a nice, big, flat, upright surface on which to write gives freedom and flexibility; I can play with the space in a three-dimensional way, take a real step back to look at the big picture, and use my entire body in relationship with the board or wall.

Making graffiti helped me develop a multitasking skill that became very useful when I started scribing. While painting on a train, a person needs to pay close attention to three specific components:

- **Execution:** How is the drawing reflecting the idea in mind, and how is that coming out on the wall/train?
- **Aesthetics:** How stylish is the image? Is there an overall beauty to the piece, in addition to the work on the letters and colors?
- **Attention:** Are the cops coming?! Who is speaking and watching, and how will they relate to the images?

Without even knowing it, I had been developing the very skillset I believe is needed for scribing in front of a wall: listening carefully for **what is said and what is unsaid**, improvising based on daily practice, keeping an eye on the beauty of the composition, and making sure to capture key meaning. It actually makes sense… and I risk so much less today!

During this transition from making graffiti to scribing, working a collaborative event, I was introduced to a "knowledge wall," a big surface used to gather inputs and outcomes of long workshop sessions. At first, I didn't know how to approach this large surface. But then, realizing I could play with it just like I had played with spray cans, letters, and colors, I found some comfort (but only some!).

I started with what I was really good at: crafting the letters. I think starting from where we are comfortable is always key. We need to establish a safe zone, a place we can return to when in crisis or stressful situations, and from which we can move into new and unknown territories. Having a bag full of tricks and habits that come out easily and quickly is, for me, key. I do love to try new things and, when challenged, know where to go: back to the basics.

Every wall, a canvas

Making graffiti taught me to look at the city with a different eye, recognizing each wall and surface as a potential canvas for creation. Everything from magazines to album covers, from advertisements to clothing designs, influences my perspective. I find the possibility of mixing styles fascinating: I think there's no such a thing as "a" style that represents us, especially if we are not able to change it. "Style" is doing the right thing at the right moment, with the right attitude and reasons. **Mixing what we see, hear, learn, and read**—that's an art itself, not to be underestimated.

These days, each piece I produce aims to be a different piece influenced by genres and arts, a reflection of my personal research through the content somebody else has provided, a patchwork of thoughts made visual.

Recently, while working with Internazionale at the annual festival in Ferrara, Italy, our team went to visually document some of the sessions without constraint (besides visualizing, the main reason to be there was to freely experiment). We came up with different challenges. We scribed

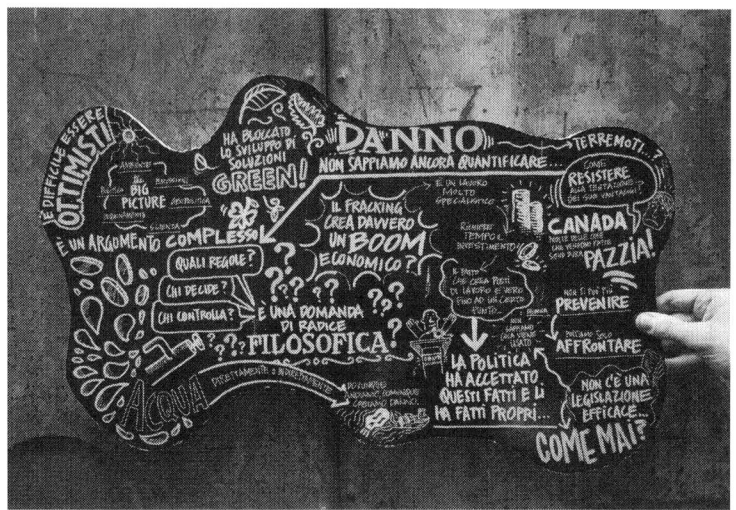

some of the sessions as a team, where each of us would draw only one level—words, drawings, or colors. We would each draw on a different piece of paper and then swap them to see what would happen. Or we would cut our canvases into shapes and use a color that would match the theme of the speech; in the picture above, for example, the theme was oil. In the closing plenary, there were ten of us scribing little bits on each other's pre-printed templates, to see how our different styles and ears would mix and integrate with each other. It was quite a messy experiment, but fun!

> Take a notebook and fill it in 10 minutes.

I love challenges. I think we learn so much more from being challenged than from being in a state of comfort. I love (and hate) the feeling of being a step away from failing because I know that's when I give my best.

> Draw a face made only out of letters.

Sometimes I scribe on a wall trying to start from the opposite side I am used to, contradicting my assumptions about direction. Sometimes I do the same with markers and colors, using those that are not in my usual range. **I often practice with different tools and sizes and constraints:** If I draw the same thing with a pencil on a big poster and then with a huge sharpie on a Post-It, what happens? How do we interact with the surfaces we face in the moment? How do we sustain a certain value, while experimenting with the same message in different situations?

> Draw something with your right arm, then draw the same thing with your left arm, and then with your eyes closed.

I believe we enter into a relationship with the surface, and our body becomes one with it through the tools we have in our hands. That's why the tool we are using is not that essential.

What is essential is to initiate that relationship and have fun. Having fun is another key component of work and life; I personally try to have fun with anything I do and, the moment the fun stops, I look for something else where I can again find it. I think fun helps creativity, and creativity can solve anything!

> Keep a journal of your practices.

Again, it doesn't matter what tool we are using (in fact, we use a lot of different ones). What's most important is the idea that the tool should always create a little bit of discomfort; that's how we find the best solutions—by adapting to the change for which we didn't plan.

For the Business School of Lausanne we re-designed the look and feel of their shared spaces and classrooms, all done using particular paints and simple designs, but all with brushes (and, yes, a little bit of spray

can here and there). We went from painting the stairs with quotes and characters to using magnetic paint to allow students to hang up their notes and announcements. We added shapes in the classroom with chalkboard paint that would allow them to use those areas to write, share, and eventually draw. Each classroom has a different color related to the topics and a keyword to name it. The school (a business school!) is now full of colors and inspiration.

I guess my point is that we are what we do, and we need to try and experiment to be able to find who we are and what we are really good at.

At the time I was running along the train rails to make a piece of graffiti, I didn't know that I was planting the seeds of my best professional future. Now that I am a graphic facilitator, I know for sure it is just a transition into something else, different but equally stimulating.

Pay attention to everything you have around you and listen to your senses to notice when the next right thing is getting close, and catch it.

ALFREDO CARLO is a graphic facilitator and a designer of collaborative processes. He bases his work on the power of collaboration, committing himself to each project in a creative and active way. He's a founding partner of Housatonic, a partner of Matter Group, and a member of The Value Web, a network of international facilitators and designers working with large and medium organizations across the world to find solutions for systemic issues.

Alfredo has a deep knowledge of silkscreen and printing techniques, as well as of scenography and environmental decoration, areas in which he has materialized his passion for t-shirts and writing. His works have been published on several books of brand design, street art and graphic design. Alfredo grew up in Rome and studied art history at university in Bologna, where he currently lives with his wife and two children.

Visual Improvisation
How improvising influences my sketchnoting

Eva-Lotta Lamm

I am a sketchnoter. I create visual notes of talks and discussions in real time. Mostly in a small format, sometimes on a large wall-sized chart. I try to capture the main points, to distill key topics in words and images to make the content accessible and memorable beyond the event itself.

Sketchnoting combines several very different skills in one intense, real-time activity. The first skill is drawing or sketching itself. This is quite a technical skill, involving motor dexterity and hand-eye coordination; making clear marks on paper that are recognizable as specific objects, people, or words. The second type of skill is more structural: breaking down information, synthesizing the important points, and establishing hierarchy and relationship between the points. The third skill involves the imagination: choosing and developing strong visual metaphors for abstract concepts.

Sketchnotes from Smashing Conference New York, 2014

I am also an improviser.

Discovering improvisation

I discovered improvisation by chance shortly after I moved to London about seven years ago. I had signed up for a free workshop about improving presentation skills that was offered through a network for women in digital design. I didn't know many people in town and presentation skills are always worth improving, so I signed up with little expectations.

It turned out that the woman teaching the workshop had prepared a day of different improvisation exercises, most of them drawn from a form of improvisation called Action Theater[1].

Action Theater improvisation is deeply grounded in the physical experience. The body and the awareness of its physicality are the basis for developing all material. The three basic ingredients that can be used in improvisation are movement, sound, and language. Any combination of the ingredients is possible—movement only, moving and sound, being still and speaking, transforming sound into language, etc. The process is very open and playful. Meaning can emerge; images can arise, become denser and more concrete in parts, and then dissolve again into more abstract expressions.

I didn't know all that back then. I just loved the exercises we did all day. We moved in different ways, played with rhythm, timing and pauses. We played with language and what words sound like when you explore every single sound in them, when you roll them around on your tongue and turn language into music. I felt like I was five years old, just having fun and freely playing around with my expressions. I had been doing this kind of stuff all my life, on my own, when nobody was looking or listening. Discovering that this was actually "a thing"—something with a name, something that people did in a structured way—was a huge surprise and a feeling like coming home at the same time.

A few weeks after this chance encounter, I began practicing Action Theater with a wonderful teacher, Kate Hilder[2]. Little by little, I discovered the full depth and structural richness of this form and began to see parallels with the visual work I had been doing.

Exploring the overlaps between improvisation and visual work

BEING PRESENT

The first and most immediate parallel between improvising and sketchnoting is that both are happening in real-time. In improvisation we develop material on the fly. We don't know beforehand what we are going to create. We trust the skills we have practiced and the instincts we have developed as an improviser to respond to the material as it arises and shape it into a meaningful experience for the audience.

One of the key things we practice in improvisation is "being present." But what does this mean? For me, it all comes down to become extremely good at noticing. Noticing what is going on around you, noticing what is going on inside of you, noticing what you are doing, how you are doing it and which effect it has. Being present is the basis for being able to truly listen in a holistic sense.

In Action Theater, most practice starts with breaking things down into very small aspects and using simple exercises to focus on one specific aspect at a time to train the senses and the awareness. Little by little, we combine several aspects into bigger scores until we are able to use the practiced skills and sharpened awareness as a tool in an open improvisation.

We try to sharpen our awareness of aspects of movement like:

QUALITY
- Which body part is moving?
- Is the movement hard or soft?
- Is it tense or relaxed?
- How big is the movement?
- Is it a fluid movement?

SPATIALITY
- Where am I in the space?
- Am I close to the wall or in the middle of the room?

- How much of the space am I using?
- Which direction am I facing?

RHYTHM
- Is the movement regular or random?
- Is it continuous or do I use stillness and pauses in between?
- Am I creating a specific rhythm?

TEMPORALITY
- How fast or slow am I moving?
- How much time do I use for each movement?

RELATIONSHIP
- Am I responding to a previous movement?
- Is it the same as, the opposite of, or a variation on what I did before?
- Is my focus directed inward or towards the audience or other improvisers?

Just as a sharp awareness is the basis for truly listening and immersing myself in a talk I am sketching, a lot of these aspects of movement directly translate into sketchnoting as well. When I draw, I deal with the quality of my lines, the placement of objects on the page, the rhythm of the piece, balancing areas of density and areas of openness, and of course with the relationship between the different elements, in terms of both style and content. In my personal sketchnoting and in the coaching and workshops I do for others, I use the same principle of breaking-down as I do in my improvisation, separating exercises into tiny focus points in order to single out very specific aspects and practice them one at a time.

In sketchnoting, these basic exercises include sketching different qualities of lines, experimenting with spacing, size, and proportions, and playing with different speeds of drawing—always observing the difference in quality and expression that results from each change. The focused practice helps to internalize basic drawing and composition skills, so the mind is freed up for the listening, synthesizing, and metaphor-development part during sketchnoting. It fine-tunes our awareness of shapes, space, rhythms, patterns, balance, and textures so that we develop the necessary intuition to take all the underlying micro-decisions that need to be taken when sketching live.

RESPONDING

Another key principle in Action Theater is the notion of "responding." Once we are present and notice all the interesting details going on in and around us, it is time to respond to them, to move from noticing to doing. The whole improvisation is a constant oscillation between noticing and responding. With a lot of practice, the amplitudes between the two get so fine that both are practically happening at the same time.

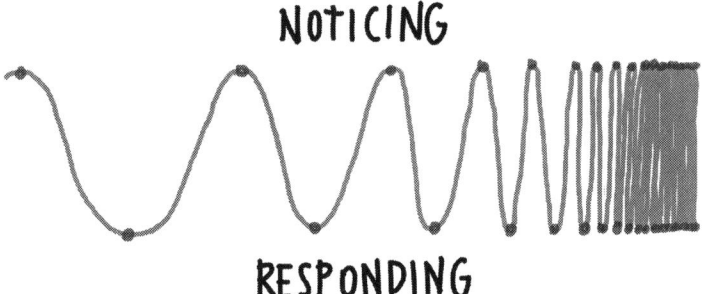

Responding can have many forms. In Action Theater, we differentiate between three main types of responding: developing, transforming, and shifting. Developing means exploring the thing we are responding to—repeating, varying, or deconstructing it—so that it becomes clearer, sharper, and richer, the way the image on a photo takes shape in the development process. Transforming refers to slowly transitioning from one thing to another by gradually changing the quality of one or more aspects at a time. Shifting means to completely change every aspect of the thing we respond to and to contrast it with something quite different. We practice the different types of responses in small, formal exercises at first (using simple movement, sound, or language scores) and extend the reach and complexity to include whole story lines.

There are various ways to practice responding in a visual sense. On a very basic formal level, it starts by exploring simple and combined shapes. The page fills as one responds to each previous shape by either developing, transforming, or shifting. Playing with a shifting focus between different aspects like shape, size, spacing, orientation, line quality, proportion, etc. in the response helps to sharpen the awareness and to broaden the range of expression.

I also like using random inputs[3] as a starting point. I use all kinds of stains—placing used tea bags or dripping coffee cups on paper, ink blotches, fingerprints, wild scribbles, scraps of paper, or some of my own random warm-up doodles. Then it's about looking at the random shape at hand and asking what does it look like, what are its qualities. It's a bit like watching clouds—imagining what this shape could be, what I could add to make it into something else, such as an object, an animal, a person, or a little story.

I try not to go for the "obvious" first idea I have, instead going down a stranger, more adventurous route. Adding a few first strokes, looking again, and responding to the changed shape; adding some more until slowly, something recognizable emerges, an image takes shape, a little story reveals itself. I like having to bend my mind around the shape, to try and wrap my imagination around its edges and to keep noticing and responding to its changing form. It's challenging and playful at the same time.

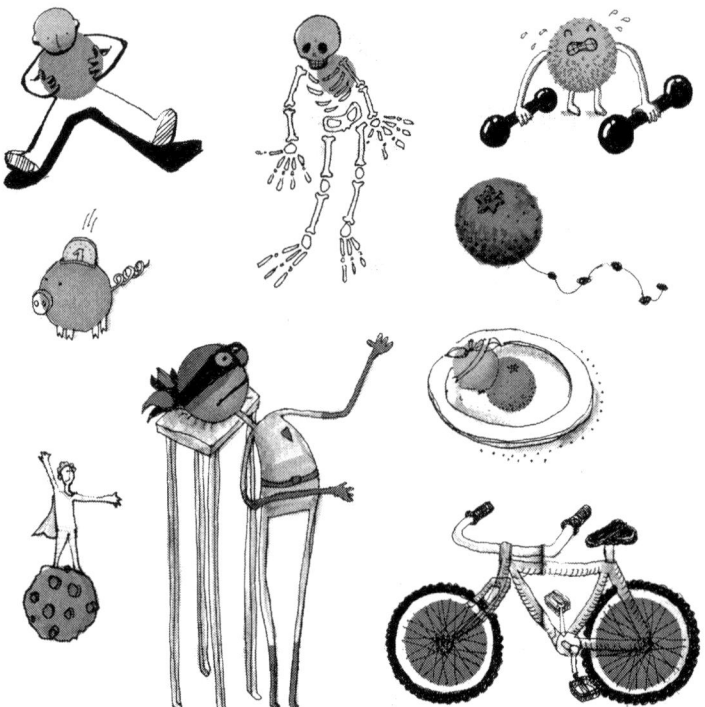

Random scribbles from ink stains from bleeding markers

The most valuable outcome of this kind of practice is that I learn to stay open and responsive while I am working. In my sketchnoting, this helps me to develop structure and balance visual hierarchy in my pieces as they develop. It also allows for visual metaphors and patterns to arise and transform while I am working. An image can change halfway through sketching, because the shapes remind me of something and give rise to a new image. Staying open to changing course at any point, to letting the work be influenced by the process, is something I enjoy a lot. It has been a source of many beautiful discoveries.

Random scribbles from tea stains

THE PLEASURE OF GETTING IN AND OUT OF TROUBLE

Developing work in real-time and responding to new and sometimes unexpected content on the fly doesn't come without difficulties, though. It means giving up control over the final piece: As I don't know beforehand what is coming, I can't plan it all out. I can't choose a perfect structure for the material. I can't develop visual metaphors for all of the key points in the talk in advance. When I work in real-time, I leave behind the safety net of carefully planning things out and iterating through several versions to get to the final solution. I have to rely on the skills I have built so far, and I have to accept that I will make mistakes.

Sometimes people come up to me to ask how my sketchnotes look so perfect and how I manage not to make any mistakes. Well, it's not true that I don't make mistakes. I make a lot of them. I misspell words, I run out of space, I mess up sketches. Luckily, a lot of my

People are difficult. Especially if they hold things. I get that wrong sometimes.

No need for an eraser. If the first line is wrong, just put another line over it to make it right.

mistakes hide very well in the visually busy notes, so that nobody other than me ever sees them as mistakes. But also, over time, I got quite good at using my "mistakes" as "happy accidents" and responding to them in such a way that they end up looking like deliberate choices.

I like to think of it as sketching myself into trouble and out of it again. Instead of being afraid of doing something wrong, I try to embrace everything that comes up as a chance to experiment and to play. It feels very liberating that I can get myself out of a sticky situation just by noticing, responding, and not capitulating.

I sometimes even step into trouble deliberately. This can mean using different materials from the ones I am used to—working in black and white instead of color, using very fat markers instead of the fine liners I usually gravitate towards, or changing the size of my format dramatically by sketching on a whole wall or a little notepad. It can also mean leaving my comfort zone in terms of sketching things I am not quite sure how to sketch. Or trying out new, maybe wacky visual metaphors instead of the tried-and-trusted, generic stereotypes that are used over and over again. It can be about injecting my own point of view or sense of humor at the risk of other people not agreeing or not getting it.

Taking a risk is taking a chance at the same time. Taking a chance to surprise myself, to discover a new way of doing things, and to grow my skill set.

Sketching myself out of trouble. If I can't get the sketches to look realistic because I messed it up, I sometimes make them deliberately non-realistic or surreal. They take on a different dynamic and start working again because it is clear that they don't have to work in the real world.

Sometimes, perspective needs to be bent to fit the available space (bed) or to make sure there is enough space for the person I already sketched before (pedestal).

I am quite bad at sketching portraits. Sometimes they work out, but sometimes they go so horribly wrong that I feel the need to apologize in the notes.

If something goes wrong, it means that there is a chance to explore how to do it better. Repetition is the best way to learn and to practice. I look at what is wrong in the current version, I try to change it in the next. Noticing and responding. Often over and over again.

My confidence in my ability to enjoy the resulting "trouble" has developed through practice. Many hours of sharpening awareness, of playfully responding to material in various ways in a safe environment, has continually built a robust basis for my work out in the wild. Paired with the

Mistakes as happy accidents: When a lack of spacing suddenly means an island in the sea can double up as a duvet or musical notes merge into a hairstyle

playful non-judging approach of improvisation, it is growing my confidence to just throw myself into doing, to dare to start without having a firm plan, and to trust my skills and the process to create an interesting piece of work. It empowers me to take bold choices in my work. Some of them work out as I imagined, some of them need visual troubleshooting, and some of them just teach me to accept my own mistakes. But I am always up for the challenge.

Calm seas don't make skillful sailors after all!

EVA-LOTTA LAMM is a user experience designer, illustrator and sketchnoter. She grew up in Germany and worked in Paris and London for a few years before packing up her backpack to go travelling the world and sketching her journey for 15 months. She has over 12 years of experience working on digital products as an in-house designer for Google, Skype, and Yahoo! as well as freelancing and consulting for various agencies and her own clients.

Besides her daytime mission of making the web a more understandable, usable, and delightful place, she regularly takes sketchnotes at conferences and has self-published her notes in several books.

Eva-Lotta also teaches sketching and is interested in exploring the area of Visual Improvisation — looking at the parallels between sketching and improvisation to explore how some of the principles from her regular theater improvisation practice can be used to inspire visual work.

Eva-Lotta's books and work can be found at www.sketchnotesbook.com and you can follow her on twitter, flickr, or instagram under the name @evalottchen.

References

1. Action Theater was developed by former dancer Ruth Zaporah. More information on her website: www.actiontheater.com

2. Many artists have used random inputs as starting points. Some beautiful examples are Marion Deuchars' Fingerprint Art (vimeo.com/49681168), Daily Monsters made from ink stains by Stefan G. Bucher (www.dailymonster.com/344_loves_you/the-daily-monsterpapers), Coffeemonsters by Stefan Kuhnigk (thecoffeemonsters.com), tea drawings by Austin Kleon (austinkleon.com/2009/11/06/tea-drawings), and Dave Gray (communicationnation.blogspot.de/2006/01/visual-thinking-practice-randomness.html).

Solo-Practitioner Partnerships

A Conversation between Lisa Arora and Robert Mittman

We, Lisa and Robert, are seasoned solo practitioners who have been collaborating internationally since 2008. We started out as strangers referred to one another, and along the way became solo-practitioner partners, world adventurers, and dear friends. We've worked together at countless meetings, always with Robert as Lead Facilitator and Lisa as Graphic Recorder. When clients work with us, they experience a seamless team of experts. At the very core of our union as partners is a shared passion for using our skills for positive change in the world, as well as having fun while doing excellent work. We'd like to share our conversation with you about the ways in which we unite our skills to serve clients.

Partnership

Lisa: *How can we help shift others (lead facilitators and potential clients) we might work with from seeing graphic recording as a commodity, to seeing the graphic recorder as a true partner?*

Robert: This question pre-supposes that graphic recording is being perceived as a commodity. In some sense, those who are asking the question are holding a piece of the problem. I've been working with graphic recorders in my consulting and facilitation practice for more than 25 years and I have never viewed graphic recording as a commodity.

Any graphic recorder partner I work with must have the basic entry-level skills (being reliable, arriving early, handling logistics, preparation, and paper smoothly, making the charts beautiful, etc.). But then there's the quality of the listening. This is the precious part that is *not* a commodity and is dependent on the individual. The four people I work with know what needs to make it onto the page. They understand the change objectives of the meeting and they use that as a strategic filter for the content. They place the information on the page exactly as I would do myself, so that when I turn around to engage the group with the chart, I can easily make sense of it. They can handle technical, complex discussion and maintain their listening presence at rapid paces, sometimes for up to eight hours.

Clients call me up occasionally and ask, "Hey, do you know any graphic recorders who live in, for example, Omaha?" And I will never advise choosing a graphic recorder on the basis of geographical location.

L: *I agree. People looking to partner with a graphic recorder need to educate themselves as consumers because graphic recorders are not interchangeable parts. Their talent, knowledge base, experience level, listening skills, meeting design skills, client relationship skills, and many other things are far more important than choosing a graphic recorder based on geography.*

I don't think of what I do as a commodity. I show up in every stage of the work process as more than "just a graphic recorder," and so I rarely run into my work being perceived as a commodity. When participants experience the graphics as a helpful aid for structuring a conversation, synthesizing, prioritizing, and making further meaning, they see the value.

I've also focused on developing a full spectrum of skills beyond graphic recording. I understand organizational development, I have broad business knowledge, and I've studied strategy development. I am a skilled lead facilitator in my own right. I know how to form strong relationships with my clients. And then there's me... who I am. I always show up with elite professionalism. I bring my personality, my smarts, my heart, my style, my humor, good questions, good insights, a service ethic, and a full on commitment to making sure the client gets what they need and more.

R: You are often part of the meeting design calls with clients. Sometimes I contact you for design suggestions for meetings you're not even going to be at. With you as a process design partner, I can validate ideas, we can brainstorm possibilities together, and—since you're in so many meetings—sometimes you know more about facilitation processes than I do. It helps that you focus on first understanding the meeting objectives, then make visual process suggestions that support those objectives.

L: *Over time, we've built trust in each other's expertise. I've learned about facilitation by watching you, too. And, along the way, you've always been open to my suggestions about other ways to allow participants chances to interact with, review, and reflect upon the charts.*

And, Robert, I think the way you talk to your clients quickly establishes us as experts on many levels. You do a great job of insisting on the conditions we need for people to experience graphic recording as a process tool and a product.

I also consider you to be a fairly unusual facilitator partner because the visual approach is so deeply rooted in your facilitation philosophy. It's simply the way you assume you will be working and so you insist on it (with relatively few exceptions). Many facilitators who are curious about beginning to work with a graphic recorder would ask how you pitch your way of working to clients, and how you justify the extra cost. How do you?

R: When I talk to a client, one of three things happens:

1. The client trusts my recommendation that graphic recording is effective and needed and doesn't even ask much about it. These are usually clients that are referred to me, or have seen me in other meetings, so trust begins high.

2. The client has experienced graphic recording before and they love it, so they go for it.
3. The client has experienced graphic recording before and they didn't love it.

In any case, once I explain the value of graphic recording and our partnership approach, very rarely do clients object. I tell clients that it engages the visual thinkers in the room. They find it stimulating and satisfying. And more importantly, I explain that the way we will collaborate in the meeting is deeply integrated into the process so the graphics become a way of making the conversations more focused, disciplined and efficient. Some exercises/processes absolutely require the graphics. I will facilitate the odd meeting without a graphic recorder, but it's not my preference.

L: *And what about cost?*

R: I price by job, not by time. I don't have a day rate. I use value-based pricing instead. Graphic recording is part of the value proposition, so it's not a focus of the conversation.

Occasionally a client might ask, "If we didn't have the graphic recording, how much would we save?" If budget is a real issue, I am so committed to the success of the meeting that I will offer to lower my own fee (within reason) to bring in the graphic recording.

Selecting a graphic recorder partner

L: *Robert, you've worked with many graphic recorders over the years. Can you go deeper into what you look for in choosing a partner? What skills and attributes can new practitioners aspire to develop?*

R: I am looking for the "Vulcan Mind Meld." I remember having this experience for the first time when I was working with Deirdre Crowley. I was leading. She was following. Our every move was just naturally synchronized. It's like a chemistry that's either there or not.

L: *I know what this feels like from a graphic recorder's point of view, too. I think it has a lot to do with having similar thinking styles, high degrees of perception, and similar levels of consciousness. In my experience, it's a luxury when that chemistry is naturally there. In other partnerships, it can be developed intentionally between the facilitator and graphic recorder over time. It helps to work together often.*

R: I've been amazed many times at how some graphic recorders don't have even the basics down. I've seen people show up without their own copy of the agenda. I've had graphic recorders seriously disrupt a meeting by making excessive noise while attempting to hang paper. I've had awkward moments where I've had to stall and buy time in a meeting while the graphic recorder gets ready.

L: *I find commonly that new graphic recorders are usually very focused on developing the aesthetics of their work, sometimes at the expense of developing precious listening and synthesis skills. These skills are differentiators.*

R: Yes. I'm looking for someone who has these down. I also want a clean visual look to the work and I want the graphic recorder engaged fully in the process as an expert listener. Can they hear what's important to the process or meeting objective and actually capture that content correctly? Can they keep pace? Can they adapt on the spot if we need to change the process? Do they have helpful input on where we might go next? Do they bring valuable insights and observations about group dynamics to impromptu huddles during a meeting? These abilities all matter.

Meeting design

L: *What is the lead facilitator considering in a meeting design? How do you decide when to use visuals, or when to bring in a graphic recorder?*

R: I work from the presumption that there will always be a meeting design. It shows up in the proposal as the fabric of how I work. The entire first conversation occurs without even mentioning graphic recording.

L: *I think this process of helping the client get clear on what they're actually trying to do by having a meeting is a huge part of the value the consultant brings. And then, once everyone is clear on that, the conversation can shift to, "How are we going to do that?"*

Once the basis for the meeting is established, our process design choices are driven by the meeting objectives. That's where our collective creativity comes in. From the range of possibilities we conjure up, we then have to think about what is most fitting or appropriate for **this** group of people. Let's brainstorm a little list of some of the things that go through our minds.

R: Okay, here are a few things:

- What's the topic of the meeting and culture of the group or profession? What's the expected level of engagement?
- What's the necessary output? If we use a visual process, what type of output is needed? Will raw data captured into a template suffice? If this is the case, can I accomplish this with only one person in the room? Would a polished vision map (possible only when two practitioners are in the room) serve the group best?
- What parts of the meeting process lend themselves to straightforward graphic recording?
- What level of detail in capture is needed? In what way do the participants need to experience the information? Is a transcriptionist or videographer vs. a graphic recording required? Or all of the above?
- What is the client's experience with graphic recording? Do they understand the depth of the process? Have they had positive or negative experiences with it?
- Do I know any good graphic recorders who are capable of showing up professionally with this type of client and are they available on that date?
- Is that person someone who will represent my brand well?
- What is their rate and what's included?

L: When designing a meeting, we're using healthy doses of both logic and intuition. We expect it to be an iterative process that directly involves the client (or an entire design team).

Hidden value

L: When you show up as a strongly grounded, seamlessly performing pair of solo practitioners, how does that contribute to the "meeting container"? What additional value does this create for the client and participants?

R: People come up to us in meetings all the time and say, "Wow. Have you two worked together a lot? You two seem seamless." That's a huge compliment to us. We both see ourselves as integral to the container. Our relationship is wholly in service of that.

As lead facilitator, there are many things I'm doing in my role (with the graphic recorder's help) that are creating a container for the work to get done:

- My job is to get participant egos and organizational positioning out of play. Graphics help do this by not distinguishing comments by name and status.
- I'm there to ground and keep participants oriented to the content arc. The visual agenda helps, as do individual charts that each contain one part of the flow of the meeting.
- I need to make sure everyone understands each other. This means I must identify and address miscommunication. A recording can show the group or me where something is muddled.
- I'm also there to keep the conversation at the correct and most useful level of abstraction. Getting something that is "recordable" helps avoid useless contributions.
- As an objective facilitator, I'm there to see the over-pattern that specialists or internal people can miss. The graphics can provide a supporting panorama.

There's a lot of hidden value we're bringing by combining our talents.

L: *To go on a little more, I think participants can better trust the process when they're supported by a strong duo that models the collaboration implicit in the facilitator-graphic recorder "dance" in the room. When they know you're experienced, they are able to be more trusting in the meeting culture and say what needs to be said.*

R: And, last but not least, it's simply enjoyable for people to watch others who are passionate about, and good at, what they do. When meeting participants are with us and they see that we genuinely like and respect and enjoy each other. It's like coming into our "play space."

Partnership practice tips

LEAD FACILITATORS AND GRAPHIC RECORDERS

- Focus primarily on the effect your partnership has on the process/participant experience. For example, it supports the creativity of the group, improves productivity, creates group memory, allows us to extract deeper meaning, and allows non-linear thinking. Focus on the output secondarily.

- Don't associate the word *art* or *artist* with graphic recording and don't allow the client or participants to either. This is a fast way to put the focus on the aesthetics of the work and diminish the impact of graphics on the group's thought process.
- Graphic recorders, cultivate well-rounded and deep expertise (beyond graphic recording) so that you can legitimately sell yourself to facilitator partners and clients as a consultant, strategist, or meetings design expert first and foremost. Graphic recording becomes just one of the ways you go about doing what you do.
- Graphic recorders, esteem your role and inhabit it fully. Be a true partner to your facilitator partner in all ways. Don't just deliver graphic recording. Demonstrate your value by partnering in meeting design, preparation, setup, debrief, client relations, promotion of services, etc. Facilitators, tap into the depth of your graphic recorder's skills.
- Invest yourselves in being a seamlessly united team focused on helping the client solve their problem and achieve their goals.
- Invest the time early in your partnership to talk about what professionalism means to both of you. Share your expectations of each other openly and stay focused on bringing those things to the table for the benefit of the client.
- Ask each other for feedback regularly. Debrief meetings and take note of what worked really well and what could be better next time.
- Spend time together outside of the meeting. Actually get to know and care about each other.
- Continually expand your repertoire of facilitation processes.
- Pool your knowledge to give yourselves the greatest spectrum of choices.
- Be open to each other's suggestions. Don't get too attached to your own ideas or let your ego get in the way. Stay focused on what will work best for the uniqueness of your group.
- Get good at articulating the ways that visuals enhance a meeting and the added value created by having two practitioners in a room.

CLIENTS/CONSUMERS

- Educate yourself on the range of things you want to consider when hiring a graphic recorder. No two are the same.
- Expect graphic recording to be integrated into your meeting process, not just a sideshow happening in the room.
- Where possible, invest some time and thought into formulating written objectives for your meeting before you engage a consultant/facilitator.
- Expect to be a participant in a collaborative meeting design.
- Stay open to new ways of conducting a meeting. Test and then trust your consultant/facilitator team's expertise.
- Focus on how graphic recording is enhancing the dynamics of the discussion (process), and not just on the visual products themselves.

ROBERT MITTMAN is a solo practitioner in his company, Facilitation|Foresight|Strategy, which he formed in 2002. He is primarily a strategist/thinking partner with his clients. He is dedicated to the belief that the group has its own genius and it's our role to elicit that genius. Robert has taken graphic recording training, so he is uniquely equipped to think about meeting conversations in layouts and anticipate the needs of his graphic recorder partners.

LISA ARORA is a seasoned graphic facilitator and graphic recorder who uses these skills on a wide range of management consulting projects with organizations all over the world. The rich, engaging communication experiences Lisa and associates of Get The Picture provide result in highly productive dialog, shared understanding, alignment, and high-quality decisions.

Lisa is dedicated to the idea that visual meetings must be well designed to integrate visuals in the process as thinking tools. She's written 3 "How To" eGuides on the topic (available at www.getthepicture.ca). As a lead facilitator herself, Lisa is uniquely equipped in the graphic recorder role to listen and filter information like a facilitator and anticipate the needs of her facilitator partners. Currently Lisa is pioneering the field of private visual mediation. Find out more about how you can work with Lisa at www.getthepicture.ca

Sensemaking through Arts-Infused, Person-Centered Planning Processes

Aaron Johannes

Sensemaking has been a useful concept to bring to planning for people with (or without) disabilities, team building, and other projects. As a mode of being, it involves intentionally listening for clarifying questions and directions. From these, diverse groups create "future forming" plans and the skilled person-centered planning facilitator uses processes that can be (after years of practice) as light as a feather. Simple person-centered planning processes can be used by amateurs and professionals in the places where people live and life happens. Each event changes the world just a little and shapes a future that welcomes diversity.

I had no idea what I was getting into when I took the job with an organization that had made person-centered planning central to all its work. I'd heard about Planning Alternative Tomorrows with Hope (PATH) as a planning tool, and it sounded great. The kinds of planning processes I was used to involved stacks of papers, forms to fill out, and a bunch of

professionals telling people how they could live. In contrast, the PATH process involved identifying the dream, locating what was "positive and possible" within a given timeframe, and then moving from what was happening now through a sequence of questions. These questions were: who might be involved, how everyone would stay strong enough to accomplish these goals, some first steps to take right away, and then a step-by-step action plan. It was simple, elegant, and visual—the whole thing was created in pictures and words. It invited participation and created spaces for dreaming in the lives of people who had not been allowed to make decisions, much less dream and hope for an enviable life.

I would have my own PATH as part of my learning, to feel the vulnerability of the process. I invited over friends and with our desserts perched on our knees we sat and watched my life appear in simple graphics. The facilitators led us through the steps, listening for glimpses of the future, asking questions, inviting my friends and family to speak. At one point we had to pretend to be in a time machine and then "remember" how we'd gotten to the successful places we had envisioned just half an hour before. In those memories sometimes I could hear the potential, and other times something in the plan didn't ring true: "No, that never happened." "Okay, then what did happen?"

A week later I was flying from mountain to mountain in northern British Columbia, meeting up with families, sharing great food and celebrations of their communities, and drawing their conversations on big sheets of paper, facilitated by a person-centered planning guru, Linda Perry. I'd aced art school—lots of awards, lots of scholarships, lots of coddling—but I'd never drawn in front of people like these: plumbers, miners, loggers, dads, moms, siblings, coming together after work and gathering to dream with someone with a disability who had captured their hearts.

Listening to the stories of a young nonverbal woman who had almost died, again and again, and used a wheelchair to get around in a mountaintop community, I was amazed at how well they knew her and how certain they were of her dreams and their shared dreams—and I was also just having fun drawing. When they talked about her going swimming, I drew David Hockney pools, and when they talked about her love of dressing up I went all Holbein. She was in a supported skiing group, so I got into portraying some Turneresque slaloming. When it was done, everyone was thrilled—this graphic plan represented her (and those who cared about her) in a way that deficit-based, bureaucracy-centered planning never had.

Her grandfather came over as I packed up. "We appreciate this so much," he said. "That you would come here, into our home—and with our family and friends make her... dreams... come alive for us." He waved at the drawing. He sniffled. I beamed. I was good at this. I might have been waiting for this. He nodded and said, "Especially that you're willing to stand up in front of all these strangers—my goodness...." I shrugged, humbly. "I could never do this... I mean, just look at it—you can't even draw a real person and it was just so brave for you to try, in front of strangers!" I blinked. "It made us feel like we were part of it all as we watched! If you could really draw we would have just felt left out!"

I started laughing—I'd been surrounded by people who loved everything I did, for a long time, in classes and in galleries where my work hung behind glass, already judged by some curator as special and significant. But this was what I'd always wanted out of art and never been able to identify: a dialog. I was smitten in that unexpected moment. Twenty years later I can remember those first drawings exactly, and I continue to be just as fascinated by these planning processes.

Deborah Ancona of M.I.T. says that sensemaking "refers to how we structure the unknown so as to be able to act in it … coming up with a plausible understanding—a map—of a shifting world; testing this map with others through data collection, action, and conversation; and then refining, or abandoning, the map depending on how credible it is" (2012). I work with various kinds of groups, visually mapping what's credible within constantly shifting dynamics, and their responses lead us towards different "truths" which become potential plans—does this look like what you want? Does this seem possible? Like something everyone can work on together? The graphic mirrors the dynamics of the people in the room, and plans rendered to their essential parts in simple graphics become the visualization of a changed world.

In another meeting, Brent, a young fellow with autism, is sitting at the center of a circle of about 20 people who care about him. He's got his family, some of their friends, people from his school, people who have supported him from every period of his life, including when he was a toddler, and they've all been invited in to dream of what his adulthood might be. I've been warned he hates meetings and he came in glowering at me, but now he's grinning, hugging, delighted to be here with people who love him and snacks he likes!

He doesn't speak in ways we expect. He's decided to trade in his voice for a xylophone and now he plays songs. In the old days we might have ticked off "voluntary mutism" on a form and left it at that. He plays along with his boombox to three songs he's lined up to introduce this topic of planning his adult life, but when the second song is done, he suddenly shakes his head "no," goes to the boombox, and then plays this Elvis Costello song, instead of whatever he had intended:

Oh it's not easy to resist temptation
Walking around looking like a figment of somebody else's imagination
Taking ev'ry word she says just like an open invitation
But the power of persuasion is no match for anticipation
Like a finger running down a seam
From a whisper to a scream
So I whisper and I scream
But don't get me wrong
Please don't leave me waitin' too long
Waitin' too long
Waitin' too long
Waitin' too long
Hey
Oh oh oh oh oh (Costello, 1981)

He hits the keys with perfect timing and most of those who care about him have tears running down their faces. When he's done, his mom says, a little shakily, "Thank you for coming out to support 'Brent's Big Dream'—now I want you to meet Aaron." And I begin to draw...

The "purpose-driven life" that they describe includes going to university, being part of his community, doing varied work, being with animals, and playing music. I sketch the life that is already partly happening, and also the part that hasn't yet been clear. As one mom said, "In this process we are creating the future we want by leaning into this vision as we create it."

I am drawing as fast as I can, trying to keep up with the accruing vision of his friends and family—a job, music school, friends, communication, safeguards, an apartment, a roommate. Three typical kids who have shared inclusive classrooms with him for most of his life have come tonight to propose that they share a place together. "Why not?" they ask. I am drawing apartments, parks, musical instruments, a dog—someone stops me. He doesn't like big dogs, only small dogs. I use a sticky label to cover up the big dog and draw a smaller one. Brent smiles and nods. He's been heard. Other corrections come fast and furious—the boys don't want to live on the tree-lined suburban street I've drawn them, they want to live downtown. The trees become street lamps and buildings. His parents frown a little, but stay brave. They'll get behind whatever he really wants and this is obviously it.

It all means he will not attend the small local college they planned for, but the bigger urban university. Given a clearer vision, they're happy to let go. I draw Brent in the big city. Ideas are hurtling across the room at me, people are laughing, their voices soaring, coming together in a kind of web of hope that catches me up. Brent is laughing too: his life is looking amazing.

Sometimes I am surprised to see what I've drawn when it is done. I am not the only one. Brent, expected to stay for a maximum of 20 minutes, three hours later is still grinning and nodding and high-fiving his friends.

In how many situations are we given the gift of spending time talking about a kind of heartbeat life—music, people, connections, meaning? These are the kinds of icons I get to work with:

And when people have agreed that this kind of icon can represent them, we arrive at a PATH that looks something like this:

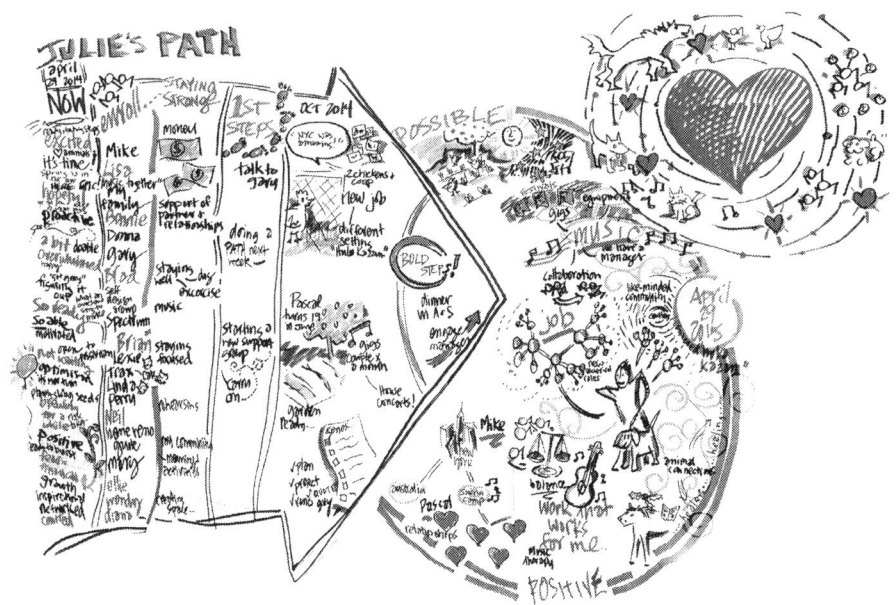

A year later, I run into Julie, who does not have a disability but has been stuck for a while, without clear aspirations. Since we last saw her, she's quit her job, she's created a different role in her community, she's got more animals, and she's part of two bands, both playing lots of gigs. As people do, she wants to report back on the progress of the vision we shared that day. We often are gifted with calls from people we've planned with to tell us where they are in these newly clarified plans.

PATH was invented by Marsha Forrest, Jack Pearpoint, and John O'Brien in the 70s (Sanderson, 2000). As with many transformational discoveries for people with disabilities, PATH comes out of the work of Inclusion Press (www.inclusion.com). It was one of the early alternatives to the kind of planning that was happening in special education and services—planning driven by professionals, filling out pre-determined forms using "specialist" language embedded in rigid roles. The role families and folks with disabilities had been given was to passively attend as professionals worked through a number of domains by tallying up at what was problematic in each one. In comparison, PATH was a sequence of open ended questions that assumed everyone in the room—including the person with the disability—had input that mattered.

The originators of PATH wondered: What might happen if people were encouraged to dream? If there were ways to record their dreams which everyone could see and understand (no matter what their literacy levels) and ways to plan to get from where they were to where they wanted to be?

PATH is almost always co-facilitated with a graphic recorder and a facilitator and is designed to be a simple process that amateurs can use (amateurs—from *amat*, to love).

Begin with a dream: A PATH starts with the facilitation of the person's (or group's or project's) dream: what does it look like? If you could have anything—no holds barred—who would be there? Where would it be? What would surround it? How would it feel?

Looking back from a future time: The facilitator then moves to the "positive" and "possible" section. Sometimes we do a quick guided meditation about taking a time machine into the future and looking

back on what dreams we've accomplished in a given time (say, two years). While the dream section might have included things that seem impossible—someone who can only move one finger wants to work and be self-supporting—in this section things must be doable. Within two years what might be accomplished towards this dream? The person might "remember" (from their future time machine) that they got a part-time job. Questions to deepen this might include: Who would they be working with? What kinds of things might they be doing? Someone in the group remembers that their church needs someone to staple the newsletters each week—it only takes one finger… Possibilities accrue and each question, each detail, builds a picture of a desirable future.

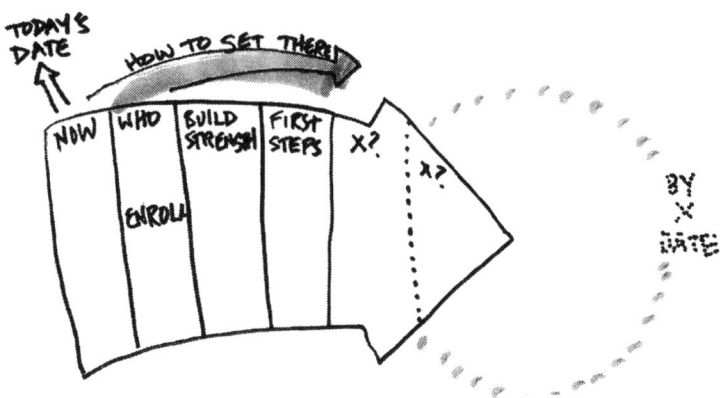

NOW: We move down to the "NOW" section—how are things right now? What feelings are people having? For Brent's family, speaking out of their knowledge of him, there was excitement about the future that felt even more "positive and possible" given the full house of all the people who responded to the invitation to his meeting – this act of planning for the future is in itself an act of creating that future by bringing these people together.

WHO: Social constructionist Kenneth Gergen writes,

> ... virtually all intelligible action is born, sustained, and/or extinguished within the ongoing process of relationship... [and] there is no isolated self or fully private experience. Rather, we exist in a world of co-constitution. We are always already emerging from relationship; we cannot step out of relationship; even in our most private moments we are never alone. (Gergen, 2009)

When I am teaching the idea of "theory" to college students I start here. The "theory" of capitalism is that we are individuals, alone, competitive, responsible only for ourselves; the theory of social constructionism as defined by Gergen and his colleagues is that we are each part of a network of relationships. A PATH is an opportunity to invite those others in, often for the first time, and welcome them to take roles in people's lives. Person-centered planning activates our tribes.

Building strength: As we look at the emerging PATH graphic it becomes clear that a new picture of a possible future that matters is happening before our eyes. We are looking at real "positive and possible" change. Gergen has recently written about "future forming research" and this is a small domestic example of that larger idea.

Step by step: The first of these is "first steps"—what few things might we do in the next week or so that will lead us into this future? After this, things are broken down into manageable chunks—it might be four months, or six, or even a year. The idea is to create the milestones for the emerging plan, as if one is looking back from the viewpoint of having accomplished those goals.

In these sessions, which can be a few hours long, new relationships are formed, and old relationships are transformed. A new future is depicted,

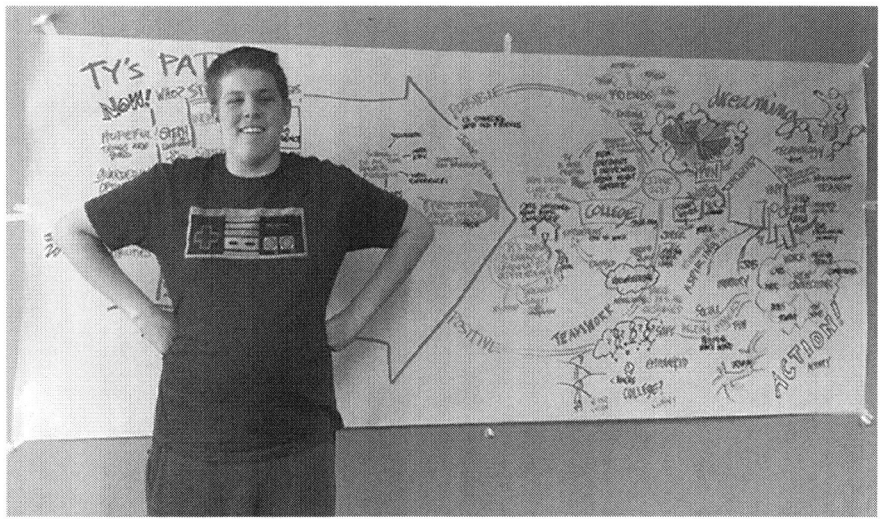

and it is one that the person (with their network) can visualize with the help of graphics and facilitation.

What had seemed impossibly ambitious becomes, somehow, possible. A few years ago, Liz, a woman with Down syndrome learning to facilitate PATH in one of our workshops, ended up facilitating a PATH for me. I began talking about my work-life and she put up her hand and said, "Stop: Let's come back work later if we need to." So I started talking about holidays I hadn't been able to take, art galleries and countries and cities I hadn't been able to see yet… we never did talk about work. And, over the next 24 months I went to 11 different countries, took 18 holidays with people I loved (using up all my vacation time for the first time in decades) and saw thousands of works of art.

While it was my ambition to travel the world, in the PATHs of people with disabilities we realize that our assumptions of what our lives can be like—that we're going to work and have jobs and relationships, for example—are not true for everyone. What we think of as a given wealth of choices is really a privilege. Thus, a PATH, for one person and their network, becomes an emancipatory action—part of a political movement that clarifies, on the wall of someone's home, with people who care about them, that we might become more equal, in just a few steps. The insanity of supports that do not allow for choices about where people live, who they live with, where they spend their days, and who supports them becomes evident, and radicalizing. PATH is part of a social transformation movement.

Sometimes I imagine all these wall-sized drawings layered over each other and coming together in a kind of infinite collage of possibilities that create a kind of chorus, demanding systems and governments to change and foster a transformed and welcoming world for us all.

AARON JOHANNES, Director of Spectrum Consulting Collaborative, partners with people of all kinds to provide workshops and community based research and is an instructor with Douglas College's Child, Family and Community Studies faculty, where he is constantly amazed by the students. His MA is in Integrated Studies in Equity and Education and he is a PhD candidate with the Taos Institute / Vrije Universiteit Brussel, researching what works best to support marginalized people in leadership. Facilitating planning for people, teams, and projects, problem solving through dialogs, graphic facilitation, and world cafes are some favorite activities. Tweet me at @imagineacircle, visit www.imagineacircle.com, or email ajohannes@me.com. All graphics are licensed under creative commons and may be shared, unaltered, for non-commercial purposes with attribution unless they feature other persons than myself.

To learn more about PATH check out www.inclusion.com for books and tools.

Dancineering, Researchals, Bodystorming, and Informances

Movement-based approaches to sensemaking and transmediation through contemporary dance

Christopher Knowlton

I started dancing while studying engineering as an undergraduate, which led me to ask: Can we understand the body the way we understand engineering and science? After all, isn't the body just another physical system, governed by the same rules as the rest of the universe? After plenty of "no"s, I found an enthusiastic "yes": a burgeoning field called bioengineering. After graduating, I moved to Chicago to pursue a PhD in biomechanics and to research orthopedic joint replacements. Thanks to Chicago's terrific dance scene, I kept performing as a freelance dancer and creating my own work. But I never thought I'd merge the two fields. Here's my exploration of movement-based sensemaking through contemporary dance.

Dancineering

Two years into my studies, my dancer and scientist friends alike bombarded me with a link to John Bohannon's brilliant 2011 TED talk *Dance vs. PowerPoint, a modest proposal*.[1] In it, he suggests that speakers could abandon slideshow presentations as visual aids and replace them with dancers, while the stunning yet simple collaborative choreography of professional dance company Black Label Movement swirls around him to demonstrate precisely this point. Having sat through years of tedious lectures and an equal number of frivolous performances, this choreographed talk affected me like few before—and obviously appealed to people in both fields. The talk mentioned a contest called Dance Your PhD, an international competition run by *Science Magazine* that asks PhD students in science-related fields to explain their thesis to a broad audience through a dance film. I eagerly took up the challenge.

After assembling a cast from a collective of dancers known as The Dance Team, we got to work in the studio. I briefly summarized my thesis, let the cast ask questions, and then described a different aspect in more detail to each dancer. I pointed out specific words I found important and let each person independently build a movement phrase based on that information. After about ten minutes, I would circle around to each dancer, observing, asking how they were understanding what they were doing, answering questions, soliciting feedback, or suggesting movement and edits. Toward the end of rehearsal, we taught phrases to the entire group that we felt had solidified. This is a fairly standard contemporary dance approach for collaboratively generating choreography through improvisation, simply adapted to the subject matter of my thesis.

I encouraged them to disregard familiar dance aesthetics for something more demonstrative, matter-of-fact, and straightforward. In fact, my dancers laughed when they caught me praising them by saying, "That's effective." At the time, I only knew I wasn't looking for "good" or "pleasing"; I was looking for useful and communicative. We had three rehearsals, each two and a half hours long, before filming the entire work in six hours on the final week. Taking cues from John Bohannon's talk, I scripted subtitles that would more precisely frame the choreography to guide the viewer's understanding. Though the final film utilizes many cuts, we intentionally choreographed the dance so that it could be performed live, with one or more of the dancers speaking the subtitles.

Our film *Multiactivity Wear Testing of Total Knee Replacements* became a finalist in the 2012 Dance Your PhD contest and can be viewed on Vimeo.[2]

Researchals

Not long after finalists were announced, we were invited to perform at the 2013 TEDxWindyCity talks in Chicago. I proposed that instead of my thesis, we would summarize every speaker's idea in one live performance. If we could make a dance about the mechanical testing of orthopedic implants, why not these subjects?

Unlike my thesis, I was not intimately familiar with these topics, and I certainly was never going to become an expert in microeconomics, gender studies, education, entrepreneurship, environmentalism, photography, and more within a few months. But I didn't need to become an expert; we had set out to help make these speaker's ideas more accessible to the broader public. I met with each speaker to hear them informally explain their work and to ask my questions. All the while, I paid special attention to the gestures and imagery they used. I often asked what a given idea looked like or what an abstract concept felt like. Mostly, I tried not to let learning get in the way of understanding.

Concurrently, my dancers and I worked in the studio, in what they fondly began calling "researchals." I assigned two topics to each dancer and provided them with speakers' blurbs, bios, videos, conversation notes, and the internet. After they studied for a while on their own, I answered their questions as best I could and relayed what else I knew. Using different colors, I asked them to highlight words or short phrases that 1) helped them understand, 2) they could see or do, and 3) resonated emotionally. Once they felt able, I had each dancer explain their topics to another dancer, encouraging them to physicalize the gestures and images they had encountered while learning. These conversations led to the dancers discovering parallels between vastly disparate topics, either between some mechanism of two systems or between the imagery used to portray them. One example of this can be seen on the following page. In one talk, graphic facilitator Brandy Agerbeck drew stacked lines to represent the inundation of linear textual information that we experience daily. A video for another talk showed workers stacking boards in a warehouse as Elise Zelechowski of Rebuilding Exchange described diverting useful resources from landfills.

Photo courtesy Pivotal Productions

Photo courtesy Pivotal Productions

Photo courtesy Rebuilding Exchange

With the simple action of stacking dancers on top of each other, we embodied the constant streams of texts, the accumulation of waste, and the sense of overwhelm and unsustainability from each. We were at once language, materials, feelings, and people. This is the power of abstract contemporary dance performance: the ability to have multiple meanings simultaneously. We found these moments crucial in delivering a high density of easily understandable information, as the final performance would have to transition chronologically and cohesively from talk to talk.

In 12 researchals of two or three hours each, we repeated the process of transmediation that we had discovered for Dance Your PhD by translating the ideas on the page into movement phrases in order to realize our live performance. We again framed the choreography with a script, spoken by a live orator, and used costume colors to help the audience demarcate our transitions between topics. A film of 10 *Talks in 10 Minutes Through Dance* is available on YouTube.[3]

Three months later, we were invited to produce a new, similar performance for the Illinois Art Council's 2013 One State Together in the Arts, a biennial state-wide arts conference modeled on the TED format in Moline, IL. A film of this performance is available on Vimeo.[4]

Bodystorming

Unbeknownst to us at the time, the methods and choreographic tools that we had been playing with in the studio for transmediating ideas bear some striking resemblances to an emergent practice in the mobile design world known as "bodystorming." As a juxtaposed complement to brainstorming, bodystorming asks that designers of technological solutions (i.e. mobile devices, apps, and ubiquitous computing systems) observe or embody the user experience in a setting similar to the one in which it will be used.[5] Trust me, the irony of using an embodied practice to develop a disembodying product is not lost on me. However, the three modes of bodystorming described in literature are thought to reinvigorate the creative process in many ways. By being there (so-called "design in place" or brainstorming "in the wild"), designers can better understand the nuanced contextual factors where people might use their technology.[6] Bodystorming also allows for rapid implementation of rudimentary versions of ideas ("prototype in place" or "strong prototyping") that can provide immediate and insightful feedback in a way that a studio/office setting cannot.[7,5] Finally, experiences can be simulated, investigated, evaluated, and communicated by instructing end-user representative, role-playing designers, trained actors, and even children with a simple prompt, scenario, or narrative and allowing the "scene" to play out ("embodied performance," "use-case theater," or "experience prototyping," depending on whom one asks). Overall, bodystorming is thought to provide a more directly observable and explorable problem space, help prevent ideation and groupthink, facilitate rapid group communication and consensus, elicit tacit knowledge of the problem, provide immediate feedback of ideas, improve empathy, and create a memorable and productive experience for all participants, all of which may spark new ideas that were perhaps undiscoverable through traditional brainstorming.[8]

As a dancer, it is apparent to me that these experiential methods hinge on limiting one's reliance on symbolic language and encouraging exploration, play, and improvisation—all of which are experiential, enactive approaches to cognition. Not coincidentally, exploration, play, and improvisation are the tenets of contemporary dance. By choosing to step back from verbal and graphical representations in the process of bodystorming, we may discover the following:

1. Freed cognitive resources that would otherwise be spent decoding and maintaining constructed language. Researching TEDxWindyCity took significantly more time outside of the studio, since technical jargon familiar to each presenter—such as "graphic facilitation," "resource streams," and "silos in inefficient markets"—were unfamiliar to us.
2. Tacit knowledge that provides insight to the material at hand. Once my dancers were armed with preliminary information, they continually synthesized information and discovered new connections between sources that had not been made before.
3. Multiple simultaneous meanings that can change in time and according to context. Dancers stacking themselves became lines of text, building materials, people in these systems, and the emotions of those involved.

4. High bandwidth of information by communicating and experiencing through multiple layered, dynamic contexts. We used movement, gesture, body shape, spatial relationship, facial expression, narration, costuming, color, sound, voice, and setting concurrently in order to convey all 10 presenter's ideas in 10 minutes. In comparison, each presenter was allotted 20 minutes to explain their idea with the aid of a slideshow presentation.
5. Intimacy and empathy with the information being conveyed. My dancers and I were surprised by a standing ovation and a number of audience members who said they cried or became emotional during the performance.

Informances

Our performances for Dance Your PhD, TEDx and One State are hardly novel. The Dance Your PhD competition is inspired by Stanford University's *A Protein Primer*, a 1971 dance film that describes protein synthesis.[9] In 2006, professional company Liz Lerman Dance Exchange explored genetics in their breathtaking *Ferocious Beauty: Genome*, collaborating with scientists in the field. As mentioned, our performances emulated a 2011 TEDx performance by John Bohannon and Black Label Movement, who collaborated again in 2012 for the impassioned TED-Ed Original *Let's talk about sex*.[10] The mobile design world has also coined a term for these types of presentations: "informances"—informative performances.[8]

While we had made our informances to educate specific audiences, I had overlooked how quickly my dancers were understanding complex subjects. Black Label Movement had similar findings from *The Moving Cell Project*, a collaborative effort with bioengineer David Odde. By providing professional dancers with a set of rules governing their movements, the group was able to rapidly prototype, explore, and troubleshoot proposed models of diffusion, microtubule catastrophe, and macromolecular crowding.[11] Moreover, they found that when abstract concepts were put into concrete physical terms, the dancers easily understood them. This suggests a high degree of untapped potential for learning through embodied practices. As one dance researcher wrote, "exponents of contemporary dance epitomize cognition that is multimodal, embodied and distributed."[12]

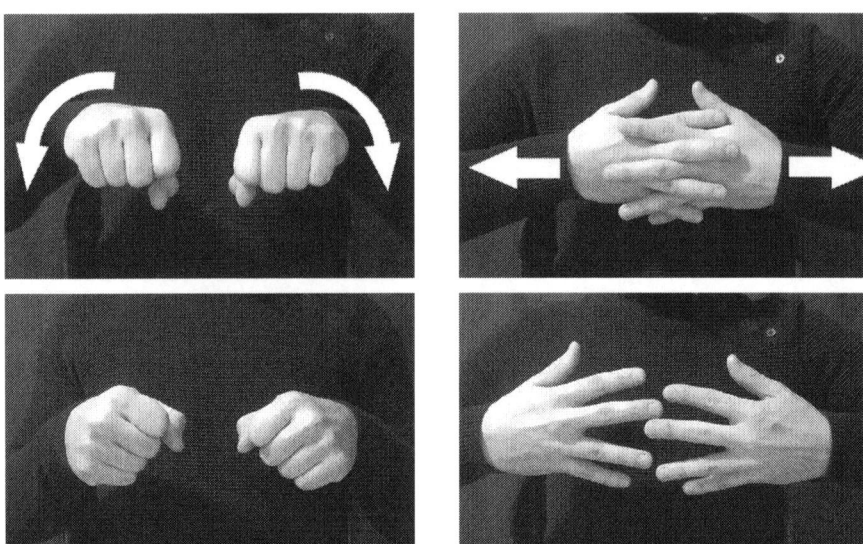

Which hand gesture best helps you understand how chemical bonds break?

Consider the chemical process of "breaking a bond." When you say the word "break," you are likely to make a hand gesture similar to snapping a pencil, as seen in the images above, on the left. "Dissociation" better describes the process, but like most scientific terminology, the word is cryptic and cumbersome. However, the process can intuitively and more accurately be demonstrated by interlacing your fingers and pulling your hands apart, as seen in the images on the right. Why? Like all symbolic language, "break" is simply a metaphor referencing something in the real world. A physical medium like movement is better suited to represent a physical phenomenon.

Even this type of small-scale arts integration could have profound effects on education, especially for students who gravitate towards enactive modes of learning. As the dearth of enrollment in STEM fields (science, technology, engineering, and mathematics) consistently makes headlines, initiatives to reinvigorate interest by integrating the arts into STEM to form STEAM—excuse the pun—gaining steam. Despite these fields producing the most exciting, life-changing, and ubiquitously available innovations in the last several decades, students consistently describe STEM fields as "boring" and "difficult." I believe dance is uniquely suited to reduce barriers to participation and understanding, help the public realize the creative potential in these fields, and continue to drive innovation.

Imagine a dance company in residence at a science museum. The group could bodystorm the subject matter of exhibits to create public informances that augment otherwise static installations. Additional interactive workshops and hands-on experiences would improve understanding, participation, and engagement. Their movement expertise could help collaboratively develop movement-responsive exhibits using motion-sensing devices such as Microsoft Kinect. The studio itself could be put on display as a fishbowl exhibit of contemporary dance and the creative process. Performances and workshops could function as outreach education in the form of "traveling exhibits" to institutions which have limited or no access to the museum. In doing so, the company could learn more about barriers in science education, share best practices among teachers, and develop a movement-focused arts integration training for educators. As Carl Flink wrote, "a future science classroom might look more like a dance studio or gymnasium."[11] Ultimately, I feel the need to invert my initial question and ask: Can we understand science and engineering the way we understand the body? Based on our work so far, I firmly believe we can.

CHRISTOPHER KNOWLTON is a PhD candidate in Bioengineering at the University of Illinois at Chicago and currently researches orthopedic joint replacements at Rush University Medical Center. Chris is also a professional choreographer and movement artist. The dance work herein was created collaboratively with The Dance Team, a rotating pick-up collective of Chicago-based dancers. Email: chrisknowlton@gmail.com. Copyright © 2016

References

1. John Bohannon and Black Label Movement. 2011. *Dance vs. PowerPoint, a modest proposal*. TEDxBrussels, filmed Nov 2012. www.ted.com/talks/john_bohannon_dance_vs_powerpoint_a_modest_proposal
2. The Dance Team. 2012. *Multiactivity Wear Testing of Total Knee Replacements by Christopher Knowlton*. Dance Your PhD 2012. www.vimeo.com/50507963
3. The Dance Team. 2013. *10 Talks in 10 Minutes Through Dance*. Performed and filmed at the TEDxWindyCity, Feb 23, 2013 in Chicago, IL. www.youtube.com/watch?v=cJPHzIgA6Qc
4. The Dance Team. 2013. *The Dance Team at One State Together In the Arts 2013*. Performed and filmed June 25, 2013 in Moline, IL. www.vimeo.com/130515499
5. Smith, B. K. (2014). *Bodystorming mobile learning experiences*. TechTrends, 58(1), 71-76.
6. Oulasvirta, A., Kurvinen, E., & Kankainen, T. (2003). Understanding contexts by being there: case studies in bodystorming. *Personal and ubiquitous computing*, 7(2), 125-134.
7. Schleicher, D., Jones, P., & Kachur, O. (2010). Bodystorming as embodied designing. *Interactions*, 17(6), 47-51.
8. Burns, C., Dishman, E., Verplank, W., & Lassiter, B. (1994, April). Actors, hairdos & videotape—informance design. *Conference companion on Human factors in computing systems* (pp. 119-120). ACM.
9. *A Protein Primer*. Directed by Robert Alan Weiss, 1971. Department of Chemistry of Stanford University. www.youtube.com/watch?v=u9dhOoiCLww (Uploaded on Jun 6, 2006, retrieved Jan 1, 2016.)
10. John Bohannon and Black Label Movement. 2012. *Let's talk about sex*. TED-Ed Originals. ed.ted.com/lessons/let-s-talk-about-sex-john-bohannon-and-black-label-movement (Published on Dec 3, 2012, retrieved Jan 1, 2016.)
11. Flink, C., & Odde, D. J. (2012). Science+ dance= bodystorming. *Trends in cell biology*, 22(12), 613-616.
12. Stevens, C. J., & Leach, J. (2015). Bodystorming: effects of collaboration and familiarity on improvising contemporary dance. *Cognitive processing*, 16(1), 403-407.

Stories and Storytelling

Anthony Weeks

On the first day of my Documentary Methods class in film school, the professor wrote a word in big letters on the board: PROFLUENCE. I had never heard the word before. Profluence, in brief, is about flow. It means movement, tension, propulsion, unexpected twists, and resolution. All good stories, whether narrative or documentary, are profluent because they create an experience of starting somewhere, and by the end of the story we arrive somewhere else. We are moved. Profluence is the narrative connective tissue that transforms moments into scenes, scenes into acts, acts into stories, and stories into connections.

In 2005, I was seven years into my career as a professional graphic facilitator. While I had built up a respectable cross-industry, international practice and developed both my business acumen and graphic skills, I was not happy. I had lost the newcomer's zeal for experimentation, play, and fun.

As I became more professional, I bargained away my fresh-eyed naïveté for the joyless rigidity of "this is the way I work," "this is the way I draw _____, no matter what the context or content," and "this is my style and this is how my stuff looks." I felt stale, uncreative, and stuck.

I needed to step out of my professional life and immerse myself completely in another creative pursuit. A fortuitous glance at an ad in a San Francisco free weekly newspaper revealed my opportunity: "Documentary Media Studies: The New School in New York announces a new graduate-level certificate program, beginning in Fall 2006. Applications now accepted."

That is how I ended up in that classroom. The notion of profluence changed my life. Once the meaning became apparent to me, I began to see movement, connection, and story in beautiful, disturbing, curious, and unpredictable ways.

My sabbatical, intended to be a temporary, one-year immersion at the New School, stretched into three years. I couldn't get the documentary thing out of my system. While I took an occasional graphic facilitation gig to stanch the hemorrhaging from my bank account, I began to think seriously about a career change to "filmmaker." I enrolled in the MFA program at Stanford in documentary film and video. I reveled in the pursuit of story. I made films about an unemployed Mexican immigrant who saw the Virgin Mary in a rock and built a shrine to it in his garage; a Chinese hotel housekeeper who ruminated about the family she left behind as she changed sheets and scrubbed toilets in a San Francisco boutique hotel; actors with disabilities in Hollywood who scrambled for bit parts while their able-bodied counterparts won awards and accolades for playing characters with disabilities. Individual lives, mostly unrevealed and invisible. In every film, there was the question: Where is the profluence?

How do stories *become* stories, though, not just data points? How do they move? Where do they go? Who cares? Is the artifact of meaning the film itself—or the way that it makes people think and feel after it is over?

As a newly-minted Stanford MFA, my transition into work was rough. Documentary film is a competitive business—and a potentially impoverishing one. The "occasional" graphic facilitation gigs became more frequent, yet my re-entry into graphic facilitation was fraught with feelings of failure and resignation. What was this whole madcap filmmaking escapade about if I was just back doing what I was doing before?

While becoming reacquainted with former clients and collaborating with new ones, I discovered that my graphic facilitation work looked different. It felt different. I worked differently. Perhaps I had learned something, after all.

Whereas my work circa 2005 had been a collection of aesthetically pleasant scattergrams, replete with bullet points and orphaned icons and text, my new work unfolded in flows, currents, arcs, arrows, dotted lines, and pathways. I asked new questions: Who is the protagonist here? Who is going to do all these bullet-pointed items? Who will be glad about it? Who will hate it? What are the bumps in the road? How is all of this going to be memorable and repeatable? Who is the audience? Why should anyone *care*?

This professional and creative reboot that began in 2006 finally made sense when I ordered new business cards. Struggling to find the right descriptors for my services offered, I ended up with a too-long list: "Graphic facilitator. Illustrator. Process consultant. Filmmaker. Producer. Information designer…" Frustrated, I deleted everything and just wrote:

"Anthony Weeks. Storyteller."

This fit me. The word "storyteller" elegantly encompassed the services I could competently offer while sending a signal to the people with whom I hoped to collaborate. Now I was less interested in being the quiet scribe on the side (or in the back), furiously scratching away in an effort to capture every word. I wanted to be a partner in helping groups to think about moments as building blocks of stories. Connect the dots. Discover intellectual and emotional resonance. Tell a story that felt like a story, not just a collection of disparate data points. Reveal the profluence.

While we know that good stories have value for engagement and connection, we still harbor skepticism about the idea that stories have currency. They might be frivolous. Or too personal. They might be—gasp!—emotional. We are daunted by story because we still hold on to the notion that stories, somehow, cannot possibly be as rich with content and data as a spreadsheet or a PowerPoint presentation. We are afraid of our own subjectivity. We are afraid of the sound of our own voices.

Discovering our own voices requires deep and intentional listening—to ourselves and to others. Storytelling necessarily depends on *storylistening* because stories derive their meaning in their re-telling. Both storytelling and storylistening invite the exchange of experience, the awkward yet skillful dance of faithful interpretation, honorable subjectivity, and graceful authenticity.

Our subjectivity as storytellers and storylisteners *is* our calling card, our differentiator, our way of creating value. For facilitators, graphic recorders, and visual storytellers, no matter how quiet, unobtrusive, faithful, and seemingly clear our respective channels, we are always making choices: what we include, how we write it, where we put it on the page, the juxtapositions of chunks of content, the graphics we draw, the colors we use, the size of the paper, our position in the room, and the ways in which the graphics are (or aren't) used in the facilitation. Objectivity is a myth.

I question our role. Is our charge to "capture information" or to liberate stories?

"Capturing information" is problematic. To me, the capture of information seems like closure and restriction of possibility. If we hew closely to the notion that our primary role is to just write down what people say, we become glorified note-takers—and thus, easily replaceable. Information capture is a phone book, a grocery list, or a video clip of a soccer game. We know, though, that a phone book is not a novel, the recitation of a grocery list is not a soliloquy, and video footage of a children's soccer game is not a film. It is context and meaning that transform our work into an experience and a narrative.

Our subjectivity as storytellers and storylisteners is not the problem. It is our strength, our virtuosity, and our ability to embody humanness. Those qualities are irreplaceable.

As I experiment and grapple with making story an integral part of my work, I am reminded of the words of media psychologist Dr. Pamela Rutledge:

> Stories are how we think. They are how we make meaning of life. Call them schemes, scripts, cognitive maps, mental models, metaphors, or narratives. Stories are how we explain how things work, how we make decisions, how we justify our decisions, how we persuade others, how we understand our

place in the world, create our identities, and define and teach social values.[1]

Isn't this how we value and legitimize our role as facilitators, process designers, and graphic recorders? We are in the room with teams who are talking about things that are important to them. Our marks on the page are not for entertainment. We believe in the power of understanding how things work, the value of making good decisions, and the translation of decisions into meaningful action that will hopefully change the world. Our role is to help groups accomplish those very noble and crucial objectives. Telling good stories—and listening well to stories—is essential.

The International Forum of Visual Practitioners conference in Austin in 2015 set me on a path of inquiry about the deeper practice of storytelling and storylistening. I met people from all over the world who were doing gorgeous work with beautiful colors, impeccable calligraphy, and ingenious graphics. While humbled and inspired, I noticed the conversations tended to center on the aesthetic value of our work, not the listening value.

After the conference, I pursued the discussion online in the Graphic Facilitation Facebook group by asking, "Pretty chart… but how did you *listen* in this particular conversation?" Amidst the vague and inchoate responses, the question remained: "Are we doing all we can to be good storytellers and storylisteners?"

I asked myself, "Who do I know who *listens*?" I began to compile a robust list from my networks. Psychotherapists, 911 dispatchers, clergypeople, investigators, judges, musicians, conductors, ASL interpreters, marine bioacousticians, doctors, HR specialists, futurists and forecasters, historians, and museum curators. I knew a lot of listeners.

After I asked people in my network ,"Who do you know who listens?", the list grew longer. I began interviewing these people. Each session began with three simple questions: "How do you listen in your work? How did you learn to listen that way? How does listening matter in the work you do?"

My research thus far has been rewarding and surprising. I'm discovering a variety of qualitatively different listening styles. Once I learned how others approach listening, I began to realize I needed additional information about the context, purpose, and intention of my own listening. Merely saying "I listen" was no longer sufficient.

Take my interviews with Larry and Shannon, for example. Larry is an emergency response dispatcher while Shannon is a psychotherapist in private practice. When I began reviewing the first transcripts, I began to tingle all over. Through their wisdom and experience, I heard a vocabulary and taxonomy around listening begin to emerge.

Initially, Larry offered multiple disclaimers about his lack of suitability as an interview subject for my project: "I'm not a good listener! I'm a terrible listener. Even my wife doesn't think I'm a good listener!"

When we finally spoke by phone, Larry issued his protest once again.

"Okay, okay," I said. "You've told me that. Tell me how you *do* listen in your work."

What he described was a methodical and efficient process of asking questions about the emergency, the current location and status of the caller, the urgency of the need for response, the resources (if any) already at hand, and the type of response that would be most appropriate and helpful.

"I'm not a therapist," Larry laughed. "I don't get into a lot of history stuff, and I'm not interested in all the other things in their lives that might be going wrong. I just don't have the time to get into it. I do try to calm them down, though, and stay calm myself. Otherwise, I won't get the information that I need in order to respond. It's a transaction, really."

Transactional listening.

"I don't think the people who call you would want you to be a therapist," I offered. "It sounds like you have some pretty specific filters in place for how you listen."

Larry and I arrived at the epiphany at the same time. Transactional listening is still listening—and useful listening, at that. In Larry's case, this type of listening—specific and goal-oriented, relying on filters and prescribed intentions—might literally mean life or death.

"Ha!" Larry said triumphantly. "I *am* a good listener, then. How about that? I can't wait to tell my wife that I'm a good listener... maybe just not to her."

In the early 1990s, Shannon and I were both on the therapy staff at a small Minneapolis non-profit serving survivors and perpetrators of domestic violence. While my path led me to facilitation and visual storytelling, Shannon continued to work with survivors of trauma and pursued a doctorate in clinical psychology. She maintains a private practice, consults with agencies and organizations, and teaches psychology graduate students.

When I asked Shannon, "How do you listen in your work?", she paused for a few moments before saying, "Sometimes, the listening *is* the work."

When I asked her to explain, she offered an insightful observation about her work with survivors. "Often, people who have been traumatized are isolated, have few social resources and connections, and have been disbelieved by family, institutions, and service providers. They are conditioned over time to understand that speaking out leads to further traumatization, abuse, and marginalization. As a result, being *listened* to is therapeutic unto itself, even if there is not a stated 'therapy goal.'"

"I don't start out by asking people what their goals are," Shannon said. "Sometimes, they don't know. Sometimes, they just need to talk and be listened to. They're so used to being shut down and told that they are crazy that they haven't experienced being listened to in an open and non-judgmental way. Eventually, we may surface some needs that they'd like to address in more depth. Initially, though, a lot of my clients' primary need is to be listened to, heard, validated, understood. I listen to what they have to say and stay present with them so they know it matters."

Open. Non-judgmental. Validation. Being present. What do we call this kind of powerful listening? I would call Shannon's style *empathic listening*. It is the creation of a space and forum where the listening itself is the priority while goals and objectives are deferred. Empathic listening is not "efficient." Listening for the sake of listening would likely make a task-centered meeting facilitator or a goal-oriented executive go absolutely mad. Moreover, empathic listening, as Shannon practices it, is exactly the wrong kind of listening for the time- and need-sensitive work Larry does.

As I continue my exploration, more modes of listening emerge. Forest, a marine biologist, studies the sounds of tiny shrimp and crab footfalls in order to assess the health of coral reefs. His listening is data-rich, populated with millions of data points from which the story emerges. It's quantifiable, data-informed. Systemic listening. Mike, the audio engineer, claims that listening to music in groups is one of the best ways of learning how to listen. This is social listening. The social experience of sharing a piece of music reveals new understanding and learning, based on the subjectivities of the individual listeners.

How do I listen?

I am a work in progress. In the past, I might have advertised myself as a versatile listener. "Yeah, I listen, and I draw out the key content points, quotes, questions, relationships between ideas, blah blah blah." Based on what I am learning, my listening is one type. It is selective. While my graphic facilitation clients are dazzled by the fact that I can listen, synthesize, write, and draw at the same time, sometimes I question how effective my listening is in the context of my work.

Personally, I despise being a transactional listener. You talk, I listen and "capture" every little bit of what you say. It's a day job, but it isn't what I am good at nor what I love to do. What I really love is this storylistening, most prominent in my work with scenario development groups, forecasting-for-strategy sessions, and conversations based on ethnography and user experience. When we are talking about emergence, disruption, discontinuous storylines, and points of divergence and convergence, I light up. I am both scared and excited because I don't know where my chart is going to go. I don't know how the next 60 minutes will unfold, much less the next 10 years!

This is when I turn around and ask the group: "Who are we talking about here? Who is the protagonist? What is the tension? What's the *story*?" If there is still some confusion, I might say, "Let's start with 'who cares?'" The listening becomes social, empathic, and open to unpredictability. If my charts in a discussion about the future of work look the same as those from a meeting about a civil rights educational program, I have missed my mark. Each is a story in its own right, revealed by a process of intentional listening best suited to the conversation at hand.

We need more models of storytelling and storylistening in our work. The field of graphic recording, graphic facilitation, and visual storytelling has become mature enough that simply picking up some markers and saying, "Okay, I'm going to listen and capture the conversation" is not good enough anymore. We must think more rigorously about *how* we listen. Are we transactional listeners? Empathic listeners? Systemic listeners? Social listeners?

Who are the storytellers and storylisteners you admire? What can you learn from their approach and experience? What do you bring back to your own listening practice?

As storytellers and storylisteners, how do we make our charts different from scattergrams of bullet points, with some nicely conceived but essentially inert graphics thrown in for good measure? A scattergram assures that you aptly captured the information. Still, it misses profluence, a sense of the story's flow. A story makes people feel something that they had not felt prior to the conversation. It reveals something, rather than capturing something.

When I approached Refugio (the worshipper of the Virgén de Guadalupe rock), Kitty (the immigrant housekeeper), and Diana (the actress with cerebral palsy) about making films about them, they all said, at one point or another, "Why do you want to make a film about me? I'm not that interesting." Just like Larry the emergency response dispatcher, Shannon the therapist, and most of the people I spoke with about listening.

Ultimately, they were all fascinating. More than that, they inspired me because their stories were so much more than I ever expected, and invariably, their stories were more fascinating *to them* than they ever expected, once we began the conversation.

Certainly, we can dutifully record what is said, be faithful to every letter and word, and maintain our dignified silence on the side of the room as we write, write, write away, with a picture or two for visual interest. At some point, though, there could be a breakthrough, a flash of recognition, a collective bolt of insight when we ask the simple question: "Yes, and what's the *story*?"

Are we capturing information and data or are we liberating stories?

This is the role of the storyteller and storylistener: to elevate the disparate moments, data points, and comments into something bigger. Every conversation, no matter how seemingly mundane and banal, contains a story—or a multitude of them—waiting to be revealed.

ANTHONY WEEKS After a masters degree in social work, an MFA in documentary filmmaking, and 18 years as a narrative facilitator and illustrator, Anthony Weeks decided to just call himself a storyteller and storylistener and leave it at that. He is based in San Francisco and travels globally to help others discover what "profluence" means.

Reference

1. Rutledge, P. "The Psychological Power of Storytelling," *Psychology Today*, 16 January 2011. www.psychologytoday.com/blog/positively-media/201101/the-psychological-power-storytelling (accessed 15 June 2016).

The Secret to Long-Term Impact in Your Engagements

Mary Alice Arthur

Every meeting—whether it is focused on business, community, action, or relationship—is predicated on hope. We are hoping for understanding or mutual agreement. We are coming for action or to create something together. We are longing for the resolution to a conflict or the easing of some need. Often, even with the greatest will and intention in the world, we are disappointed when nothing seems to come out of the time and effort we have invested. And sometimes, even when we sense that something significant has taken place, we are blind to the potential waiting for us. Something is missing in making the most of our time together.

Over more than 25 years of facilitating groups of all kinds I've grappled a lot with this myself. Why is it that sometimes action happens and sometimes nothing happens? Sometimes it seemed like all the reports or Post-It notes in the world didn't add up to the sparkling promise we seemed to see together. I began to realize that it didn't depend on leadership or a single person; it depended on what we could see *together*. Then, in 2007, I learned about the **Art of Hosting**,[1] which has a strong practice of creating ways to help people capture what they are learning and thinking about. Something clicked into place.

I found out that every meeting holds the potential for collective intelligence to create wiser action. The key to long-term impact lies in paying attention equally to what comes before, during, and after a meeting or event, and getting strategic about it. What is that special something that helps us to capture "the magic in the middle" that happens when groups discover something together? What is the practice that helps us to move from meeting to manifesting? The secret lies in *harvesting*.[2]

Harvesting and the art of hosting

The word "harvesting" was coined by the Art of Hosting network. *Hosting* is what we call the art of working with a group to support them through inquiry and emergence into the co-creative work that leads to focused results. Hosting and process design support participants to bring what they have in experience, worldview, expertise, and curiosity to the table. Good hosting is like the difference between carrying tea in a teapot and carrying it in a shallow saucer. Either way you are transporting tea, but if you trip, the tea stays in the teapot, but sloshes all over the floor from the saucer. A teapot just makes a better container in case of turbulence.

With a solid container, we can tease out our different ideas, stay together when new perspectives arise, and then create something helpful together. A well-hosted event supports people both to step into supportive relationship and be more effective in the tasks they want to undertake together.

All of this I knew from my background as a facilitator. What I learned about *harvesting* means I now take a totally different approach. Harvesting is more than reporting on or documenting the outcomes of a meeting; it is treating the things we uncover and experience together as the important puzzle pieces they are. Harvesting acts like a group's collective brain, creating both a group memory—which is valuable when you want to dive back into the stuff you worked on together—and a way of analyzing and synthesizing information to make new meaning. It is both a skill and a practice that supports and enhances the individual and collective sensemaking that leads to wiser action.

In a very real way, doing the work of synthesizing and sensemaking together makes a group into a community because they have created and are holding something together. It helps to make it possible to look for patterns, meaning, and actions that will help us move forward, and we become more committed to a collective future and our stake in it. Just think about the last time you had a challenging work experience, but made it through with the others and got results. Since you had to struggle together, you have ownership of what you created, and most likely a deeper relationship and a greater sense of responsibility for your results. You are prepared to do something because you grappled with it and you care about it. You've seen something together and now you have a collective meaning around it that gives energy to your actions.

Harvesting is a companion to hosting in the same way that the black and white halves make up the yin/yang symbol and it is a strategic asset in the healthy life of any group.

When I begin working with a group, I always ask first about the harvest. What is it we want to get out of this meeting, event, or initiative? I ask about the purpose, both in a tangible and an intangible sense. **How** we feel about the work we're doing and the results we want to achieve, the strength of relationship and trust we can create together, is equally important to the **what** we are creating together. As that very simple African proverb says, "If you want to go fast, go alone. If you want to go further, go together." But this "going together" is difficult if we don't know both **what** we want to do and **how** we want to do it. Discovering and understanding what we hold in common is the beauty of harvesting.

What is harvesting for?

At first glance, most of us in organizational, community, or group settings might be surprised with both the word and the concept of *harvest*; it seems to be a word

Maja Rotbøll works on a picture book to accompany the story of Denmark going bankrupt in 1813

that belongs with gardening or farming. My father was an amazing gardener and for most of my youth he had a big garden and produced embarrassingly many zucchini. I was too young to appreciate it at the time, but now I see how the work I'm doing with groups is similar to how a gardener needs to have an intention, be tuned into the growing cycle, and tend their patch well in order to produce what they planned for.

If you think about it, good harvesting makes good community and business sense too. After all, why have a meeting if you have no intention to produce something in the end? It might be something tangible, like an action plan or a strategy, or it might be intangible in the form of relationships, trust, or simply the goodwill to explore together and see what happens.

For me, the overall purposes of working like this are:

- To capture and illuminate collective achievements and results;
- To make collective knowledge visible, accessible, and useful;
- To give back energy to the group to continue working and to support keeping people together and resourceful in the face/space of complexity for the life of the project.[3]

A focus on harvesting also helps to:

- **Create the foundation for the work of the group.** What results do we want from this event, initiative, or meeting, both on the tangible and intangible levels? Our focus helps to indicate what group processes are needed to create the results we seek. Another way to think about this is: our harvesting *intention* helps to create the way we focus the group's *attention*. I've seen things dramatically shift when participants realized we were moving away from keynote speakers to keynote listeners, and they were being asked to become sensemakers themselves. The group paid attention in a different way, and showed greater ownership and commitment.
- **Remind those who participated what happened and what was achieved.** The harvest reflects both the process and results of the process. It makes the invisible visible. Sometimes people leave a meeting feeling really engaged and on fire, but quickly the fire dies down. When harvest comes in the form of videos or graphics or photos or the plan they created, they remember how they felt and the fire comes back. We need the emotion to help move us into action. I've especially noticed that when we uncover an important story or metaphor for a group, it keeps working for them and begins to uncover a more promising potential.
- **Help those who are important to us, but were not in the room, to support and come with us.** If we've been thoughtful and strategic about how we've included those who couldn't be there, they will be more likely to be able to come with us in the journey ahead. Many harvests I've been part of were intended to help important others to understand what happened and how we came to conclusions we did. We want to show them how they can be involved in the future.

First page of the "Pixie Book" created for the Denmark 1813 story

- **Leave a trail for those who come after.** Engagement and motivation depend on "line of sight"—being able to see how my work supports and enables our goals. Understanding the work that came before and the story you are part of builds a solid foundation for continued motivation. In one merger process I was part of, we had a summit with a representative group from the larger system. A graphic facilitator captured the story of the gathering. It was printed as an accordion card for each of the participants, who then went out and told the story of the meeting to all their colleagues. Enthusiasm spread like wildfire.

What form should a harvest take? That depends on what will serve the results you want to create and what is most meaningful to the group you are working with.

The harvesting cycle

Using the metaphor of gardening is a great way to understand the nature of harvesting. Every serious gardener is focused on a harvest. Whether it is food for the table, beauty for the eyes, profit for the pocket, or the regeneration of a place, the work a gardener does has a tangible goal—a gardener is planting for results.

Once a gardener has a result in mind, then he or she turns to preparation. The ground needs to be prepared, the seeds need to be planted in the right timing, and the garden needs to be tended during the growing season. The gardener works alongside the land they are tending, making an intervention when needed and responding to what emerges. Once the growing cycle is over, the results are picked and then the second phase of harvesting begins. Will the apples be eaten fresh or will they be turned into a pie, or applesauce, or apple juice? Will we keep the harvest for ourselves or share with a wider community? It all depends on what results we want to create.

The harvesting cycle has these steps:[4]

DESIGNING FOR HARVEST: BEGIN WITH THE END IN MIND

There are some main coordinates that offer focus and foundation for a good harvest:

1. **Need:** What is the real need and how compelling is it?
2. **Context:** What is the context we are working in (e.g. a school, a company, an NGO, a municipality, etc.)? Context determines tools, methods, and applications.
3. **Purpose:** What is the purpose of the event, process, or meeting?
4. **Deliverables:** What are the tangible and intangible results[5] needed to be able to move forward?
5. **Focus:** What harvest is needed by whom and when? Often there are multiple end users and they may need a different form of harvest in different timings. How will they be catered for?

Once these have been defined they become the sounding board for planning the harvesting process. A clear focus makes it easier to create a solid interface between process and harvesting.

STEPS:

- Get a clear picture of the purpose of the event, the participants, and what results are intended.
- Work with the caller[6] of the event to brainstorm a list of tangible and intangible harvest goals.
- In what form do the target audiences for this event—both participants and others—need to receive information before, during, and after for greatest impact?

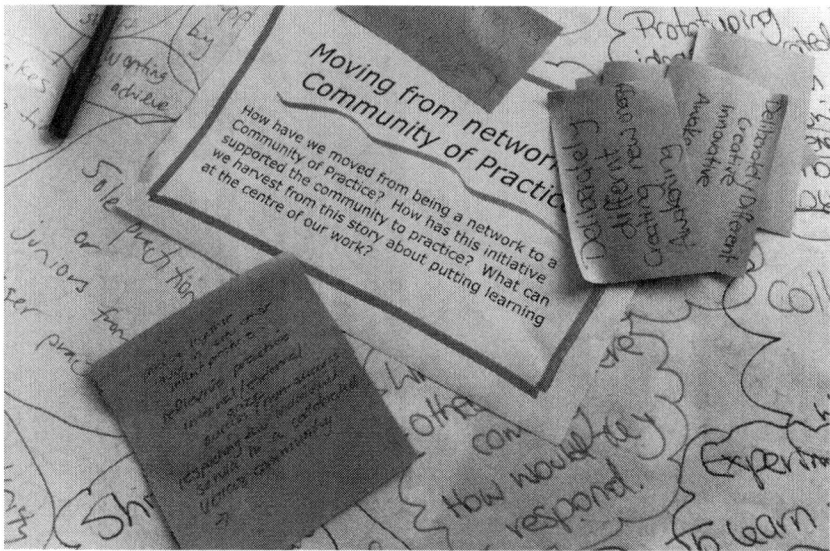

Results from a Collective Story Harvest for a children's initiative in Queensland, Australia—this was one of the listening arcs a team prepared

- What input needs to be gathered prior to the event? How do participants need to be invited so they arrive ready to participate?
- In what ways can the expertise/creativity of the group be focused during the event for sensemaking and further action?
- What audiences do you need to cater to? In what form will they need to receive the harvest?
- What is the timeline for delivering the harvest? What needs to be delivered when?
- What resources—in terms of people, skills/talents, materials, technology, etc.—are available for this project?

BEFORE THE EVENT: SET YOUR STRATEGY

Next comes the focus on creating the team and planning the elements of the harvest. Develop your harvesting strategy. Make sure harvesting is built into the process and that hosting and harvesting support each other well. Test your inquiry questions with your target audience. Think about how the team will work with the group and in the event space.

STEPS:
- Create a plan that includes a strategy around each harvest goal. What focus is needed to create the results you are after?

Part of the graphic harvest of a storytelling process

What resources are needed? Who might take responsibility for each part?
- Build the Harvesting Team and begin aligning the overall harvest plan and specific elements. Brief the team on the purpose of the event, the harvesting goals, and the participants.
- Work with the Hosting Team to create the process design and align how the group—and the harvesting team—will work to create the harvest. Is the Harvesting team part of the Hosting Team or working in the background of the event?
- What mediums will you use to deliver the harvest? What physical results are needed (report, document, newsletter)? What digital results are needed (website, photos, videos, Prezi/PowerPoint, SMS harvest, etc)? What graphic results are needed (visual recording, images, illustrations)?
- Create templates and source other materials needed. If you are supporting a new group, create a glossary so the team can smoothly harvest concepts and terms unique to this group or industry.

DURING THE EVENT: HOST THE HARVEST

Harvesting as a team gives you more ability both to capture the intended harvest and to be aware of emergent harvest. Create a clear harvest around each process (clustering, synthesizing, prioritizing, visuals) and wherever possible work with these to help inform the next stage of conversation. Where content matters, use templates or computer capture. Support the Harvesting Team to work seamlessly alongside the event and do as much harvesting work as possible during real time.

Visual or graphic recording can bring strategies to life and make it easier to stay focused as an initiative unfolds. It can be key in helping to flesh out the unfolding story of an event or initiative, making it easier for those who were there to share what happened with their colleagues or community members. Digital harvesting, in the form of interviews or event video, can help to give a feeling of what happened and reinforce key points. Harvest websites make it easy for geographically scattered groups to participate as an event is unfolding. Choose your media wisely.

Talk about how you will act on what emerges in the moment. Not everything can be planned for, so being present, awake and curious is the best strategy.

STEPS:

- Set up your harvesting space.
- Support the Harvesting Team to work with the plan you developed around harvesting. If this is a multi-day event, when and how often will you meet to check in with each other?
- At the same time, be open to what might emerge as a group goes to work and begins a conversation that will unfold over the course of the initiative.
- Find points in the event to bring the harvesting back in, demonstrating to participants their contributions have been heard and incorporated. Point out underlying patterns that are surfacing as the work continues.
- Find the balance of harvesting the content and the spirit of the event, as well as the amount of harvest.
- Continue to stay alongside the Hosting Team as the event continues, making sure the process and harvesting goals and plans are in alignment.
- Where possible, engage the stakeholders in making sense of their own harvest and invite them to help surface patterns.

AFTER THE EVENT: MOMENTUM FOR NEXT STEPS

As soon as possible once the event is finished, complete any outstanding harvest and distribute the results. Gather whoever will be involved in the next level of harvest and take a look at deeper patterns. Create the next level of sensemaking and action planning together. Implementing concrete results leads to the change that can impact a system or organization.

STEPS:

- Finish off the harvest artifacts and distribute to the target audiences.
- Once the event is over, bring a selected group together to sort through the harvest and look for deeper patterns and next steps.
- Feed forward what you've found out and see what next steps and next harvest opportunities arise.

> Many years ago I worked with the Information & Knowledge Management (IKM) Team at the Inland Revenue Department in New Zealand. The leadership team wanted both to be able to work well together and to establish their identity within the organization and within the much larger IT group. We decided to harvest a metaphor that could help both to orient their work as a team and to position them in the wider organization.
>
> We began by looking at the organization itself—what did it remind us of? In listening to our stories, we realized it was like a city made of islands connected by bridges—like Stockholm—where the bridges were the conduits for the flow of information. When the bridges broke down, or got jammed, areas of the city were effectively cut off from each other. We looked at all the parts that made up the system. The group agreed that they were not the bridges and didn't want to be the controller of the flow. Nor could the group expect that everyone wanted the burden of being forced to contribute. They needed to find a way to encourage all the little bits of information held by individuals to flow in continually, rather than depending on the slow flow of information through reports and the usual channels.
>
> In the end, the group realized that the IKM team needed to be a guiding hand. We began to see that it was like the editorial board of the Lonely Planet Guide (or in our case the "Plan-IT Guide". Notice how we got IT into the picture?), and everyone in the entire organization was, in fact, a reporter for the Lonely Plan-IT guide. And what was the potential for IKM? Just as you can either order the entire Lonely Planet guide for an area, or just the piece you are most interested in, data within the department needed to work the same way—just in time and just as you need it. The focus of our harvesting together enabled us to see a whole new way to position the IKM group.

The harvesting mindset

So how do you bring harvesting into a process where no one has ever heard about it? Harvesting is both a skill and a practice, so I take on many roles during an engagement[1,6]. At the outset, I act as a *consultant*, helping to set the foundation for the fusion of hosting and harvesting that will bring the best results. Next I am a *strategist*, helping people to see that what and how we choose to harvest are important strategic choices. I can also be the *host* of the harvesting process, tending the team of harvesters and the engagement of the wider participant field. And finally, of course I am a *harvester* too, helping to capture data and supporting the sensemaking process.

To build your practice, focus on some core capacities

One of the foundation stones is *listening*. To be a good harvester you have to be able to stay present and to listen on more than one level. Of course you have to be able to catch what is being spoken. But you also have to be attuned to the energy around what you're hearing and be alert to the deeper context underneath what you're hearing. Then there is the ability for *synthesis*—to be able to take in a variety of inputs and see how they fit together, offering it back to the group—"Is it like this?" A third element lies in *pattern recognition*—can you look over all that is being offered and see patterns showing up now in the group, those from the past, and those of the future?

Over the years I've really learned that harvesting is both the foundation for, and the fruition of, collective intelligence at work. It is the bridge between the conversation or inquiry we are in and the wiser action we want to create. If you want to make the most of your event—and create long-term results—make harvesting part of your plan from the start.

Ten questions to a great harvest
1. What is the purpose of the event or initiative?
2. What do you want to harvest and why? What are the tangible and intangible harvests you hope to create?
3. What resources do you have to create a harvest? What else do you need?
4. What processes might be most helpful to the harvest(s) you want?
5. Who is on the team? Who will harvest the hosting? Who will host the harvest? What other support is needed?
6. Who are the stakeholders?

7. What invitation will help people show up ready to participate?
8. How and when will the harvest be shared? What needs to be shared during the event? After?
9. What is the next level of harvest? Who will take part in the deeper sensemaking?
10. How will you stay together as a harvesting team to create the next level of meaningmaking and action?

MARY ALICE ARTHUR is a Story Activist, using Story to help make positive systemic shift and for applying collective intelligence to the critical issues of our times. Her art is in creating spaces where people can find the stories that take them to their most flourishing future. Building the capacity for participatory practice supports people to take back the power of their stories so they can make wiser choices. She is a sought after process consultant and event host, and an engaging speaker. As an international steward of the Art of Hosting she teaches participatory practice around the world. Through The Story Dojo, she is spreading the meme of Story Activism, supporting people to develop their skills and practice and engaging in leading edge conversations about the power and potential in our world. Contact her through www.getsoaring.com, also The Story Dojo Facebook page or The Story Dojo Vimeo channel.

References

1. From "Applied Practice Harvesting", Monica Nissén, 2015

   And appreciation to the Art of Hosting community, which continues to explore, develop and promote the joy and the art of harvesting. Thank you to all you practitioners out there continually moving the edge!
2. Properly "The Art of Hosting & Harvesting conversations and work that matter." www.artofhosting.org
3. From "Applied Practice Harvesting," Monica Nissén, 2015
4. Adapted from "Applied Practice Harvesting," Monica Nissén, 2015
5. Examples of tangible harvest:
   - Model an engaging way for people to work on their projects together and come up with an implementation plan
   - Create the next strategic plan
   - Set priorities for the coming year and make them highly visible in a graphic form
   - Produce a policy statement on community development

   Examples of intangible harvest:
   - Reawaken commitment to the organization's mission
   - Strengthen relationships and connections across functions, geography, and experience levels
   - Give people the sense that their contributions are valued, respected, and instrumental to moving forward
   - Offer a space for synergy, energy, and enthusiasm to be expressed
6. A "caller" is someone who is holding and naming an intention with a group of participants. Often a calling arrives in a compelling fashion—you cannot not do something. As a friend once said: "I thought somebody should do something about this until I realized my name is Somebody!" And it might be that as part of an organization you are tasked with creating an event. You have received this task from someone who is "the caller" and you would also be in the calling team

Using Perspectives to Build a Practice

Bryan Coffman

Fossils and facilitation

Next week I will facilitate 70 participants from a large organization through a process of discovering solutions to a thorny strategic challenge. Success will rely upon innovative thinking. I've done all the usual preparation—design, agenda building, logistics—but I'm also reading Donald Prothero's book *The Story of Life in 25 Fossils*. In particular, Chapter Seven captivates me. It briefly covers the emergence of plants from the seas onto the land. Understanding how this happened may be the most important preparation I can do for my upcoming session.

Why?

Reflecting on an article from a completely different domain forces me to make connections and uncover insights that would otherwise be impossible. I ask myself, "How does the emergence of plants onto the land 1.2 billion years ago relate to solving a thorny strategic challenge?" It turns out that the first life to colonize the land was likely in the form of symbiotic associations between algae and fungi. According to Prothero, the products of this association "served to help bind and stabilize the land against erosion by wind and rain, even as they helped marine algae and cyanobacteria pump more and more oxygen into the atmosphere." This is the kind of metaphor that I need to keep in mind for this session. Moving into new strategic territory may take a *symbiotic association* between unlikely groups, while in the meantime, the people and systems from the old strategy need to continue to *pump more oxygen into the atmosphere* because ultimately the oxygenation of the atmosphere enables all of the life that follows. I now have a principle—in metaphor—upon which to base my practice and thinking next week.

This kind of reflection and combination has informed my practice as an illustrator as well.

Before I was a facilitator I was a real-time illustrator, or scribe. I'd listen to people talk and build diagrams in real time that showed their ideas and the relationships between them. I also undertook more conventional illustration projects where I would work with a client over a period of days or weeks to build a visual model of their ideas to help them gain insight into, and communicate, complex or sensitive concepts. Later on I took up the practice of facilitating events where groups of people designed solutions to complex problems. I ran the three practices in parallel for many years. Today I'm mostly a facilitator, but illustration is still a significant part of my personal design process.

Using perspectives to build our practice

At the level of a lifetime of work, combinations of perspectives shape one's entire practice. A new discovery often emerges by reflecting on the intersection of two themes, two disciplines, or two perspectives. Creativity and personal growth both rely on exploring such combinations. While drawing, one may experience this discovery by combining different colors or using different media together, like markers and pan pastels. Or the artist may combine a visual metaphor like a river, with a topic of discussion like the trajectory of a company's history, to provide insights about how the company experienced dangerous competitive rapids or meandered through periods lazy market dominance.

The visual practitioner may also find inspiration to guide their work from other, completely unrelated domains. In my case these domains included geology, engineering, cartography, painting from the imagination, the 4,000-year-old strategy game of Go, the field of pattern recognition, the mathematical principle of recursion, and cybernetics, among others. I've summarized their influence here.

Perspective 1: Engineering and problem solving

I started this work in 1984. At that time, we visual practitioners called ourselves scribes. I was working for Matt and Gail Taylor at the Acacia Group in Washington, D.C. In the small Radiant Room that served as a plenary for our DesignShops, or collaborative events, there was a long expanse of marker boards at the front of the room and a shorter one set on the left side at right angles to it. The other scribe on our team templated the main wall with bridges, dragons, or other visual themes. The participants copied key ideas from their breakout group areas onto designated spaces on that wall. During the reports from each breakout group and the conversations that followed, I listened and drew a synthesis—a visual set of insights and conclusions—on the shorter wall.

Since the main board already held a visual representation of the content from the breakouts, I was freed from the need to capture what was said. Instead, I made sketches to help me understand the whole system that the participants were talking about. I had studied geological engineering and systems engineering in college. Engineers use diagrams to map out and solve problems. I was taught to clearly state what variable I was trying to solve for, list the givens and assumptions, and then to draw a diagram that showed the elements and their relationships to one another. The diagram would help me understand how the system worked—what forces were at play and where. Once I understood the system, I could solve the problem. I used this diagramming technique as a scribe to depict future visions, plans, the interplay of conflicting forces, the flow of information, and the relationships between departments.

Perspective 2: Recursion

In addition to scribing, I sometimes offered a walkthrough of my ideas to the participants following the reports and conversation. Great value may lie in affording scribes the opportunity to explain their work to the group live, either immediately after capture or at the end of a block of work. Most participants in a collaborative session appreciate the illustrations that scribes create, but if you ask participants to describe the content and meaning of the art, they often find it difficult. A brief description or guided tour helps.

Following the DesignShop I often authored an analysis of my illustrations for distribution to the participants. This forced me to review and iterate my work in more depth. Part of the review was technical, focusing on improving my drawing ability, and part was concerned with understanding the content and searching for deeper insights that might help the reader. This twin practice of describing the work to the participants and then generating a follow-up document provided the opportunity for valuable self-reflection and input from others—insights that I folded and hammered back into my practice and work over and over like the Japanese swordsmith folds and hammers steel while forging a sword.

Perspective 3: Requisite complexity

Around that same time, I spent a day with Jim Channon. Jim was a former Army officer, visionary, storyteller, and illustrator. He had an ability to clearly convey very complex ideas on paper, but not by simplifying them. His brand of illustration invited the viewer into exploring the complexity of an idea. One or more visual principles anchored each drawing and everything else was organized around those principles. The organizing principle might be a circle, or a 3D arrow leading off into the future, or the inside wall of a vast cylinder etched with interacting elements of a new organizational structure. He used this approach to convey the relationships between elements that collectively formed a complex, multi-dimensional whole. Successive images in a storyboard allowed him to move the viewer laterally, deeper, or up to a higher vantage point within the same universe.

Much like an architect of the day would create a roll of blueprints illustrating all the many facets of a design, Jim could create and manage a complete set of blueprints for complex ideas. This was a mind-blowing metaphor for me. I had been drawing ideas as sets of relationships among visual actors (words, glyphs, or larger visual structures). Now I knew I could hunt for a visual organizing principle and then assemble all of its component elements within and around it without losing the viewer. Layering became part of my pattern language. By using the visual organizing principle, I could embrace more complexity on the marker board or page. Most of the problems clients face are incredibly complex. Finding a way to express the complexity requisite for insight often trumps simplification.

Perspective 4: Mapping

During a summer job as an intern geologist I had used well log data to map the sub-surface geology of a gas storage field in eastern Colorado. Gas was leaking out of the field somewhere under the surface. In order to solve the problem, I had to jump back 150 million years or so and create a map of the Mesozoic landscape as it appeared then. This allowed me to trace the meandering paths of the rivers that would later become the sandstone that held the gas my company was storing. I used this map to determine that our gas field was leaking where the ancient river had been breached by flood waters carrying sand, which then connected to a subsequent river system that cut into it millions of years later. The gas was therefore leaking into an adjacent field that our company did not own. Armed with a portfolio of maps drawn from many perspectives and time periods, I was able to see the problem and outline a solution.

Interlude: Synthesis and the organizing principle

I began to slowly build a synthesis for my practice. I combined my problem-solving and mapping experiences in engineering with a recursive approach to analyzing and improving my work. On top of this I added Jim Channon's complexity-embracing style of idea mapping and visual storytelling. The map became the primary metaphor for my work. A map allows me to display complexity in two, three, and four dimensions (by adding change over time) without losing applicability. It also could be used as a problem-solving tool.

When I shared a few drawing tips with participants in sessions I sometimes tipped a marker board over on the ground, inviting them to think that they were uncovering a landscape of their ideas viewed from the sky, currently shrouded by clouds, but ready for exploration. This jolted them out of recollections of drawing on a marker board in a classroom at school or a conference room at work. Ideation became revelation instead of genesis, peeling back layers of obscurity to reveal what had been there all along.

In addition, I recognized the need to find and apply an organizing principle to my drawings. This principle could be visual, like a set of concentric circles, or it could be a theme crafted from words. It could be a metaphor, like that of a river, where each feature relates to one of the speaker's ideas. Tributaries might show how several ideas joined to become one. Towns or villages along the river might represent major turning points. The organizing principle provides a vehicle for the arrangement and connection of most or all of the other elements of the drawing. Note that organizing principles don't have to be patterns; they can also be key words, or the use of key colors. Whatever helps the viewer to make sense of the composition.

Perspective 5: Thumbnails from imagination

I took a painting workshop at Idyllwild Arts Summer Program from Max Grover, an accomplished author and illustrator of children's books. He taught us to work creatively from our imagination and rapidly express these ideas with acrylics on paper. For each exercise, we selected a theme and drew several small thumbnail sketches in pencil. Each thumbnail suggested a different treatment of the theme. Then we transferred aspects of one or more thumbnails to the final painting using acrylics. The whole process might take an hour or two.

Up to this point, most art classes I had taken presented me with a physical subject to study and then asked me to capture what I saw using some medium (like watercolor paints) on some surface (like canvas or paper). This was a very different process from the scribing I was used to, where the subject consisted of a flow of words from one or more speakers. Scribing is an aural process more than it is a visual process. The speaker's words in the moment inform an internal process of creating mental images that the scribe attempts to transcribe. I don't scribe the speaker's words. I scribe my thoughts about his or her words. Finding the time to study the flow of speech is not possible.

In Max's class, where thought was the subject, I honed my skill of thinking in thumbnails. I began to see scribing as a multi-layered set of thumbnails captured through observation of a dynamic subject residing fleetingly in thought.

Perspective 6: Creative tension

I learned another valuable lesson from Max. He told our class that the first brush stroke on the paper creates a problem. Once all the problems are solved, the painting is finished. For me, the first stroke began the dance between hearing, insight, and expression. Sometimes these flowed together like currents in a river and other times they wrestled with each other in creative tension. Maybe my insight couldn't find proper expression, or what I heard challenged my insight. Often the tension emerged as a feeling that something was missing. Or maybe a shadowy organizing principle that could connect many different elements of the composition eluded my grasp. This sense of tension may lead either to frustration or curiosity. Curiosity enables exploration that solves the problem. But it took me years to embrace this.

Perspective 7: Pattern

In the 1990s I learned to play the rudiments of the game of Go—Igo as it's called in Japan, or Weiqi as it is known in China where it originated. It's very easy to learn, but mastery requires superhuman dedication and talent. Western chess mimics warfare, but Go is a game of market share. Capturing the opponent's pieces is not the primary goal. Instead, during the course of play, the black and white stones build patterns across the board. Where the relationship between the different colored stones is unstable or undetermined, ownership of the territory is in question and the pattern is fluid. Where the relationship is determined, the pattern settles. When all of the unstable relationships are resolved, the game concludes and the final pattern has emerged. Either black or white has won. Good players develop the ability to recognize and build winning patterns.

Scribing isn't quite the zero sum game that Go is, but pattern recognition plays a role. Scribes use certain images or patterns over and over. They recognize patterns in the way that speakers work through a topic (one year the recurring theme might be innovation, and the next it might be customer centricity). They learn that certain images or visual structures communicate better than others. For instance, most scribes have used a light bulb as a stand-in for "ideas." Or a causal loop motif to show the mutual influence that several forces have on one another. Or a tree structure to show the branching of ideas. Or a storyboard set up as a series of boxes. Many patterns are small in size or limited in scope, but patterns that dominate an entire drawing are a form of the organizing principle that I mentioned earlier.

Conclusion: Building a framework

I don't stand in front of a group and actively call each of these perspectives to mind when I scribe. Like many other scribes, I tend to enter a state of flow while drawing. A landscape *unfolds*, influenced by the speaker's words. However, once or twice while scribing I feel a thrill when I *consciously* uncover an organizing principle around which I can construct a map. Or I step back and try to *consciously* understand how a whole system works and then draw that. Once the insight is attained, though, I'm back in the flow.

In the late 1990s I was a partner with Jay Smethurst in Sente Corporation and we began to create a synthesis of our thinking. We viewed real-time illustration as a combination of actors, relationships, frames, and annotations. The actors and relationships formed the core of the work much like nouns and verbs in grammar. Actors were the ideas that emerged, expressed as pictures or words. Relationships connected actors with one another, represented directly by lines, proximity, color, visual interaction, or some other technique. Frames provided the visual sectioning or emphasis of larger sets of actors that shared a common theme. Framing could also be done using lines, color, or shading. Or it could simply emerge as a part of the composition without any specific delineation. Finally, annotations comprised the textual descriptions, labels, and comments required to clarify the diagram for the viewer.

This taxonomy was general enough to support application of the seven perspectives I described above. On top of them all lay the organizing principle—that word, theme, image, or shape that could knit everything together.

BRYAN COFFMAN · USING PERSPECTIVES TO BUILD A PRACTICE

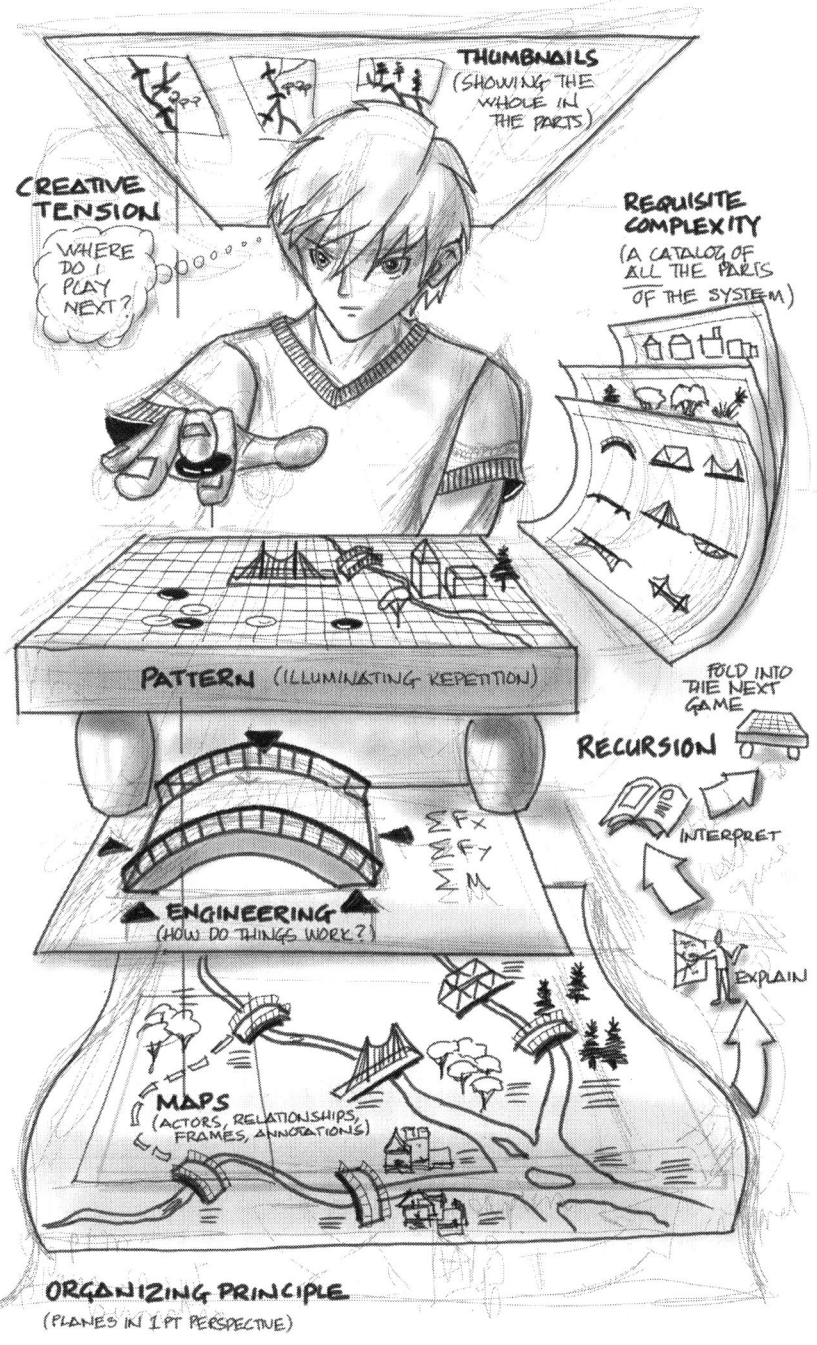

Synergy

The behavior of the whole is not predicted by the behavior of the parts. I've always liked that definition of synergy. The shorthand version that reads, "1 + 1 > 2" doesn't quite capture the excitement or uncertainty experienced in the presence of synergy. Combining the seven perspectives led to an unpredicted expression of this work across my career. They became more valuable to me as a collection than they were individually. Mapmaking and creating thumbnails overlapped in interesting ways. Embracing complexity while looking for patterns kept the work clear without oversimplification. Acknowledging creative tension made problem-solving fun, even when performed in front of a live audience.

Employing the perspectives involved study. A casual transference of ideas from one perspective to the practice never cut it. It took effort to get deep enough into a subject to discover that at its source lay a valuable connection to every other subject and therefore to my practice. I sensed intuitively that scribing was like mapmaking, but to create value from the connection required practice in making maps as a geologist, an activity apart from scribing.

No doubt the reader can list the perspectives that have served them in their career and note the synergy between them. But what new perspectives should you or I learn that will lead to greater insights and abilities? What subjects should we study? What activities should we pursue? Should we simply allow them to emerge from life without intention at all? And how do we fold these back recursively into our respective practices?

BRYAN COFFMAN is a Director in the Experience Center at PricewaterhouseCoopers LLC, where he currently practices as an architect of multi-day co-creation experiences. Prior to joining PwC he was a partner at Sente Corporation and InnovationLabs where he practiced as an illustrator, real-time scribe, and facilitator. Before that he was a knowledge worker with MG Taylor, an application developer, a geological engineer, a video producer, and a combat engineer. Variety may be the spice of life, but in Bryan's case it's been more of a main course. He has practiced yoga and meditation for many years. He shares boundless curiosity in common with cats and a tendency to be distracted by squirrels in common with dogs. He currently lives in Orlando, Florida with his wonderful wife, Lida, who is the inspiration for everything good that he does.

Cultivating Cultural Safety

The visual practitioner's role in motivating positive action

Sam Bradd

I'm a graphic facilitator, and I want to plant a seed for other non-Indigenous practitioners who work with First Nations, Métis, and Inuit communities. The seed is *Cultural Safety*. Cultural Safety means that I work in a particular kind of way—with Cultural Humility—when I work with Indigenous people and others who are different from me.

Many visual practitioners work cross-culturally, and it's never been more timely to grow our collective skills together around an issue that is complex, challenging, and also deeply rewarding. Visual Practitioners use our considerable visual and facilitation skills to create—and see!—a more profound level of behavioral, interpersonal, and structural change. For these reasons, I believe Cultural Safety is an emerging core competency for visual practitioners.

Let me tell you a story. Participants' hearts are tender after a workshop on Cultural Safety from an Indigenous-specific perspective. I've just finished graphic recording this workshop and a white, middle-aged nurse approaches me and my drawings at the front of the room. After workshops that explore the inequities that First Nations people experience from mainstream society, I feel like I'm a magnet for people to spill their guts. She says,

> "One night, late in the emergency room, I was the nurse on duty. An Aboriginal man was slurring his words. I figured he was drunk. But it turned out he was a stroke survivor. I chalked it up to a mistake and brushed it off. And now I feel ashamed. Where did I learn that?"

The nurse is looking directly at me, with urgency. So we talk. I point to a small part of my larger image and say, "We're all on this learning journey. We make mistakes but we have to try." I feel her discomfort, but shame and guilt only take us so far. I invite her to take three steps to the left with me. Now we stand before a giant interactive wall where participants are writing their "Commitments to Cultural Safety" in their health work. Offering my markers, I say, "Do you have a small action you can take today?"

She says, "no, I don't." It might be three steps, but some people feel resistance in going from reflection to action. So we read some of the other statements together.

And finally she says, "I do have something. The next time my colleague says something about 'those people,' I'm going to speak up." And she grabbed a purple Sharpie and wrote her commitment in big letters on the wall. And then she underlined it. I felt something shift in that moment.

Like with many moments of transformation, it's not the *what* that changes us. It's the *how*. Getting her to take those three steps towards her own commitment wall took a very long 10 minutes. It also takes two lifetimes—because transformation starts with me, too.

Planting a seed for cultural safety and humility

Recently, I graphically recorded four health events in seven days. Three Indigenous health events referenced the impacts of Residential School and separation from culture as a current social determinant of health. The fourth event, about province-wide seniors' health, made no mention of Indigenous patients at all. Afterwards, I wanted to put all the people in one room to show the gaps in who and what we're talking about.

Using graphic facilitation is an opportunity to learn about First Nations cultures, different ways of facilitating meetings, and the richness that visuals can bring to group conversations. I listen for stories of resilience, success, and ways to connect to culture: illustration can model holistic ways of knowing in powerful ways, better than a linear list. Graphic facilitation can create an environment that encourages dialog and helps people explore difficult issues that a more "traditional" meeting may not be able to probe. Indigenous community members, leaders, and clients have commented that graphic facilitation approaches connect to the rich oral and artistic traditions of First Nations cultures, and that this art-based approach is an effective way of supporting traditional ways of meeting and talking together.

Guiding the work: A national agenda for reconciliation

It's an important time to consider my context. I'm writing from Canada, as a non-Indigenous, specifically White, graphic facilitator located on the traditional, ancestral, and unceded Musqueam, Tsleil-Waututh and Squamish Territories (Vancouver, British Columbia). In 2015, Canada closed the Truth and Reconciliation Canada Commission (TRC) and provided 94 recommendations, many related to health and education. This was a national process to address the impact and legacies of the Indian Residential School era. This opportunity for national soul-searching enables us to see what else is connected – the inherent right of Indigenous self-government, honoring treaties, restoring education, child welfare and wellness systems, dismantling unjust funding models – and take action.

The journey of cultural safety and cultural humility starts with self reflection

Graphic facilitators can use our whole selves in service of cultural safety. There are moments where we can't rely on drawing tokenistic concepts of "multiculturalism" or "diversity." Instead, we can draw from a deeper, more informed place. As a start, we can enlist our heads, hearts, and hands to support this work. I'll use this structure of heads, hearts, and hands to outline a non-comprehensive set of tools that have helped me.

The head: Understanding context

Understand history. Keep learning. Celebrate strong, diverse, and vibrant Indigenous cultures.

Cultural safety asks us to examine our own cultural identities; it doesn't ask us for the impossible task of understanding everyone else's cultures.

In order to support a group in building cultural safety, I have to see myself as part of—and not separate from—the journey of cultural safety as well.

My work starts before I arrive in the room. Even though I know race is socially constructed (that there is no scientific basis for racial differences), I know that race and Indigenous-specific racism shapes people's lives. Cultural humility helps me question the textbooks that taught me the winners and losers of history, and helps me understand Canada's colonial history and how my family has benefited from laws and Indigenous-specific racism. By this re-learning, I uncover what shapes my worldview.

Suggested tool: Historical research

The Truth and Reconciliation Commission report is an excellent place to start reading (or listening—you can find people reading the TRC report on YouTube videos). Indigenous-specific racism is not about "unintentional harm." Visual practitioners don't intend to draw the wrong thing. In the same way, health care workers don't intend to create inequalities in health outcomes for Indigenous and other racialized people, yet Indigenous people die sooner. Further, discrimination is clearly a part of our systems, with a legacy of inequalities ranging from the Indian Act to clean water. The Truth and Reconciliation Commission report connects these systems. Cultural safety asks us to examine our own cultural identities; it doesn't ask us for the impossible task of understanding everyone else's cultures. I know I will never understand every indigenous culture, so working with a sense of humility, I bring to the work an open mind. This makes me aware of how much I don't know. However, there is a wealth of knowledge to be learned: there are over 600 First Nations in Canada with unique histories and experiences. Remember to research what is to be celebrated, along with learning past injustices: these are strong, vibrant, and diverse cultures despite the intentional efforts of colonialism and racism.

The heart: The role of emotion and empathy in this work

Be aware of what triggers me emotionally. Build my own resilience. Define my role in the room. Show stories of success, not just trauma. Be humble.

Graphic recording intense stories and histories requires empathy. My colleague Kelvy Bird wrote to me that "the work we do is not emotional, but generates emotion in us and others, and involves accessing empathy through it all." Developing empathetic listening and relational skills as part of cultural safety is more important than a new set of icons.

> The work we do is not emotional, but generates emotion in us and others, and involves accessing empathy through it all.

It's important that I am not swept up in strong emotions that pull me out of the meeting and into my own inner world. The first time I heard an elder tell me about their traumatic experience in Indian Residential School while I was working, I froze. I knew the histories—but how could I make art that did this justice? I needed to come back to center quickly, because my role was to make images, and capture her story, not mine. The key is building my own resilience.

An approach that keeps cultural safety to the forefront is to introduce myself in a culturally respectful manner where I describe where I am from and acknowledge whose territory we are meeting on and thank my hosts. This builds relationships based in the processes of cultural humility, and believe the graphic facilitator holds an ascribed position of authority in the room, similar to any instructor or facilitator. Working live, I can explain that I can make adjustments to the posters as needed, and confirm with keynote presenters one-on-one about the way I've captured their words. Contractually, I ensure that First Nations organizations retain ownership/copyright of the images, using the principles of OCAP™: Ownership, Control, Access and Possession.

Engaging with participants while self-reflecting about visual processes is a praxis: it can lead to more questions, which lead to new, better approaches to the work. Participants may experience legitimate doubts about raising "concerns" with the graphics—they might feel their feedback would "ruin the pretty picture," they may know race or culture is visualized incorrectly but are unsure how to "fix it," especially around a sensitive issue such as race. Therefore, the responsibility is up to me to actively check with participants about their experiences: I can create the safety for people to approach me. While doing studio work and developing imagery, I often ask my clients if we can directly engage community feedback via elders, an advisory group, or an informal network, and I am open to feedback during all stages of creating illustrations.

Suggested tools: Build capacity for respect, and find ways to stay grounded

When I work from a place of empathy, it gives me joy. There are as many ways to build empathy as there are people. We can build empathy toward others by being honest about our own culture, and strive for open-mindedness through cultural humility to learn, honor, and respect other cultures. We can demonstrate empathy in our actions: giving people our full listening focus, or being attuned to body language. We can nurture our spiritual selves so we arrive to our work balanced, and have the capacity to build even more empathy. When we are thrown off balance or triggered, we need tools to become re-centered and return to the present moment. Breathing, moving my body, self-soothing with a drink of water, anchoring my feet by pushing them into the floor, or engaging in self-talk help me while I'm working. When I'm engaged in community-led processes it helps me move from reflection to action, and gives me joy- listening and taking direction from leaders in the room about what's needed.

The hand: Drawing visuals to support cultural safety

Although it will always be faster to draw simpler icons, what is gained in speed may be lost in distinction when ideas are distilled to universal concepts. Illustration can model holistic ways of knowing. Drawings can show us a strengths-based approach.

It's important today to reflect on how our work is representative of the people with whom we're collaborating. Because graphic recording and graphic facilitation are fast work, there is no easy answer. The important part is that as a practitioner, I am aware of the choices I make. Most practitioners use familiar ways of drawing people—often as "everyman" stick people (star people, bean people, and other shapes). This "Everyman" idea is meant to be a stand-in for a universal symbol—and in North America, we consider all other differences to be compared against Whiteness as the default.

It's important today to reflect on how our work is representative of the people with whom we're collaborating.

A question I've come to consider is how can a stick figure (if it doesn't have a race or ethnicity) represent, or support, cultural safety?

Although it will always be faster to draw simpler icons, what is gained in speed may be lost in distinction when ideas are distilled to universal concepts. I find myself asking in a graphic recording or facilitation session, what is more important: cultivating cultural safety or how I draw this stick figure? This may mean in some cases, I decide it is appropriate to use stick figures, because there are other drawings or text that create imagery or processes that support cultural safety. Sometimes on the same poster I will have a number of "everyman" stick figures balanced with other types of images. Overall, I challenge myself to go beyond different skin tones in what I draw, avoid reinforcing stereotypes, and utilize all resources to ensure respectful representations.

Sometimes I draw culturally relevant images, and I also avoid being inappropriately reductionist. For example, while working with specific First Nations on the west coast of British Columbia about their traditional herring practices, I was able to refer to each Nation's unique fishing traditions. But while graphic recording at a national First Nations data conference, I was careful to not choose one symbol (not a tipi, nor a medicine wheel, etc.) to represent the diversity present. Using one symbol would be applying a pan-Indigenous graphic and would potentially be received as disrespect. It's an important moment of choice that needs to be made quickly while working. The strength or limitations of my decision is based on my own knowledge.

Suggested tool: Be an anthropologist about yourself

Take personal notes during a session, similar to how teachers-in-training keep journals or how anthropologists keep field notes. This is a reflection-in-action project. It was challenging to take time out to make notes, but later on, while I reviewed them, I was amazed at details that I had already forgotten. For example, one of my blind spots is feeling I need to capture new-to-me information as fast as possible. Being confident that I can wait, and use that time differently, is one of my reflection-in-action learnings. I've noticed times where I drew a list, but a diagram or model would have brought more meaning.

Suggested tool: Graphic facilitation portfolio review

For my graduate work, I designed a research study about my own practice that is easy for other practitioners to duplicate. I selected five illustrations from my portfolio over a period of 10 years and analyzed my design and content choices about how I drew issues of race, gender, or other markers of difference (or how I avoided it). Educators will recognize this as a self-study, or action research. Next, I kept a journal to better understand my biases and my worldview. I shared this journal with a trusted reader or group to deepen the learning. Then I wrote up the research findings and adjusted my work based on my learnings.

Core competencies in cultural safety for practitioners

Graphic facilitation has the potential to enhance knowledge and build on the self-awareness necessary to advance meaningful change. As professionals, we can help the groups we work with by developing our core competencies, just as we work on other aspects of our practice. Here are suggested core competencies to support building cultural safety in our work:

1. It starts with me. Each of us has to do our inner work. Arrive with humility. Research and understand my own history in the context of colonization of this country and the impact colonization has on the indigenous people and cultures here in their own land.
2. My relationships with others in the room. How I introduce myself in a culturally appropriate way, and how do I behave. Who are the leader in the room? For this engagement, have I established appropriate networks in advance?
3. Understanding my biases and worldview. Start from an assumption that things are not equal, institutions are not neutral, and that at the same time, people inside them may be very well-intentioned.
4. Review my body of work as a critic. Pull out a selection of my images, and examine my work with a lens of cultural humility. What patterns do I notice? What choices did I make?
5. Become an anthropologist-about-myself. Make field notes during a session one day. Use reflection-in-action. Take time out of the work to reflect on it and write down in as much detail as I can.
6. Go beyond multiculturalism on the surface, and don't limit myself to drawing different skin tones. How do I avoid reinforcing stereotypes in my images?
7. Listen for the paradigms of colonialism, systems of class, gender, privilege.
8. Support traditional Indigenous knowledge, connect stories to land and place.

Core competencies in cultural safety: Supporting organizations

Graphic facilitation can help support an open type of discussion for challenging issues, bringing art and conversation together in a room. Organizations can adopt graphic facilitation as a change methodology to tackle tough issues such as cultural safety, while learning about First Nations cultures with the richness visuals can bring to group conversations.

Here are some implementation ideas:

- Cultural safety depends on people understanding **histories** they likely weren't taught in schools; graphic facilitation is an engaging way to explain histories.
- Encouraging people to **learn**—starting with self—is key to building cultural safety because competencies are not developed overnight. Information from keynotes or presentations is synthesized into smaller, bite-sized chunks.
- Graphic facilitation creates **reflection** tools that create a natural conversation or solo reflection area which can prompt people to examine their cultural identities.
- After the event, the visuals can be **shared** by email, newsletter, intranet, and in reports to continue to engage people emotionally and intellectually.
- Graphic recordings can support **organizational change**: saving time by quickly summarizing meetings, identifying next steps, and mapping out change processes such as assessment tools, trainings, and human resources policies.

I believe each mark we make is an opportunity to reflect in the moment and adjust the course forward, together. In writing this, my intent was to share my personal learning with others, to ask for and gather feedback, and always consider how we can challenge our own work to go deeper.

With gratitude to Cheryl Ward at the San'yas Indigenous Cultural Safety Training Program (British Columbia, Canada) and Harmony Johnson and Janene Erickson at the First Nations Health Authority (BC, Canada) for support and feedback on this draft and along my learning journey.

SAM BRADD is a graphic facilitator and specialist in information design. He uses visuals for people that want to engage, solve problems, and lead. Together, we're drawing change. In the last 15 years, Sam has collaborated with the World Health Organization, Google, indigenous organizations, and researchers on three continents. In 2016, his side project the Graphic History Collective published a new book of comics because how we tell histories can change the world. He has a Masters in Education (University of British Columbia). Contact: @sambradd and www.drawingchange.com.

References

OCAP™ principles: via the First Nations Information Governance Center

Rockwood Institute, sketchnotes on triggers:
drawingchange.com/new-rockwood-art-of-leadership-sketchnotes

San'yas Indigenous Cultural Safety Training Program: www.sanyas.ca/home

Schon, D. *The Reflective Practitioner: How professionals think in action*, London: Temple Smith, 1983.

Smith, L.T. *Decolonizing Methodologies: Research and Indigenous Peoples*, London: Zed Books, 2006.

Truth and Reconciliation Executive summary:
www.trc.ca/websites/trcinstitution/index.php?p=893

Williams, R. (1999). "Cultural safety—what does it mean for our work practice?" *Australian and New Zealand Journal of Public Health*, 23(2), 213-214.

The Use of Imagery in Conflict Engagement

Aftab Erfan, PhD

For the past decade I have lived a double life as a conflict resolution practitioner on the one hand, and as a visual facilitator on the other. The invitation to contribute this chapter was a call to bring the two sides of my work together and make an attempt at describing their often-productive and occasionally explosive intersection. These pages are a starting point for an exploration of the central question: **how do we imagine an expanded role for imagery in service of productively addressing group conflicts?**

What is conflict?

My work in conflict engagement has encompassed settling a fight between three colleagues who felt they could no longer work together, assisting a leadership team at a difficult crossroads regarding their organization's future, and bringing Palestinian and Israeli students together to dialog about their coexistence on a Canadian university campus. Each conflict is unique and it is difficult to find a commonly accepted definition for what conflict is. What we know from the literature is this:

1. Conflict hinges on real or perceived incompatibility between opinions, principles, objectives, interests, or desires of the parties involved. In other words, there is an element of *difference* at play.
2. Conflict arises when the parties are not willing or able to settle their differences in a fully rational argumentative manner. Most people feel angry when they are in conflict. Others feel sad. And many feel afraid. Conflict is disagreement that has the potential to *mobilize emotional resources* in a way that can be destructive to people, relationships, properties, or systems.

As shorthand: **conflict is difference that matters enough to activate our emotions.**

How do we view conflict?

There is no single view or perspective on the nature of conflict. The traditional view has been that aggressive conflict is part of human nature and therefore unavoidable, while the alternative view is that humans are naturally cooperative but caught in a historical narrative of hostility (Clark 2002). The dominant view is that conflict is generally a bad thing, that a group in conflict is a malfunctioning group; the alternative view is that conflict is inherently good as manifestation of diversity, and that it is the seat of a group's creative potential (Lewis 2008). Finally, the traditional view is that conflict should be dealt with primarily at the rational level through discovery of mutually beneficial material solutions, while the alternative view is that engagement with the emotional and symbolic layers of conflict is essential (LeBaron 2003).

How one views conflict is very important because it determines how one approaches engaging with conflict. **The various methods of conflict resolution are pinned on implicit views on the nature of conflict, which in turn influence how imagery and visuals may or may not be helpful as companions to these methods.**

A warning: If you are going to use visuals in conflict resolution, it is important that you have clarity on the approach to conflict that informs the session. The imagery used needs to be consistent with the philosophy and aims of the approach. Visuals that are not well aligned—for example, a visual that makes everything look pretty and harmonious while a facilitator is trying to surface tensions, a chart that includes too much detail while the facilitator is drawing out a dominant dynamic or relationship, or a metaphor of building something new while a facilitator is working to dismantle the existing situation—might add to confusion in the room, and will likely become irrelevant to the process.

The approach to conflict engagement that I am most fluent in, called the Lewis Method of Deep Democracy, takes the view that conflict is unavoidable, that it is fundamentally a good thing, and that it needs to be engaged at the emotional and symbolic levels. Within this view, conflict is seen as a doorway to wisdom and personal growth, so we speak about "mining the gold of conflict," we search for it in the course of a meeting (any meeting—not only a conflict intervention), we bring it out as early as possible and explore it in the most personal and emotionally-engaged way available to us. We also acknowledge that conflict is uncomfortable for many people, and that conflict engagement processes can be unsafe unless people go into them with awareness and readiness. The job of the facilitator is to speed up or slow down a process at appropriate times, to give structure and to let go of structure at appropriate times, and to hold the group with a non-judgmental attitude that creates safety. What I describe below are some ideas for how imagery can be used to assist with this specific approach.

How can imagery help as we work with conflict?

I see two primary ways in which the use of imagery can be helpful in this work, addressing two primary difficulties we tend to have with conflict:

Giving form: Most people are not big fans of conflicts and many people experience significant anxiety in conflict situations. One reason conflict is so difficult for most people is that it feels so disorganized: we just don't know how to get our head around it, let alone what to do with it. Conflict is perhaps the most familiar form of chaos in the realm of human relationships. We know from the new sciences that chaos and transformation tend to be linked to each other—thus the amazing potential in conflict—but for most people chaos is uncomfortable because it is disorienting and unpredictable, making us feel vulnerable and on shaky ground. **Visuals can help give us the forms, the language, and the structures we need to make sense of conflict, making it feel less chaotic and more approachable.**

Making visible: Since we are so uncomfortable with conflict, we usually tend not to want to look at it—or not be able to look at it—until we absolutely have to. What we know about the process of conflict development is that there is a typical progression (Mindell 1995). Generally conflicts begin as a small disagreement, but since we don't see them and deal with them they tend to brew for a long time until they gain momentum and become explosive. It is usually not until they blow up that conflicts become visible to us, at which point they are already too big and scary to deal with. **Visuals have the possibility of making conflict visible earlier in the process, making them available for working with before they grow too large.**

Another warning: Sometimes the people you are working with may not be happy with you for making a conflict visible. Sometimes they will accuse you of having "created" conflict when everything was fine. The accusation may not be true—you are in fact only reflecting the group's existing issues to it—but if people are afraid or not ready to see a conflict, bringing attention to it may be unwelcome. If you're going to make conflicts visible, you better have a way to make it safe to work with them. Visuals will often accelerate the process. That is their gift and their danger.

How to use imagery to give form to conflict

First things first, remember that imagery can appear in different forms: it can be literally and explicitly put on paper as a drawing, or it can be spoken in the form of metaphor and other verbal imagery. **Imagery can be very potent when we are in the presence of conflict because people in conflict tend not to be fully in their rational mind and need instead to draw on imaginative resources which give access to the irrational mind** (LeBaron 2003).

Much work has been done on the power of metaphors as organizing structures that help create meaning and therefore help shape and shift our reality (Lakoff 2003). One of the advantages of metaphors (particularly when used verbally) is that they are understood *not* to be a literal representation of what you are talking about, so they tend to be flexible and intuitively clear. If I say to a group of people in conflict that we are going to "jump in the deep end" they will know what I mean and may even suggest that we instead "put our toes in first". If the metaphor isn't working I can change it on the spot and say "let's start peeling back the layers of the onion," and again people will immediately have a sense of what I mean.

I use metaphors to frame what I am doing, explaining to people what is going on as I take them through a conflict resolution process. The following are the two most powerful metaphors I use, both central to the Lewis Method of Deep Democracy:

1. THE ICEBERG

The metaphor of the iceberg is familiar to most people, indicating a reality that is only partially apparent. Freud used the metaphor of the iceberg to distinguish between an individual's consciousness (top of the iceberg) and subconsciousness (below the water line) and suggested that an individual needs to "lower their waterline" (by going to psychotherapy, for example) to resolve their psychological issues

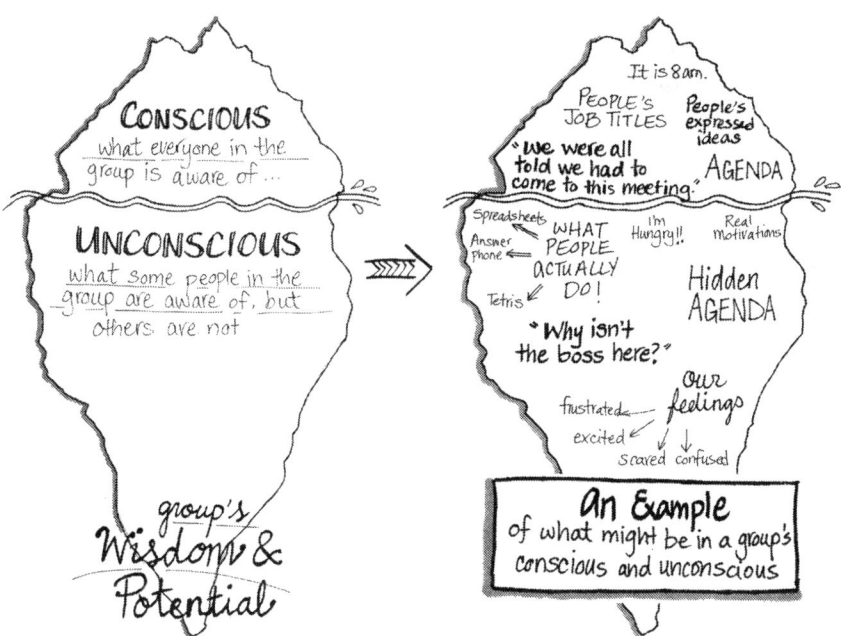

and achieve their potential. Jung applied the metaphor of the iceberg to groups, suggesting that when two or more people gather there is a conscious part of the group (e.g. the meeting agenda, the materials and issues on the table, the relative positional power of people in the room) and an unconscious part of the group (e.g. the hidden agendas, the gossip before the meeting, the emotional state of people involved, issues seen as taboos in the group). I use Jung's articulation of the iceberg to describe to people in a meeting that I am attempting to "lower the waterline" as a way to get to the hidden solutions, wisdom, and potential of the group. I may draw the iceberg on a flipchart and ask: "What do you think is in the consciousness of this group now? And what's just below the waterline?" This simple imagery, which takes only a few minutes to present, often makes it easier for people to begin to talk about what is really going on for them. The difficult-to-talk-about realities often very quickly pop to the surface.

2. THROWING ALL THE ARROWS

Various war metaphors are often used in talking about conflict. I use the metaphor of throwing one's arrows: When we are in relationship with other people, things tend to happen that annoy us, but very often we don't mention them because we prefer to keep the peace. However, we take our little annoyance, turn it into an arrow, and put it in our metaphorical quiver that we carry around until the next time we get into a fight with the person. When we fight we take out the arrows that we gathered over time and shoot them at the person (e.g. "You don't respect me: You're always late at meetings!") We typically just shoot enough arrows to win a fight! That's fine if we want to win fights, but if we want true peace we need disarmament. We have to throw not only our little arrows, but also our big ones. I invite participants to take turns throwing all their arrows, holding nothing back. Once everything has been thrown, I ask each person involved which arrows hit them and what insight, lessons, or truths those piercing arrows hold for the individual. The metaphor calls in bravery and invites an emotional release in a slightly more dramatic manner than most people are used to. The highly structured nature of the process makes it more safe and more likely that people walk away from the conflict having learned something new.

How to use imagery to make conflict visible

While the above examples illustrate how specific imagery can be used to give directions and help groups make sense of what we are doing, the following are some examples of more subtle and fluid ways that we might use visuals to make conflicts visible. What typically happens to me is this: The discussion is going on, I may be taking visual notes, and suddenly I begin to pick up on a disagreement in the room, perhaps far before people in the group are aware of it. I use my lens on group dynamics (in my case the lens of Role Theory from Deep Democracy) to draw out and visually highlight what is emerging, then ask the group if they want to do anything about it.

THE ELEPHANT IN THE ROOM

It is often there and I very often draw it as I become aware of it. The elephant in the room is the issue that people tend to speak around but not go into directly because it is charged with conflict. We experience

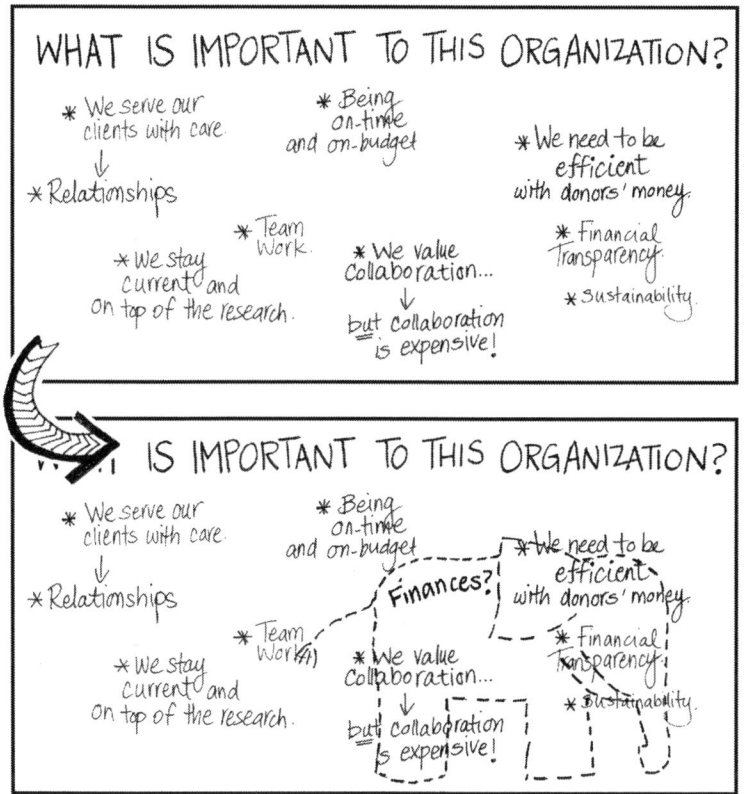

the presence of an elephant when it feels like we are cycling around something, saying the same things over and over again but not getting anywhere. We may also experience the elephant through our body symptoms, sometimes called "edge behavior" (e.g. I get a headache when a group is stuck around something they are not quite naming.) When working with a group I may not know exactly what the elephant is, but I can put a light outline of one on our chart as I am drawing, then ask people "If there was an elephant in the room, it feels to me like it would be right around here, around the word "finances". Does that sound right?" If I haven't got it right, then people usually point me to the actual elephant in the room instead. Either way, I now have the elephant to work with. If I have caught it early enough, hopefully it is a smallish elephant and easy to work with.

POLARITIES

Deep Democracy is one of several approaches to conflict resolution that works with polarities. Polarities are formally defined as an interdependent pair of notions that may be simultaneously correct and at the same time antithetical to each other, and if managed well can support one another in pursuit of a common goal (Johnson 1992). In Deep Democracy we see them less formally as any two notions that are in opposition to each other in the context of the conflict (e.g. the idealist view vs. the pragmatic view, managers vs. workers, we should do this vs. we shouldn't do it). Polarities often emerge around the elephant in the room. I bring attention to them on my charts by drawing an infinity symbol around them, to suggest their relationship and the tension between them. When polarities emerge on my charts, I point them out with as much objectivity as I can muster. I check with the group to see if one of the polarities might be interesting to explore, and if they decide to go into one I use my conflict resolution steps (e.g. the throwing of the arrows describe above) to work with that polarity. Sometimes, the group may decide not to work any further with a polarity, but I find that even just pointing it out, even just making it clear—and making it okay—that there are paradoxes or elements in natural creative tension within the group allows people to relax into them, making the conflict less scary and a little more simple to wrap one's head around.

The combination of musings and illustrations above introduce a conversation about practically and responsibly engaging imagery in

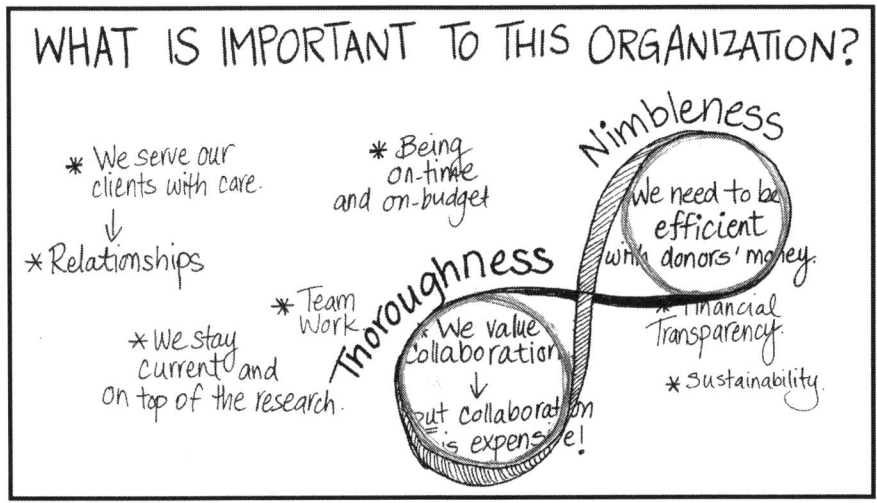

conflict resolution within groups. **In my estimation, the potential to harness the power of visuals in the service of addressing conflict is great, and so is the risk.** Without a robust approach to conflict and actual skill in holding a group through a tense situation, the intentional (and even unintentional) use of imagery to give form and visibility to conflict can ignite emotional fires we cannot manage. However, if we know how to manage the fires, the field of conflict resolution offers exciting possibilities for visual practitioners wanting to make a real difference in groups and communities in which they work.

AFTAB ERFAN teaches at the School of Community and Regional Planning at the University of British Columbia, and consults as the principal of Whole Picture Thinking. She specializes in helping groups work through conflict and come to decisions, whether around the boardroom table or in large public forums. She draws on several schools of facilitation including graphic facilitation. Her go-to approach for working with conflict is Deep Democracy, a psycho-social method developed in post-apartheid South Africa. Aftab's PhD research, defended in 2013, is a pioneering scholarly effort to apply Deep Democracy in the context of a small Indigenous community on Vancouver Island. She is one of a small handful of master practitioners and teachers of Deep Democracy in North America, and is the author of many articles and book chapters.
www.deepdemocracy.ca

References

Clark, M.E. (2002). *In Search of Human Nature*. Routledge.

Johnson, B. (1992). *Polarity Management: Identifying and Managing Unresolvable Problems*. Amherst, MA: HRD Press Inc.

Lakoff, G., and M. Johnson (2003). *Metaphors We Live By*. University of Chicago Press.

LeBaron, M. (2003). *Bridging cultural conflicts: A new approach for a changing world*. San Francisco CA: Jossey-Bass.

Lewis, M. (2008). *Inside the No: Five Steps to Decisions that Last*.
www.deep-democracy.net

Mindell, A. (1995). *Sitting in the Fire: Large Group Transformation Using Conflict and Diversity* Lao Tse Press, Ltd. 272.

Steady, to Scale

Kelvy Bird

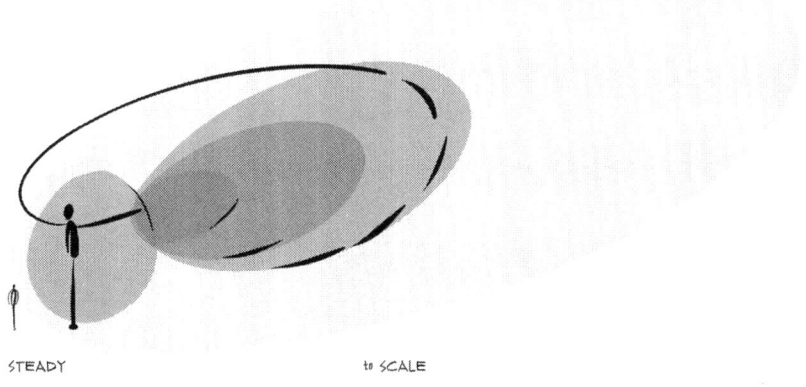

STEADY   to SCALE

Artists reflect their times through lenses that influence insight and action, in themselves and in others. In the face of truly great art, we find our spirits lifted, our views challenged, and sometimes our very foundation of understanding tectonically shifted. Art moves us, and our species evolves with this kind of internal stirring.

As visual practitioners, as artists, we aim with care and responsibility to reach people, to expand the boundaries of the assumed known. *Any reach requires steadiness*, and to ensure a stable core, we rely on support for our essential, creative selves.

Take the example of an apple tree: Weak branches yield little fruit. The stronger the trunk, the stronger the branch. The stronger the roots, the stronger the trunk. The richer the soil, the more nourishment for the roots and the fruit. And so on.

Scribing with an eye toward the orchard and the village beyond—with an intent to facilitate systems-level seeing—I experience a direct correlation between the steadiness of one's being and the range of insight that visuals can summon.

This works in a reciprocal way, where we are both held in by others to experience integrity and wholeness, and because of this, we generate visuals as a holding device for learning within systems.

This kind of support is what I'll refer to as "containers," which we can consciously form by considering how we hold ourselves, how we help others energetically through the use of images, and also how we let ourselves be held.

More attention, stronger tree, healthier orchard. Less attention, the field goes fallow.

To inhabit this kind of reciprocal zone of tending / flourishing / nourishing, I'll try to map out my thinking in three main parts:

1. An explanation of **containers**
2. Thoughts on quality of presence and **inner cultivation**
3. Two specific **examples of practice** where container intentionality directly influenced a scale of reach for the drawings and the content they carried

Containers

As my grandmother was aging, at a point when she could really only go outside with a walker and physical assistance, I recall visits where we would lunch at a local New York City diner. She would ask me things about my life, about school, about my friends, about my studies, and she would marvel at the complexity of the world in which I lived. (This was 1984, so we can only imagine what she would say about our world today!)

What I recall most poignantly is the way she would pay attention, seeming to hang on every word, and the way she made me feel safe, and loved, loved no matter what I would say, no matter what I had to share. I never felt judged. No matter what she thought about the details of my escapades, she would listen closely, look me in the eye, and continue to pursue an understanding of my life.

She provided a container, a space where I could see myself more clearly and grow as direct result of how she was holding me.

When my grandmother, somewhat hard of hearing and surely with many of her own personal concerns, was completely able to show up for me, I was completely able to show up *for her*. I could be more vulnerable, because I felt safe. She brought out the purest part of me by how gracefully she held me in her own heart.

DRAWING WITH CONTAINER AWARENESS

By listening with the following levels in mind, we can participate in a shift of awareness and possibility. My colleague Otto Scharmer[1] has described "Four Levels of Listening" that I apply here to the visual practice of scribing.

FOUR LEVELS of SCRIBING
BASED on OTTO SCHARMER'S "FOUR LEVELS of LISTENING"

1. HEAR a WORD (MAKE a PICTURE) → DRAW
2. INTERPRET WORDS (MAKE SENSE) → MAP the CONTEXT
3. CONNECT IDEAS (MAKE MEANING) → DEMONSTRATE RELATION
4. REVEAL ESSENCE of WHAT IS WANTING to BE SEEN (MAKE KNOWN) → OPEN to the UNKNOWN & HELP BRING IT to VISUAL LIFE

At Level One, to quote Otto, we "**Download** *and listen to reconfirm what we already know. What we see is limited to our own projections, reflecting the past.*"

In scribing, we draw what we hear, and it's literal. Someone says "bird" and we draw a bird. I also refer to this as "object-oriented" scribing, where the primary approach is a focus on individual, named parts.

Level Two represents "**Factual Listening.** *We notice difference, and we notice disconfirming data.*"

We see what is being spoken from a broader vantage point, and still draw what we hear, but our lens expands to make sense of what is being spoken within a context, which we can map. Someone says "The bird is flying, then it reaches the coast and joins a flock," and we enter the domain of storytelling.

Level Three shifts to "**Empathic Listening**, *seeing the situation through the eyes of another, leading to emotional connection. Listening begins to happen from the Field, or from the other person with whom you are connecting.*"

This is where containers start to really activate, where our own heart comes online as we step into the shoes of another—like my grandmother opened space to witness and feel out *my* shoes. We start to care, genuinely care, and we shift. What comes through us shifts. Our drawing shifts. (How can it not?)

We realize the story in the room is coming from a cultural frame of reference *beyond* the room; the facts coming out have causal underpinning. No bird, no story, exists as an island. Something came before the lone bird flying, and something will come after. To get at the structural dynamic, we must activate our attunement to the negative space, what is going on between the notes or objects, the subtler, quieter envelope within which the parts form a whole. We shift from noticing moments in time to sensing movements over time. As we inquire, we start to inhabit the story and make sense of it *with* the company.

And Level Four, "**Generative Listening,** *requires us to connect with a capacity to let go and let come, to connect with an emerging future possibility that helps us to connect more fully with who we are and who we want to be.*"

This can also be said for Level Four scribing: we sense into and help surface the highest potentiality for the systems we serve. To do this requires a sensitivity with the energy of what is wanting to come *through*, an energy or vibe that has started to become tangible in Level Three. What is drawn is secondary to meeting the tone accurately and crafting gestures that evoke essential meaning.

I find here that time slows, the air quiets, and a kind of creative rupture takes place in the midst of sublime stillness, where something very fine and as-yet-unnamable is coming alive, and we, as scribes, witness it. In a way we are midwives facilitating, through our being and our hands, an emergence of some communal shift and *knowing*.

This could be described as Flow, or the Zone, and is rare. It takes a well-tended container—at tiers of the self, room, and system—to reach this place, whether it be between two people or 70,000, in a window of an hour or decade. Numbers don't even really matter.

What *does* matter is the qualitative listening behind the act of drawing, the listening that comes online by orienting *within* the context of a social body, with a core intent to join an invisible place and make manifest that which wants to be seen and witnessed.

WAKING TO CONTAINER RELATIVITY

Our range of attention is ours to define, and the relative properties of containers give us choice: stay within the accepted known or expand to meet a not-yet-named reality.

An old Hindu parable, which I first heard in a year-long program called Leadership for Collective Intelligence[2] and paraphrase here, further explains the value of perspective in regards to holding capacity:

> An aging master grew tired of his apprentice complaining, and so, one morning, sent him for some salt.
>
> When the apprentice returned, the master instructed the young man to put a handful of salt in a glass of water and drink it. "How does it taste?" the master asked. "Bitter!" spit the apprentice. The master chuckled.
>
> The two walked in silence to a nearby lake, where the master again asked the young man to put a handful of salt in the water.

"Now drink from the lake. How does it taste?" "Fresh!" remarked the apprentice. "Do you taste the salt?" asked the master. "No," said the young man.

At this, the master sat beside the young man and offered:

"The pain of life is pure salt; no more, no less. The amount of pain in life remains the same, exactly the same. But the amount of bitterness we taste depends on the container into which we put the pain.

So when you are in pain, the only thing you can do is to enlarge your sense of things... Stop being a glass. Become a lake."

We are both lake-makers and salt, depending on the context. At times, we are held in by a person or group, and that enables us to show up more securely. At other times, we expand to help a group in need meet their challenge. It works both ways. And we expand or contract depending on the need of the moment.

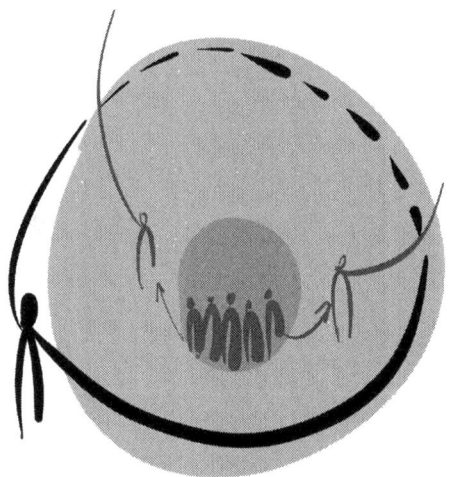
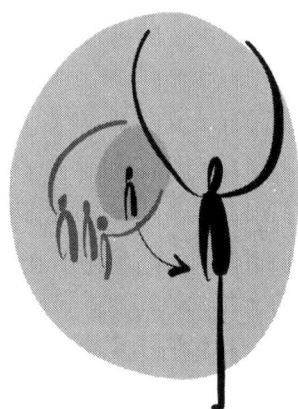

WE SUPPORT CONTAINER EXPANSION   THE CONTAINER SUPPORTS OUR EXPANSION

INNER CULTIVATION

Towards forming these types of enlarging holding spaces for others, and before even making a mark on any wall, we must first learn to cultivate a container for ourselves, opening our stance, to stay clear for what wants to "move through."

We start by locating our best self—the self that accepts, that chooses possibility over fear—the self that welcomes the new, and actually carves a path for it. In orienting with this self, we serve as a microcosm of re-orientation for every part of a system that our drawings might touch.

This can be a conscious, enlightened, spiritual choice. It's also simply a matter of relaxing into the fact that—through every gesture, every word, even every silence—we exist in a cascading ripple of touch. Our presence allows us to show up for others, joining individuals and groups precisely where they are in their process, poised in a receptive and steadying way.

A rigid stance blocks, separates, reinforces a dualistic mentality: you|them; you|content; imagined you|true you—the "you" with the most to actually offer any given situation. As we steel up we stand guarded, sectioned off. As we soften, we are inevitably moved. Moved, additional senses come online. Attunement amplifies. Range increases. Listening cascades down those Four Levels.

In this place we meet a "knowing" beyond literal understanding of words, concepts, and impressions. An intuitive muscle comes online, and it's an absorbent place, where—because of our open stance—we can facilitate a group from monologic to dialogic interaction.

The range of our attention relates to that which is taken in, received, and then that which is turned outward, revealed, through the hand. It's a mutual relation; the more open the scribe, the more received. The more received, the more revealed.

We are reflective aids and, as such, our attention to personal containers helps stabilize that of the room and systems we address. If the room feels rattled and we collapse into that, we echo rattledness. Yet if we are able to stabilize internally, we're more likely to reveal cohesion.

Draw with crystal clear intention. To make a mark before a mark wants to be made risks destabilizing the container through misrepresentation or by being out-of-sync with the true tone of the room.

Scribing is a participatory art. There are consequences to over-stacking, to overdrawing—that the image indulges the artist's needs to express and shifts away from the marks actually called for by the container.

Examples of practice

To land these concepts in very real application, I can speak to two engagements that each fully tested the limits of my practice. The data might sound extreme; I include them as an objective reference point in regards to the tides of container-building and scale. The stories evolved between 2013 and 2015 and continue as this book goes to print.

U.LAB

One example is of a Massive Open Online Course (MOOC) called "u.lab: Transforming Business, Society, and Self" offered jointly through edX and the Presencing Institute. The gist of u.lab is that, after seven years of ramp-up with experiments in online broadcasts and community-building, our team live-streamed eight times in 2015. We reached 70,000 registered participants from 185 countries—a social body made of individuals, small teams, and over 500 self-organized hubs alike.

I am such a shy person, and the notion of thousands of people watching my back made me want to crawl in a hole until the next ice age was over. To prepare, I wore soothing blackboard-matching gray, extracted chalk ink from pens to paint large-arching arrows, imagined myself one trunk in the orchard, tuned into the notion of water—extending the lake metaphor—and drew. My approach over the year, across dozens of images generated live and staged across multiple web platforms, shifted from a logical representation of frameworks to a heated extraction of some intuited field essence, which seemed most appropriate to the container that had matured globally over time.

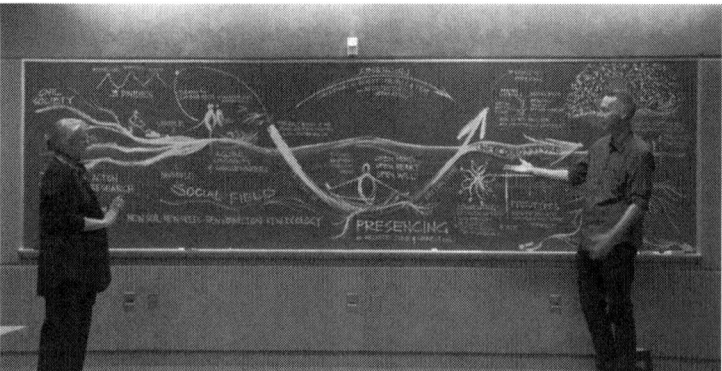

A screenshot taken by a participant of u.lab during the live broadcast, showing active use of the drawing for real-time sensemaking of course content

It would have been easy to consider the u.lab "we" as a body of "users" rather than as an alive ecosystem, since I had only had voice-to-voice or email communication with about .003% of the participants, and it was hard to tune in to the reality of those I might never know. But without attentional inclusion, I would reinforce the very pattern of societal disconnect we were seeking to address and dissolve. The stance I chose to occupy, then, was one of unbounded connection, where rather than an "out there" viewership, I was surrounded by a sea of individuals helping to hold me to the wall. I was contained by the very ecosystem for which I drew.

EXECUTIVE EDUCATION

The other practical example of container application is of a custom leadership program offered through Executive Education at MIT Sloan School of Management. MIT, with a sequential academic design approach, offered an experiment in endurance and sensemaking over long blocks of time and numerous sessions.

A highly skilled executive education team, working closely with top-level executives, customized a transformational program for senior managers from a global organization with 23,000 employees. There have been five cohorts to date—I worked with the last three—each going through a nine-month program that included an eight-day section of intensive classes, followed by a few months of applied project work, concluding with another eight-day section.

The majority of the eight-day sections involved four to six hours of faculty presentation per day, with each section leading to approximately 45 total hours of scribing onto more than 100 linear feet of dry-erase walls and sometimes extra boards. This yielded 118 unique images over the three full cycles, including on topics such as Systems Thinking, Leadership

A classroom at MIT, where drawings offered visual and content containment

and Organizational Change, Strategy, Finance and Macro-Economics, and Operations—most of which I did not initially know well or at all.

What was unique here was not the volume of time or images, but the necessary weaving of content over the educational arc. One approach could have been "one topic, one picture." The more expansive value, though, was in the wrapping of heavily-related drawings around the group, stitched nest-like, *providing a solid visual container for extended cultural learning.*

—

As initially indicated, the extension of new experience directly relates to the depth and steadiness of the soil in which it grows.

Visual practice, as a key "seeing" and anchoring device within the containers we support, serves a foundational role in our understanding of, and the evolution of, social fields. Thus, a visual practitioner's grasp of the correlation between our role as scribes and the fields in which we draw cannot be underrated. As artists participating in societal transformation, we are implicate[3] in both making apparent, and expanding, discovery.

Our times are riddled with disconnects, ideological entrenchment, crisis, fear. It is a time then, with open eyes,[4] to see. It is a time to expand, to scale, to facilitate societal sight. All inner preparation—and all holding spaces we reinforce—enable the very act of making that meets this call.

Each crooked nook, fault line, gorgeous arc, blotch of color, textured application in our drawing offers some structural integrity and some sense.

As artists, as visual practitioners of any kind, it is up to us to stretch "larger than the largest disturbance in the room."[5]

Increasing our ability to embrace current discomfort, and simultaneously represent the possible, we participate in the engagement and ushering in of tentative, emergent realities.

KELVY BIRD is an internationally recognized graphic facilitator, supporting groups by translating content and dynamics into visual formats that aid with reflection and decision-making. She leads creative design at the Presencing Institute, and is on the core team of Otto Scharmer's edX offering u.lab: Transforming Business, Society, and Self – launched January 2015, with over 70,000 students participating globally. Kelvy also cofounded dpict llc, a firm specializing in scribing to advance social understanding at all scales. Long-standing partners have included: The Value Web, MIT, Harvard, The Ashland Institute, Dialogos, and MG Taylor, as well as Fortune 500 and local community organizations alike. An artist by training, Kelvy received her BFA in painting and BA in Art History from Cornell University. Her current residence is Somerville, MA. Find more information at: www.kelvybird.com.

References

1. Otto Scharmer, "Levels of Listening," as found in *Theory U: Leading from the Future as it Emerges*, 1st ed., Society for Organizational Learning, 2007. See also a video clip from u.lab here: www.youtube.com/watch?v=eLfXpRkVZaI
2. The Hindu story and much of my understanding of containers comes from working with Dialogos, www.dialogos.com, and the Circle of Seven, www.ashlandinstitute.org
3. Here lies a subtle reference, honoring physicist David Bohm's theory of the "Implicate Order" and undivided wholeness. Any interested reader can start to lean more via: www.david-bohm.net
4. Months after the official Bauhaus closing, Josef Albers was invited to teach at the newly-formed Black Mountain College in Asheville, North Carolina. Despite knowing little English, he knew enough words to convey his purpose for teaching: "To open eyes." *Leap Before You Look: Black Mountain College, 1933–1957*. Exhibit at the Institute of Contemporary Art, Boston MA, October 2015–January 2016.
5. William Isaacs, shared during the capacity development program: Leadership for Collective Intelligence. Isaacs is the author of *Dialogue: The Art of Thinking Together*, The Crown Publishing Group, 1999.

A Learning Journey
Connecting self to planet

Stina Brown

I was on a conference call last year with 600 other people, listening to (and taking part in) a conversation on "Shaping a New Narrative for a New Economy" with David Korten and Otto Scharmer. The number of times the word *mystical* came up surprised me; I've never heard the economy and the mystical discussed simultaneously. There are—in some conversations now—people discussing their inner and outer worlds as congruent, or at the very least related. The Dalai Lama has said, "We can never obtain peace in the outer world until we make peace with ourselves." This principle is showing itself in my meetings as well.

In late 2014, the Canadian Centre for Policy Alternatives asked me to design a series of four full-day meetings over the course of two months as an engagement aspect of their Climate Justice Project (CJP), led by Marc Lee, Senior Economist. The CJP "asks how we can tackle global warming with fairness and equality. Our challenge is to build a zero carbon society that also enhances our quality of life." This series of "deliberative dialog sessions," which took place in the Metro Vancouver area, was intended to advance the outreach work of the CJP and deepen understanding of effective engagement processes. It also held the potential for expanded activities across BC and Canada to spur climate action.[1]

> "Strangers are more beautiful than I have been led to believe,"
> "climate change is essentially just a people issue." – CJP Participants

In this chapter, we will explore how I, in the role of visual facilitator, together with Sam Bradd as a graphic recorder, guided a group of strangers toward self-determined transformation—connecting their individual experiences with each others' to see themselves in relationship with the larger context of the planet and our collective future.

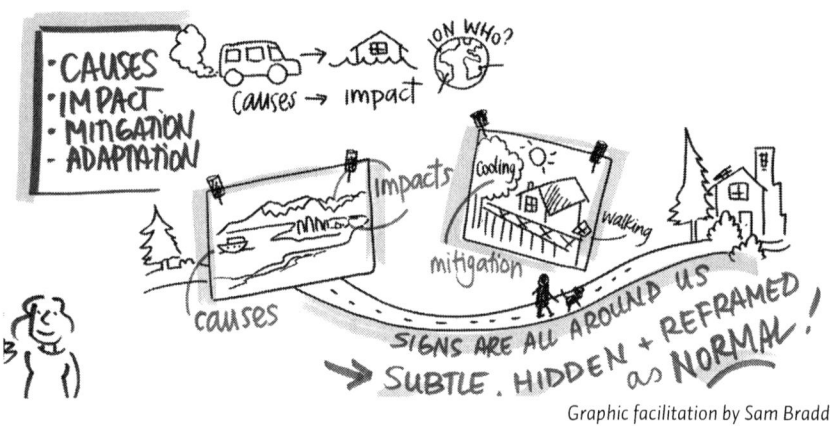

Graphic facilitation by Sam Bradd

This experience demonstrates how design and visual facilitation can create the conditions to:

- Connect to and increase awareness of the self and others;
- Build community by creating the space for conversation;
- Enable deep and empathic dialog through shared and visual awareness; and
- Help participants find new hopeful ways of relating and taking action to move their own "worlds" into a future of their own making.

Connect: awaken to a relationship with yourself and others

There is a science to drawing out and managing a group's peak energy, creativity, and participation. I believe it begins with connection—awakening to a relationship with yourself and others. Once you are present, you are available to engage in conversation with others, to share, envision, discover, grow, etc. Visuals help anchor this process.

The process we were undertaking would need to be one that would engage the whole person, whole brain, and whole group. I would need to guide the group through a mix of reflection, dialog, self-organizing, presentations, and collaborations, with many of the outcomes emergent. This was an experiment, and the participants and leaders were in discovery mode together.

Before participants arrived at the first in-person meeting in mid-February 2015, we asked them to consider the following questions: "Why are you choosing to be a part of this conversation on climate justice?" "What are you passionate about?" "What are three to five values that guide your life?" I made these "data" into word clouds and posted them in the room on the first day.

Creating the conversation: participate, share, discover, envision, transition, un-limit

The first morning of our first day together, 40 of us sat in a wide circle with Sam's graphic recording wall set up nearby, and four flipchart pages filled with pre-meeting survey answers in the middle, oriented around a green and blue fabric Earth. On the wall, in those word clouds I'd created, participants could see each other's names and job areas, and just as significantly, their new colleagues' values, hopes and concerns.

Marc and I welcomed the group, discussed our roles, and gave an overview of our time together in this "learning journey" as well as the desired outcomes. These outcomes were to:

- **Learn** about the local connections between climate change and overall quality of life today and in the future
- **See** the "big picture" with up-to-date science and research
- **Explore** participants' personal and shared assumptions and values

- **Connect with others** to ask questions, envision the future, and share stories, concerns and ideas
- **Reflect on** the participants' own role in addressing climate change

We established "Group Agreements" to create transparency around forming group norms, articulate a way to build trust, and encourage self-regulation and inclusion. Setting our group agreements became one of our most significant keys to success; we posted them on the wall and re-read them every day. We noticed over the course of the four days that as long as the group kept their agreements, they thrived.

But group conversation is collaborative—and even with my interventions, at times the group struggled to stay balanced. If people no longer feel a sense of psychological safety (because others are breaking agreements), dialog loses its diverse viewpoints and energy plummets. I learned when you bring a widely varying group of people together—strangers who are diverse in almost every way—there is even more of a need to facilitate closely and wisely and to provide variation in activities.

Learning shared awareness: exploring assumptions and perspectives, activating knowledge

Participants' awareness about reality—and their role in creating reality—can be explored more fully through conversations that invite them to see their own assumptions more clearly, bring out their perspectives, and link new knowledge or understanding with existing knowledge. They begin to see a bigger picture, to expand or shift the way they relate to themselves, their actions, their community, and maybe even their world. Through the process of dialog (both internal and external), their systemic understanding of individual and collective action grows and creates new possibilities.

Hearing about the dire state of the world can surface a wide range of emotions in a group. We wanted to offer people a chance to reflect on their response to the question, "How are you feeling about climate change?" I provided a handout with two articles: "Climate Change and Emotions: How We Feel Matters More Than What We Know"[2] by David Ropeik[3] and an article by the David Suzuki Foundation titled "Coping With Climate Change is a Family Matter."[4]

Sam Bradd

On the wall, I put images of faces demonstrating a range of emotions (hopeful, interested, helpless, worried, sad, afraid, depressed, angry, disgusted), and asked the group to reflect on them and place Post-It notes beside the expressions that resonated with them.

Stina Brown

The comments people wrote and shared on the wall revealed, to our surprise, that the majority of them felt inspired and even happy; they were experiencing feeling part of the solution already, just by participating in these conversations. Even on their first day, participants came to see that they were not alone, their opinion mattered and this conversation was just the beginning. They learned strangers "are more beautiful" than they had been led to believe, and that "climate change is essentially just a people issue."

At times I saw group members experience feelings of guilt, grief, anger, and frustration—even mild depression. This sparked deep compassion in me, related to my own waves of ups and downs in my personal awareness of climate change. I encouraged participants to ride the waves with self-care, knowing their emotions will change many times around this topic—and that it's healthy to feel so deeply.

Relating differently to the world

A key element of our agenda became shifting the focus from becoming overwhelmed by the up-to-date research on global climate change and

Sam Bradd

our own emotions, toward understanding the skills and solutions that already exist—even locally—giving us what we needed to create a compelling future vision of what our world *could* look like.

I believe hope can be born in meetings where people can relate to each other as human beings and discover new things about themselves, each other, and the world along the way. And, as hope was born on the first day, regardless of what people's ideas of what the future would look like exactly, the group's focus quickly became mapping solutions.

Reflection

Sam's large live chart work over the four days, along with his daily debriefs throughout the process, brought additional rich layers of perspective, insight, reflection, memory, and integration of the learning—literally *showing* the group their progress and new history together. *The value of this dimension cannot be overstated!* I would often benefit from chats with Sam while the group was working; his presence added a set of facilitator eyes and ears on the process.

In Sam's words, "graphic recording made visible the learning and emotional transformation that was happening in the room. Looking back over an entire room whose walls were covered in pictures, the

Sam Bradd

group could see how far they'd come together. They could see their beginning questions—layered with information and presentations by guest experts—shift into the later stages of planning for action. It was all there. The graphics grounded their reflection, it was part of their notes, and they could take the pictures into their lives to keep the conversation going."

> Hope can be born in meetings where people can relate to each other as human beings and discover new things about themselves, each other, and the world along the way.

Participants learned how to work with people with opposing or differing views in small group table conversations. Report-outs made their words visible as Sam created graphic records. They shared ideas on what solutions could look like through hands-on neighborhood energy-mapping with templates, transportation planning with large maps, visioning with visual story-telling cards, and by conducting online research, sharing their findings with Post-It notes.

Rather than focusing on the "crisis" of climate change, we encouraged the group to explore what complete communities *could* look like, making it local, visual, holistic, and fun. Volunteers whom we named "synthesizers" took notes on the meta-learning of the group to help us reflect at the end of each day. Between sessions, participants had "homework," such as talking with a friend or family member about what they were discovering, or taking photos of their neighborhood's buildings, green spaces, or places they shopped for food to create a learning gallery for the group.

By the time we met for our last session, eight weeks after our first day together, there was a sense of ease in the room. The walls were covered in over 380 square feet of Sam's graphic recordings! People were eager to catch up with each other, dive into the agenda, and meet the community "climate champions" who presented and stayed for deeper conversations. This was the day they had been waiting for from Day One, when we asked, "How do we take action in our homes, at our workplaces, in our communities, cities, province, as a country?" It was obvious: "regular folks" need to connect with people who are working every day on solutions to all of these issues—and succeeding. One "champion" spoke about change happening in a non-linear way, in "bursts," and to illustrate described how Rosa Parks had just returned from a civil disobedience training where she learned about things like refusing to give up her seat on the bus when that fateful act became a spark of profound action and positive change.

In the closing circle, the fireman in the group commented that he was so grateful to have this group to talk with about these issues. He said someone would literally throw something at him if he tried to talk about these important topics at work. Others agreed that they had no other "safe space" to have these conversations, even in their families.

Sam Bradd

It became "cool to care" in this group of strangers who had evolved into a community over the course of two months and who were now prepared to be change-makers in their own communities.

It's true, this was just the beginning of the conversation for many in this group. But now, they have a felt experience of becoming a community of people who cared enough to ask the hard questions, share and learn together, and take one step toward seeing and creating a future in which they can—and will—be active participants.

STINA BROWN enjoys spending most of her time reading, listening to music, sketching, writing, walking and in silent contemplation. Silence has so much to teach us. Sometimes she works with groups who want to take a quantum leap.

Stina is an artist who listens to her life, her clients, the present moment and the future. She designs and leads processes to create new shared awareness, expression, trust, vision and strategic plans. Stina also enjoys the role of "Artist in Residence" on longer retreats and prioritizes projects that enable the healing of humans' relationship with Nature and each other. Through visual facilitation and teaching, Stina invests in people and the planet with local and international clients. Stina lives in Vancouver, BC Canada and is Super Auntie to six amazing kids. www.stinabrown.com stina@stinabrown.com

Creative Commons (CC) license Attribution

References

1. For more information on the Climate Justice Project, see: www.policyalternatives.ca/projects/climate-justice-project. For information on teaching about climate justice, see: teachclimatejustice.ca
2. Big Think.com: bigthink.com/risk-reason-and-reality/climate-change-and-emotions-how-we-feel-matters-more-than-what-we-know
3. bigthink.com/users/davidropeik
4. David Suzuki Foundation: www.davidsuzuki.org/blogs/docs-talk/2012/01/coping-with-climate-change-is-a-family-matter/

Sharing a *Dia* Experience

Claudia Madrazo

How can we create a space in which reflection emerges?

How does deep listening happen?

How do we learn to inquire about our own perceptions and thoughts?

How do we connect our own and others' learning experiences in order to make sense of the world together?

dia® *(Development of Intelligence through Art)* is essentially a methodology and a learning process that uses works of art to catalyze ideas, encourage reflection, and promote free thought and discussion on important issues related to students' personal life experiences and large-scale, global challenges.

Centered on the power of dialog around a work of Art, *dia* helps to build a sense of connectivity between students and teachers, children and parents. In fact, the *dia* programs and methodology have an impact on all of the participants, building mutual understanding across different levels and kinds of relationships. *dia* transforms teachers from their unilateral and "downloading content" habits to a more emotionally engaged partnership of mutual learning and development.

Students and their teachers connecting through an inquiry into art

Over the past 18 years, the *dia* program has been taught to more than 40,000 teachers in Mexican public and private schools, and has benefitted more than 800,000 students in different contexts, along a continuous process of practice, investigation, and systematization. Over these years *dia* has evolved from being a "structured" educational program to a much more holistic and dynamic methodology of innovative learning for personal and social development. Even though the program was initially designed for children and teachers, it has now expanded to adults, and specifically to serving underprivileged sectors—prisons, psychiatric hospitals, Indigenous communities, and parents.

Teachers in Mexico learning the dia *methodology*

La Vaca Independiente, the company that created and developed the *dia* program, (named after a painting by Mexican artist Abel Quezada), was born in 1992 out of my dual passion for art and education. The vision of the organization was to integrate art into every day life as vehicle for personal development. Early in our history we created the *dia* program, with the intention to inspire educators to transform their teaching practices. Based on the research of Abigail Housen and contributions by David Perkins, *dia* grew out of the New York Museum of Modern Art's Visual Thinking Curriculum, (VTC) which promotes student-teacher partnership through the learning process in various New York City schools. With this inspiration *dia* was born to helps develop a broad set of skills in students and transforms classrooms at every level within a school.

In each program session, teachers guide students through a conversation about what is evoked through viewing the artwork, encouraging students and participants to share personal perceptions of the image. Through this process they learn to think about their opinions, to offer logical arguments and emotionally persuasive stories, and to apply their conclusions to personal experiences. *dia* facilitators are not specialists in art, but full-time teachers who interact with their students daily. The major outcome for students and participants is the development of communicative, cognitive, emotional, and social skills.

Through this exploration with art, participants discover their own voices and share their perceptions, learning to make sense of the world with each other through the practice of listening, understanding, and sharing. The process is about awakening an inner awareness that drives individuals to act with intentionality and gain a sense of purpose and a feeling that they are valued.

The methodology can be adapted to meet the needs of different groups and contexts outside the traditional classroom and serve as a vehicle for cultural transformation.

dia methodologies and tools can be applied in a variety of contexts, enhancing team building, organizational development, and systems change.

The art of creating safe spaces for collective intelligence, deep inquiry, and self and social development is at the core of *dia* innovative learning programs. The methodology offers a set of didactic principles that structure the sessions to guide the process, encouraging people into a space of conversation and community and into circles of deep confidence and understanding.

In activating the potential of the visual image we use five pedagogical principles to guide and structure the facilitated process:
1. **Orient:** to create a safe space
2. **Generate:** to ask questions and activate the mind
3. **Recapture:** to connect and knit all participants' ideas together
4. **Motivate:** to bring trust to the space and to every participant
5. **Close and transcend:** to expand understanding into everyday life

Mediators—or facilitators—either use the collections curated by *dia* or select inspiring works of art, paintings, or photographs for their classes or sessions based on the work's ability to be widely discussed and interpreted.

A teacher guiding students through a conversation about a piece of artwork

To get a better sense of a *dia* class in action, we invite you to activate your imagination and be transported to a slum neighborhood in Mexico City.

Our lesson today begins in a CAM—a "Multiple Attention Centre" for children with serious mental and developmental disabilities. This school has been working with the *dia* methodology for more than 15 years. Gaby, the teacher, is now performing *dia* kaleidoscope, a program focused on art history and culture awareness, where the exploration includes inquiring about the context, the techniques, and the creative process. Questions are the main tool used to generate thinking and reflection, to pull out what everyone knows and imagines.

Orient

Gaby calls a group of 16 or so 14-year-old youth to start the class following recess, inviting them to start the session by performing a physical activity that enables them to bring their attention to the present moment, feel their body, name their emotions, and be connected to themselves.

She then asks them to enact the position of a tree and first models how to do it. The tree is an exercise to develop self-regulation and physical balance. All students stand still and begin to perform the tree.

After completing the task, she asks the children to reflect on their own emotions and feelings. Whenever a child says, "I feel okay," she insists that they be more specific and go deeper to connect with their physical sensations and to share a word that more precisely describes their feelings.

Then Gaby requests that students remember and share "the rules of the game" out loud as these are the keys to keeping an organized and safe space. "Look with attention, respect others' ideas, honor silence, and speak your ideas out loud," she tells the group with enthusiasm.

Generate

After the orientation practice, Gaby asks them to attentively observe the work of art, a photograph from the Altamira Caves. "What do you see? What is happening here?" The scene shows several stamped red hands on the stone wall of a cave.

"They are cavemen," "Hunters," "The hands are painted." The children express what they see, and each of them waits for the other to finish their ideas and listens to each other's expressions (two essential rules of the game).

Recapture

Gaby continues the learning by connecting the ideas, creating and narrating a story in which each child's comment is included; she integrates and makes sense with every piece the students have given her, retaining the depth and richness of the comments.

Sensemaking is emerging.

She then asks: "Why do you think they created these hand paintings?"

"So we can see in the future how they lived in the past," says one child. Another comments, "They wanted to show us what they hunt."

And Gaby continues, "How do you think they created the painting?" inviting the children to search their minds while engendering trust in the participants and the whole space.

They answer "They painted it with the blood of the animals they were killing!" "They use their hands as templates."

The children are placed in small groups; Gaby goes to each of them, and she listens closely as they share.

"So we could know these animals existed before us – now they are extinct," quietly says a child. Another says, "They had to use their hands to hunt them..."

"Wow! That's a phenomenal idea," Gaby says.

Motivate

The generation of knowledge kicks into action and the children start naming the diversity of painting techniques inferred from the picture. They re-create with their own bodies the way they imagine the cave people created their images.

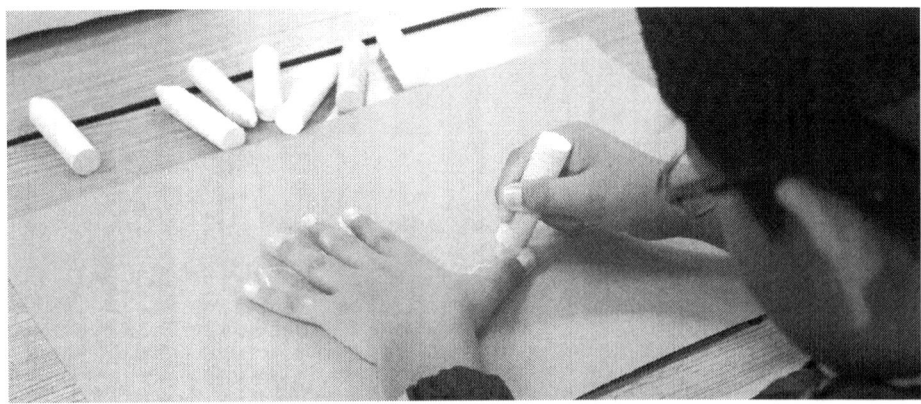

A student experiments with a process he imagines was used for hand markings in the Altamira Caves

Gaby listens. She loves them, and she comes closer. She takes time with each child. She is there, fully present. She is not just connecting their phrases, but connecting with their hearts. She is expanding the field of love and attention.

Close and Transcend

In order to close and transcend, Gaby invites the children to paint something they would like someone in the future to see, just as they are seeing the paintings of the cave people. Suddenly a girl raises her hand (another rule of the game) and tells everybody: "I am going to paint the kaleidoscope class, so in the future other people can see how we sat together in conversation to unravel how we saw the past."

All of the children open their eyes and listen to the girl with their whole bodies, and stay a little while with what they just heard, reflecting on and understanding for themselves what she said.

Gaby's smile illuminates them, she breathes, and she knows something important was understood. She holds the space, stays quiet, and gives the children time to think and reflect—to rest their thoughts on their own works of art.

In Summary

The art of mediating in education is a profound approach that helps students connect with their own passion for learning, as opposed to the traditional method where the teacher is a unilateral transmitter of knowledge and the students are passive learners. They also connect with each other at a deeper level and make sense of what it means to be human and interact within the community and the environment.

Sensemaking or making sense of the world requires a mental process that we can divide into three moments: perception, thinking, and expression. Perception is the moment that connects us to the outside world through our senses; it is the capacity to absorb, connect, and grasp the world around us. The process of thinking occurs when we reflect on what we are perceiving, and analyze our experience; expression is the interface where we communicate and share with others what we have been thinking and understanding.

Through the *dia* process we are continuously engaging the mind in these three moments of the mental act, individually and collectively, so that we become—through this journey—aware of how, and what, we perceive and how to express ourselves. Most profoundly we realize that making sense of the world is not only an individual quest, but a collective endeavor.

CLAUDIA MADRAZO was born into a family of educators and has had a lifelong interest in learning, with specific inquiry into the relationship of art, nature, and integral education for the development of human consciousness, social awareness, and social change.

Claudia has a degree in Communications and Mass Media from Universidad Iberoamericana, Mexico City, and a Master's in Museology and Semiology of Cultural Objects from Essex University in the UK. She is the author of nine books, as well as numerous essays and articles. She has founded and participated in different NGOs including La Vaca Independiente®, *dia*®, Fundación TAE®, and the Academy for Systemic Change—an initiative to enable leaders, communities, and networks in critical systems to catalyze and facilitate societal, environmental, and economic well-being on a scale that matters. www.claudiamadrazo.com

Embodied Mark-Making

The Big Brush experience

Barbara Bash

Two hundred people sit on chairs lining the sides of a large room. In the center of the space lengths of white paper stretch down the floor, buckets of ink with large bamboo-handled brushes are placed near the cushioned seats, a round rock rests on each corner of the large sheets of paper. Everything is ready.

This is the setup for the Big Brush practice I have been guiding over the years. Corporate bankers and consultants, coaches and recovering mental health patients, Buddhist practitioners, students and even children have all participated. What will unfold is an experience of natural order, learning how to begin an action, how to follow through, how to complete. Being held by this form, a fresh beauty shows up in the marks people make. What comes forth is good, worthwhile, and insightful. In this group setting the Big Brush practice joins individual embodied mark making with community art expression.

Getting ready for a Big Brush session, my preparation is focused and intense. I feel like I'm setting the table for a huge feast, every object placed exactly. Beginning with a clean, clear, uplifted environment opens and invites in the nourishment and unpredictable nature of the creative act.

The seeds of this practice began with my meeting Chogyam Trungpa, a Tibetan Buddhist meditation teacher, in the early 1970s. I had been working for a number of years as a western calligrapher, bringing my love

of the alphabet and the scripts of the Middle Ages into contemporary graphic design, bookmaking, and calligraphic commissions. I was involved in the precision, delicacy, and intense focus of the calligraphic form, but something inside was longing to take more risks and be bold. In 1978 I attended a talk by Trungpa at Naropa University in Colorado on Dharma Art. He described Dharma Art as coming from non-aggression and well-being rather than neurosis. He said the work of a dharmic artist expressed sanity and a settled state of mind, and that living an artistic life was a fundamentally human act, available to all. Then he said, "It's possible to make a brush stroke that expresses your whole life."

I sat in the middle of the crowd taking in these words, letting them land inside—"This means a really *big* brushstroke," I thought to myself. Looking back on this moment I recognize my inner teacher guiding me towards working larger, looser, involving the whole body as a counterbalance and enrichment to my precision. Over the next 10 years the Big Brush practice became my vehicle for taking more risks and getting grounded in my body. It also brought with it the companionship and delight of community art making.

Here is how it works:

Participants come up (four at a time or more depending on the size of the group) and kneel on the cushions. I introduce the principles of heaven, earth, and human as the form that we will be following in the making of our abstract strokes. Trungpa had presented these ancient Asian principles in a fresh, up-to-date, and universal way. This will be the essential structure that will hold us through the process and give our strokes strength and integrity.

To begin I ask everyone seated to bow together. A simple bow brings one into the present and bowing together is a collective act. Then each person enters the solo space of making a stroke. When everyone is finished with their strokes all bow together again as a marking of completion and a return to the larger group awareness. The strokes are then folded up, set aside, and a new sheet laid down for the next person. A new group comes up and the sequence continues.

The folding up of the strokes developed out of a logistical need to contain and manage so much wet ink, but this letting go has become a powerful teaching in itself, offering the experience of not holding on to the results of our actions. There are always more brushstrokes ready to be born. It is possible to trust this endless creative energy available to us all.

For the first stroke everyone is asked to make a circle on the page—an ancient symbol of wholeness and unity. I suggest the focus for this first stroke be on the inner/feeling experience. The principle of heaven is the sense of uncertainty one feels when facing the unknown, in this case the blank page. Trungpa called it a "positive panic," a gathering of one's energy, a natural trembling. The earth principle is felt as the movement into action—picking up the brush, becoming engaged, grounded, connected to the page. The human quality is about noticing how we feel about what we have done—curious, inquisitive, open, without judgment.

After everyone has made the first circle, the instruction for the second round is to make three strokes on one sheet—a vertical stroke for heaven, a horizontal stroke for earth, a dot for human. The focus expands now to include spontaneous design, an awareness of the relationship between the strokes, their contrasting qualities, and developing the ability to know where each mark is needed to balance, complete, and resolve the whole.

In the third round everyone makes one continuous stroke that moves through all three stages—heaven is the act of landing on the page, beginning to move, setting the tone; then the stroke shifts to earth by counterbalancing, responding, grounding. Human is the last mark before lifting off the page; resolving, completing, letting go.

For the fourth round the instruction is to make one stroke that expresses the beginning of heaven and the counterbalancing of earth. Then the human stroke is made with a small brush dipped in bright red ink—warm, direct and accurate. Now the deepest aspects of the heaven, earth and human principles are offered:

- Heaven is the basic goodness of the whole situation, a natural sacredness;
- Earth is the freedom from laziness, a natural exertion, a deep relaxation within action;
- Human is the letting go of subconscious gossip (our internal commentary) and having no regrets.

For participants the Big Brush process creates a safe space to explore power and expression in new ways. The softness of the tool combined with the directness of the stroke joins gentleness and effective action in the moment.

For artists working in smaller formats, this bigger, looser scale can breathe life into the carefulness of precision, enlivening sketchnoting skills. Broadening one's expressive range—in life and in mark making—widens the world.

Over the years I have created large brushstrokes for the ending moments of conferences. In this setting I am acting as a channel, gathering the collective energy alive in the room and bringing it down—through my body and brush—onto the page and into form.

Here is my moment-by-moment account of executing one of these strokes at the Authentic Leadership in Action conference in Nova Scotia in 2009.

Walking out into the large room I unroll a long sheet of paper in the center of the space, placing rocks on the corners and buckets of black and vermilion ink and my large brushes on the side.

I stand at the end of the length of paper, facing the room, my heart pounding. It is silent, all 200 pairs of eyes watching. I feel a stroke emerging inside me. It is just a blurred image stirring, but it draws me forward. I bow to the space, and the fullness of the moment, and walk over to the big horsehair brush soaking in the ink. Taking hold of the bamboo handle I press the hairs down and lift up, listening to the ink dripping in the bucket. I look back at the huge white sheet, my legs planted wide, knees bent. I press the brush down into the shimmering blackness, raise the dripping hairs up, down again, up, then I can't hold back anymore.

I bring the brush up and over and it lands on the page—like a hawk, talons extended, landing on prey, wings pulled back, ready to lift up and fly away, but the intention and weight is too strong, it can't pull away from the page now. The brush is connected by a powerful gravity.

The brush moves up to the right, drops down to the left, pushes through, curves around. This is all heaven, descending from above, arriving—the first mark.

The brush pauses. Now there is a turning towards the earth, the natural counterbalancing grounding energy. Mysteriously, at this moment of stillness and transition, the brush releases ink onto the paper (and the floor) in a fan of splatters. No time to wonder why.

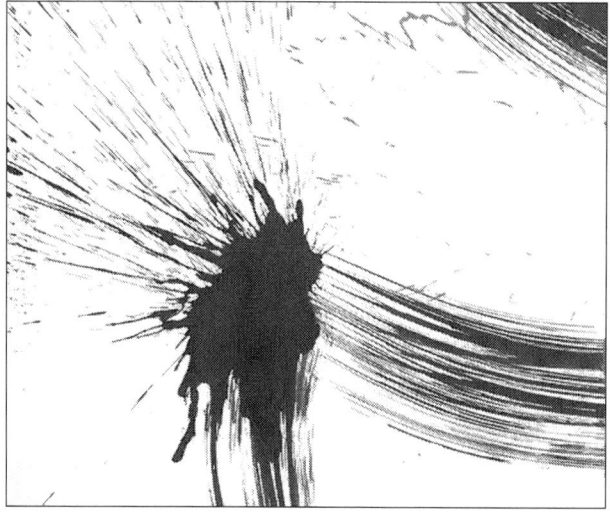

Now the earth voice is moving, speaking, slowing, steadying, drawing the brush down the length of paper, side to side, until it arrives at the bottom right corner of the big page. This is the destination, a simple stop, a quiet ending, humble earth.

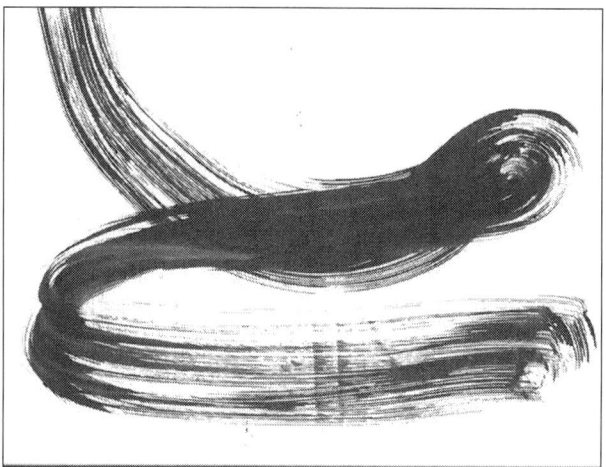

I lift up the brush, walk over and place it in the bucket, pick up the red paint bucket and smaller brush. This pigment is thick, like blood, like plasma. The smaller brush is thick too, and moist and heavy.

I scan the big glistening black stroke—where is the spot for the human mark? Where is this human energy needed in order to join and complete the act? I squint my eyes, softening the visual element so I can feel my body pull me— right into the center of the stroke—the space between heaven and earth. I step onto the page and gently, directly, strike the heart mark—wet and juicy at the core. It is another sudden landing, but this time the bird lifts off, leaving its brilliant color behind.

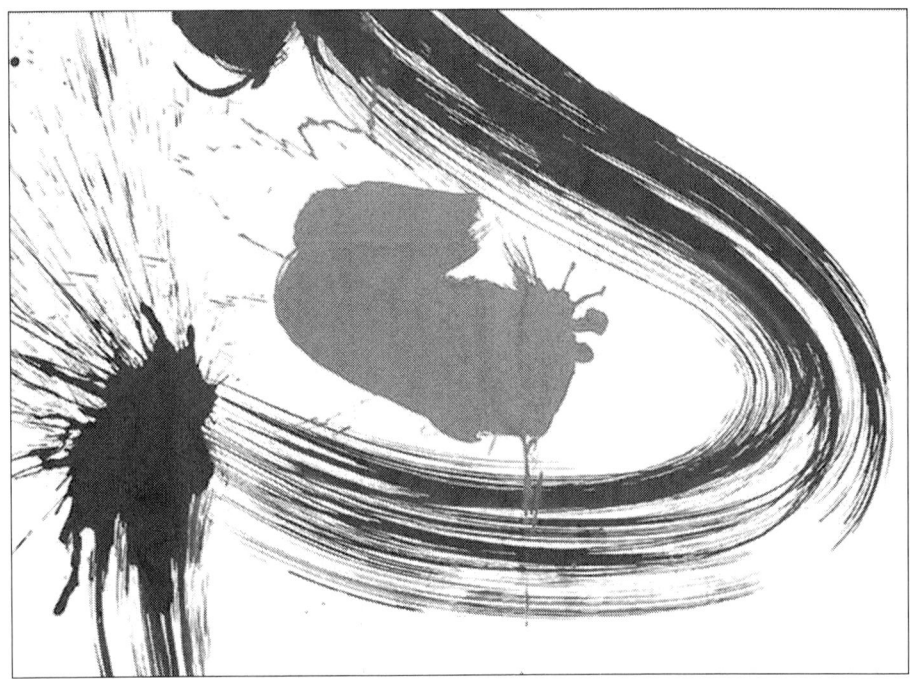

I place the small red brush and bucket on the side, stand at the end of the sheet, cool floor under my bare feet. I bow to the stroke and the space, turn, and walk away. For a moment I am caught off balance, stepping awkwardly. As the gong strikes three times my steadiness returns and the sound dissolves, slowly, into the big room.

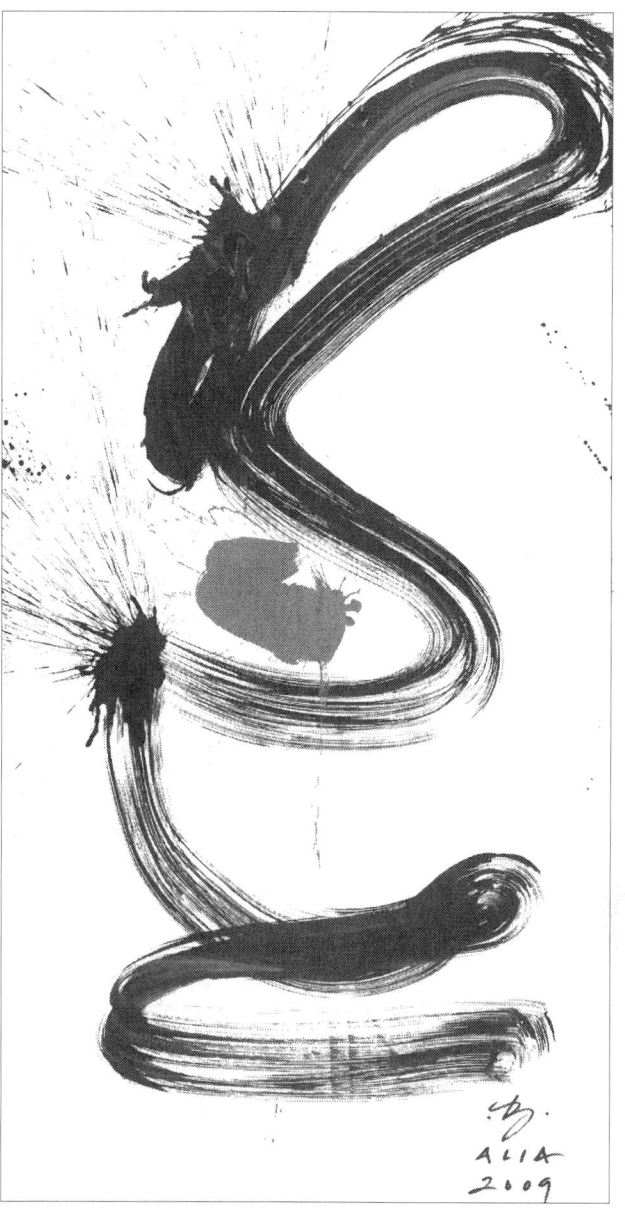

In the deepest sense, the art of calligraphy is the beautiful writing of this moment. The directness and immediacy of a brushstroke joins the space and vision of mind with the embodiment of form, body, and tools. Creating a brushstroke is the act of bringing heaven down to earth through the human experience.

Showing up fully in the moment connects us to our life. A brushstroke invites us onto this path of aliveness. The deeper the involvement in what we do, the more tenderness and compassion we have for the world. In the Big Brush practice we let ourselves be seen, and we see others truly.

This visual expression of aliveness wakes up and enlivens the viewer. This is the importance of art in the world. It is a passing of energy from person to person. The Big Brush brings everyone along on this path of art and awakening. It is possible for us all to express our life in a brushstroke and in that moment be whole.

BARBARA BASH fell in love with the alphabet as a child and has been following its creative possibilities ever since, leading her into calligraphy, illustrated journaling and alive mark making. While studying Buddhism and teaching at Naropa University she began working with larger brushes and performing with musicians, dancers and storytellers. She teaches widely and was part of the Creative Process team at the Authentic Leadership in Action conferences for many years. Barbara has written and illustrated many children's books about the natural world. Her book *True Nature: An Illustrated Journal of Four Seasons in Solitude* explored the inner and outer landscape. She is currently working on a book about the alphabet and why handwriting still matters. Barbarabash.com · barbarabash.blogspot.com · barbarabashyoutube

Discovering Wisdom Within and Between

How storyboards, portraits, and visual explanations can help us learn to solve the puzzles of our time

Jennifer Shepherd

All around the world, everyday leaders like us are working on ideas and projects we care about to address the most pressing and complex problems of our time. Respond to global warming. Improve population health. Create welcoming communities. Preserve the local watershed. While we may address different topics, we share one thing in common: a learning opportunity.

It is this: to learn to surface the wisdom hiding within us and between us and connect it with what we already know. By making the invisible visible, we can express, touch, and otherwise explore ideas and relationships until we discover the missing links in our understanding and wisely choose what to do next. This step could be to form or deepen relationships with others, to coordinate or harmonize our actions, or—like a jigsaw puzzle—to join pieces of information into a cohesive picture of the whole.

Expert navigators use instruments, maps, or other points of reference to plan and follow a path and arrive at their chosen destination. They rely on cues and information from others to see what they can't see from their perspective and add it to what they know about their current nautical position. By combining what they know with what others know, they can find their way.

We do that too. As we work to solve the puzzles of our time, we constantly navigate relationships with ourselves, others, our environment, and ideas—learning as we go. Sometimes our destination is clear to us, and we rely on each other to get there. At other times, we're steadfast in our determination to take a different approach. We have no idea where our actions will take us or what consequences await. In either case, when the winds are still, we're enveloped in fog, and our communication systems are down, what are we to do? Learn to see the wisdom hiding within and between us.

Often, we can't access this wisdom on our own. It may be explicit, tacit, or not yet formed and we don't know what we don't know. We may not even know it exists until we start to explore with others what we know about ourselves, each other, and our work. Given that we come to the work with different backgrounds and perspectives, we can offer space to each other to sit in "I don't know" and discover and learn together.

One approach is to create a storyboard, portrait, or visual explanation with others. These new images act like containers with three core functions:

1. to hold and organize what we know
2. to identify what we don't know
3. to draw out (literally and figuratively) ideas and concepts that help us make sense of the complex problem, the shared work to be done, and our place in it

Everyday leaders often share stories with me about their struggles working on simple, complex, and complicated problems. As part of my visual engagement practice, I've used a variety of co-creative processes to help clients, colleagues, and community members access hidden wisdom. Starting from a blank page, I ask questions to evoke stories, use these stories to unearth buried treasures, and invite intuition to guide us. As the visually descriptive objects take shape, something transforms within these leaders: they are no longer confused and they understand their topics differently. Their struggles dissipate and they deepen connections with themselves, others, and the world around them. Their inner awakening is also made visible and tangible; the leaders feel relaxed, energized, or empowered to make their next move.

I've discovered several patterns by following this approach. The stories I hear often reveal that everyday leaders are thirsty for clarity in at least one of four areas:

1. **Calling:** Who am I? What is my work to do?
2. **Connection:** Who are we? What do we wish to create in this relationship?
3. **Community:** What is my role within the whole? Where do I belong and what is my contribution?
4. **Coherence:** What are we together? How does our work across difference serve the greater good that grows and nourishes life?

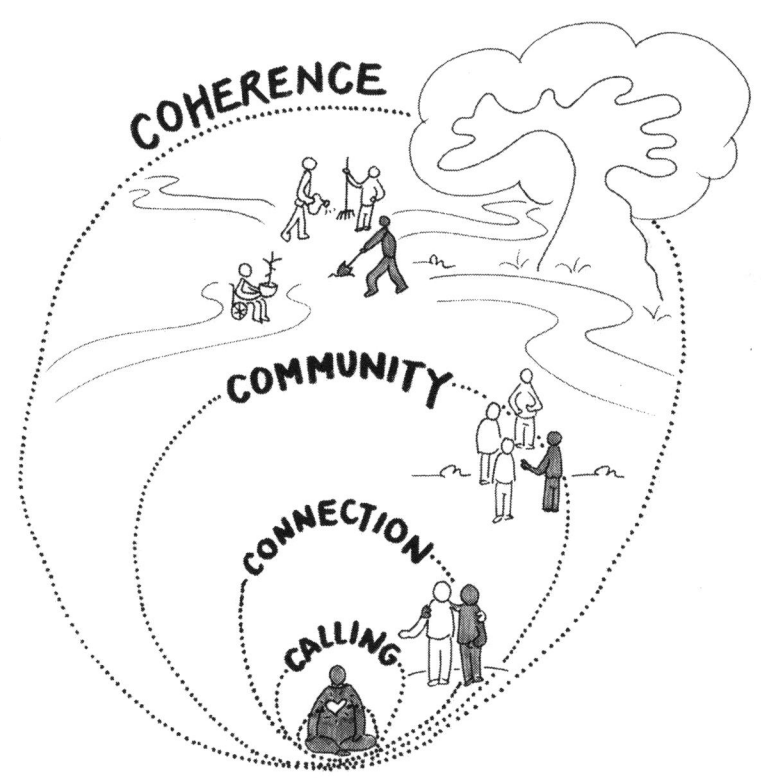

I offer the following three stories to illustrate these points and suggest why making storyboards, portraits, and visual explanations with others can help. For the purpose of this chapter, I've created my own definitions to describe these visually descriptive objects:

- **A storyboard** contains a narrative of a journey over time, or contrasts the present with the future.
- **A portrait** depicts someone or something in a particular way. It represents this person or thing at one moment in time through the lens of one or multiple perspectives.
- **A visual explanation** helps an audience to understand a complicated or complex concept. It reveals relationships among ideas that are easier to grasp visually than through the written or spoken word alone.

How storyboards clarified calling and strengthened connections

When we first met, my client "Jane" told me she felt anxious and nervous and didn't know what she was doing. Her plentiful ideas and energy were all over the place and she felt pulled in different directions at once. The opportunities she faced to expand her business, relocate, and strengthen relationships with family were overwhelming. Jane and her partner had been struggling for months to make decisions that would affect them both and they were frustrated with talking in circles. Their stress was also growing with the added pressure of looming deadlines.

Jane and I created two storyboards: one of Jane's calling and another of Jane's personal and professional vision. Jane wanted to help girls and young women to make a shift in their lives through the medium of dance. I asked Jane questions, listened for the essential ideas and details that Jane cared about, and began to illustrate these ideas on a large sheet of paper using proximity, color, and lines to show how they were related. As the storyboards took shape, Jane's concept of "Who am I?" and "What is my work to do?" began to make sense to her.

In our third meeting, Jane reflected on her inventory of competing demands for time and energy. Looking at the storyboards we created, Jane was able to confidently and quickly sort out for herself what she wanted to do and instinctively let go of the things that didn't fit with her idea of a beautiful life. Within a week of our final conversation, Jane informed me that she and her partner had made important decisions and started to plan for their future. Why did the storyboards work?

First, the process of creating the storyboards helped Jane to access her inner wisdom by making the invisible visible. Jane connected with her own intuition and could see how the parts of her life she had been treating separately—her calling, her work, her family life, and her own interests—came together into a whole. Instead of reacting to outside stimuli pulling her in different directions, Jane could easily choose what to do, guided by her clear connection with personal purpose—her inner beacon.

Second, the conversation helped Jane to interact with the storyboard as it developed. This helped her to generate insights and transform how she felt inside. Now feeling grounded, happy and peaceful, and literally seeing what mattered to her, Jane could clearly choose what to do.

Third, Jane had something tangible to show to her partner. This shared point of reference helped them to identify what mattered to them both and discover what they wanted to create in life together.

How portraits clarified community connections

In a second instance, I was approached by a funding agency to create two portraits over the course of a two-day meeting. The first would depict the perspectives shared by invited staff, volunteers, donors, and grantees on how to fund for community impact. The second would capture the board members' reflections on the topic as they contemplated a strategic change of direction for the organization. They took stock of their purpose, promise, and history, reviewed priority goals, identified considerations for focused giving, and identified implications of shifting to contributor-centric engagement.

After the gathering, staff members who were not part of the process were asked to look at the portraits. Turning to a senior leader, I heard "John" say: "I get it. I can see what I need to do now. I don't need to wait weeks for your written report of the meeting or the executive summary." The portraits made immediate sense to him and he felt inspired to take action right away. Why did the portraits work?

First, the portraits made the multiple perspectives visible to John and tied the shared wisdom together. Comparing the depiction of others' ideas with his own enabled John to instantly make sense of the new direction.

Second, the portraits helped John to connect with what he cared about: Where are we going together? How do I fit into this work? Where do I belong, and what's my contribution?

Third, referring to the tangible object enabled John to give voice to his own work and talk about it with his colleagues. Presumably, these conversations—supported by a visually descriptive point of reference—helped the agency's staff as a whole to see how their work in different departments was related to funding for community impact and to coordinate their actions going forward.

How a visual explanation clarified the coherence of a proposed project

A third client approached me with a different problem. Her organization had collaborated with successful businesses, non-profit agencies, and government partners to develop a viable model to address a complicated issue: how can we source and purchase more healthy food in the face of rising demand and rising food and fuel costs so that our neighbors in need have access to healthy food? The puzzle "Francine" was working on was complex and the response was complicated.

Francine needed a visual explanation to tackle two issues. First, she had spent years developing trust and relationships with partners to understand what was needed and design a systems approach to meet the needs. She was too close to see what someone on the "outside" saw and what they needed to understand to support the initiative. Second, to win a start-up grant in a funding competition, Francine needed to quickly explain the business model to potential funders so they could easily grasp what the new enterprise would do and where it would create value within the local food system.

Being new to food system issues, I spent over two days reviewing documents in piecemeal and engaging in several long conversations and concept development sessions with Francine to uncover the salient points to communicate in the visual explanation. Many related storylines began to surface as we explored: what's really at the heart of the problem, supports and assets, the pain points in the system, and how the new enterprise can relieve the pain or create new gains. We also explored how the various organizations in the food system are related, what relationships are missing, and where and when the money will be invested and why it is needed. We sketched and re-sketched concepts. We shuffled and re-shuffled a plethora of sticky notes. We talked, listened, asked questions, and challenged each other with a refreshing intensity until the mess of ideas gelled into a cohesive whole. We pared down the details to the bare essence and illustrated the flow of work and value.

Creating the visual explanation with me helped Francine to achieve her two goals. By clarifying her thinking along the way, she improved her ability to present her ideas coherently. She found the simple language she needed to explain a complex topic after seeing and hearing me explain how I saw and understood the problem and noticed what really wasn't clear to me as an outsider. Francine transformed her complicated proposal that made sense to those on the inside of the project into a clear and concise funding request that made sense to everyone. As an added benefit, she came to understand the food insecurity problem better, even after years of dedicated focus on it.

And although another organization ultimately won the grant, feedback on Francine's presentation was positive. Other funders in the audience saw the value in the project and wanted to support it. In fact, three different funders in the audience funded the project within three months of the presentation! Another leader, who had been hearing about the problem and the proposed business model before, told me this was the clearest he had ever understood the problem and the project. Why did the visual explanation work?

Let's peer through the Johari Window, a model developed in 1955 by Joseph Luft and Harrington Ingham, to explore this together. Francine knew what she knew, but she didn't know what others didn't know. Our conversations helped us to create a new, shared understanding of the problem and express it in a way that neither of us could have done without tapping into each other's knowledge, ignorance, and perspective. We explored *blind spots* that revealed what the other person knew but we didn't know ourselves, *hidden areas* that revealed what we knew but the other person didn't, and we made these invisible areas of knowledge visible to complete the picture of what we both knew. From this new place of shared understanding, we were able to clearly articulate Francine's social enterprise concept to improve others' understanding of how the various people, organizations, actions, and ideas involved fit together in a coherent whole to respond to the food insecurity puzzle.

What do we do when knowledge doesn't yet exist?

Storyboards, portraits, and visual explanations excel at helping everyday leaders to access, organize, and illustrate what is known to help us make sense of the puzzles we wish to solve and see opportunities to coordinate action with others. As I walk my own path in this learning journey with you, I wonder: What is their role when knowledge doesn't yet exist? How can they help us to sit in the great unknown and work across purposes, not at cross-purposes, to bridge the boundaries of relationship, purpose, or knowledge that divide us?

Answer: to focus our attention on learning *how* to work together. As we develop storyboards, portraits, and visual explanations collaboratively, we can use the visually creative process:

1. to nourish deeper conversations with each other and listen with empathy and compassion;
2. to change the object of focus;
3. to question existing practices; and
4. to develop new practices and models that shift our approach to solve the puzzles we care about.

My thinking on this topic has been deeply inspired by the work of Yrjö Engeström (2001). In applying the five core principles of activity theory, he introduced a new approach to expansive learning by exploring why, how, and what we learn as we work inter-organizationally on a common problem.

Take, for example, the complex problem of remediating the health of Muskrat Lake in Ontario, Canada. Those of us who are working on this puzzle are not well connected with the other leaders, networks, and organizations who also care. It's not clear who is ultimately responsible for stewarding this care or the lake's health for the greater good. And despite good intentions, in the absence of these relationships and a process for coordinating our actions, we don't have the means or capacity to inform others about what we notice, plan, and do. The lake is dying and its ecosystem will carry the burden until those of us who care enough or depend on it learn to solve this puzzle collectively.

Moreover, though we all depend on the lake's health, we may not all know about or respect how our different interests are interdependent. Some people want to drink the water, eat the fish, and swim in the lake. Others wish to earn a living, produce food, maintain property values and shoreline use, permit new development, and enjoy recreation and tourism assets. Still others wish to preserve habitat for flora and fauna, assess and monitor the lake's health, and better conditions in the watershed as a whole.

As we gather facts about the lake and debate what's making it sick and who's to blame, we can create portraits that show us mired down in our separateness and reinforce the divisive boundaries of what we currently know and understand. Alternatively, we can use the visually creative process to *listen to each other with empathy and give voice to and make room for our multiple perspectives*. A portrait developed in this way can reveal what connects us and help us choose to take shared responsibility for communal stewardship.

As we open ourselves to see the lake's health *through multiple viewpoints and through the context of history*, we begin to create shared understanding of the lake's situation and the conditions that create lake health. Instead of focusing on what divides us, we can now *focus our attention on what unites us*: learning what will make the lake healthy. When we ask what each other knows and sees, we make our respective blind spots and hidden areas of knowing visible. In the process of creating a visual explanation of what is making the lake sick, we deepen our knowledge of interconnected dynamics and begin to reflect on our own contribution to the lake's impending demise. As our shared understanding of the situation grows, we can begin to *question existing practices*—including our own.

Armed with two tangible points of reference about our shared purpose, we're now well primed to *notice and map contradictions* between current practices and conditions that create lake health. The act of identifying and noticing such contradictions inspires us to change and drives us to develop different ways of being and acting. Now we can create a storyboard that reveals tensions between current practices and the vision for lake health. By exploring these tensions, we begin to *identify and make sense of entry points for change*.

Others have written about the power of visual practice to nourish innovation and design prototypes, so I won't say more about that here. We know that visualization helps us to look at and see situations from different perspectives, imagine what is possible, and show and share our ideas with others. Images we create through such processes can help us to reflect on and realign practices and consolidate what works.

In summary, we can turn to storyboards, portraits, and visual explanations to gain clarity about our purpose, our relationships with one another, our communities, and the complex problem of lake health remediation. We can also use the visually creative process to help us learn how to be in this work together.

Opening to the power of not knowing

As we work with others on complex problems, it is helpful to explore our learning stance. When making visually descriptive objects like storyboards, portraits, and visual explanations, we are called to be with our vulnerability and open to the power of not knowing. We need to attend to what we are sensing in our body—not just what we are thinking—to begin to see and touch the essence of wisdom awaiting birth.

Have you ever been part of a gathering and had a feeling that something "big" is developing in the room but you can't quite put your finger on it? Staying with that energy, following it, and inviting it to speak through you is part of the process. The images we draw—or that others draw for us—can be messy because we're just starting to get a sense of what is emerging. When we allow that messiness to be as it is without judgment, we create space for new, shared wisdom to grow in the space between us and discover what we can learn from it collectively.

In these times, we are *all* called to be visual practitioners—whether we hold the pen or not. Through our presence and attention to what we notice arising inside and between us, we form an energetic container to hold the essence of wisdom as it begins to emerge. We must open to it, voice it, and begin to give it just enough form that we can work with it and come to understand it together. Co-created messy drawings are good examples of "form"; they show ideas in development and help us to see the big picture of our shared work and make sense of what is ours to do.

Conclusion

As everyday leaders, we are on a learning journey to solve the complex puzzles of our time. When our path or destination is not clear, we can surface the hidden wisdom within and between us to quench our thirst for clarity and understanding. We do this by creating visually descriptive storyboards, portraits, and explanations with others. These objects reveal patterns in what we collectively know and don't know. They become a shared point of reference as we explore: our calling, personal connections, community relations, and next steps to take with coherence of identity and purpose. We live in a relational world. By working with others to make the invisible visible, we can navigate through unknown waters and find our way.

JENNIFER SHEPHERD makes it easy for everyday leaders to clarify what matters, discover new possibilities, and intuitively make their next move. She believes individuals, organizations, and communities can achieve great things when they tap into the latent wisdom within and between them. Jennifer inspires leaders like you to access this wisdom and use it to generate insight and collaborate well. Jennifer is the Principal of Living Tapestries, a consulting practice based in Ottawa, Canada. She holds a Master of Arts in Human Systems Intervention and is an IAF Certified Professional Facilitator. www.livingtapestries.ca Copyright © 2016

Reference

Engeström, Yrjö. (2001). "Expansive Learning at Work: toward an activity theoretical reconceptualization." *Journal of Education and Work*, Vol. 14, No. 1.

Sensemaking, Potential Space, and Art Therapy with Organizations

Moving beyond language

Michelle Winkel, MA, ATR

Art-making is a deeply personal process. As artists, we may begin drawing lines or forms on a blank page without knowing how the image will evolve. We initiate the potential space of the paper or canvas. At some point, most of us become concerned with the final product of our creation. We may even consider who will view the piece, and how, when it's done. Will our viewer find it meaningful and valuable in some way? Will they construct a story for themselves about what they see?

I am an artist and an art therapist. When I step out of my artist role and into my art therapist role, I look at client artwork from a viewer's perspective. I invite the client to project their internal experience onto the blank page, and make meaning for themselves as they work. We look at the final product together. I am a witness. I am not making the art but rather participating in the creative process silently by holding a frame to support the art maker. It becomes a collaborative and co-created potential space that differs from the space I create alone in my studio. The space is full of possibilities, a psychological vessel for innovation and creativity.

The creative process in art therapy has a structure that facilitates interpretation and healing. The art therapist and client can respond to the images, giving room to digest the conscious and unconscious content safely. Visual interpretation is also a key principle in graphic facilitation. While graphic facilitation is not art therapy, I write this chapter from my cross-disciplinary perspective. Although these roles differ and usually involve separate client groups, I will speak about the overlapping concepts of the professions and how each informs the other for me.

Graphic facilitation is often conducted with, and for, organizations. Based primarily in systems thinking, they have structures and goals that differ from therapy of any kind. However, organizations have a psychology, much like an individual or a family system, which is expressed through behavioral dynamics. This shared assumption makes well-trained art therapists very skilled at interpreting and understanding organizational dynamics. Translating these dynamics into visual imagery is the graphic facilitator's arena.

Some graphic facilitators use images and words in their work, but they describe it differently from my interpretation of graphic facilitation; they often add words and diagrams to help elaborate on the content of the material. Increasingly, facilitators are knowledgeable and sensitive to visual learners in a group and want to capture their attention. They know that imagery can add an important dimension so that more of the group will engage with the material.

However, some facilitators and graphic facilitators do not, or cannot, address the latent and unspoken material which emerges through the group process. For example, novice graphic recorders usually respond to the overtly stated requests of their clients exclusively, such as drawing the conference or event content they hear. They are unable to listen to and hear the equally important story underneath the manifest, some or all of which may be unconscious material. Or they may sense the real story and be hesitant to represent it on paper without following the client's lead. However, I have found that this expression is always beneficial to the growth of the group. In my experience as both a therapist and an organizational consultant, I would argue that we add significant value to the process by **naming** emotional content in the room with our markers and our imagery.

Like making art within the safely held space created by an art therapist, effective visual practice moves beyond language. The decision-making process from moment to moment must quiet unnecessary noise on the drawing or, as art therapists sometimes call it, the mural. The choice of which images and words are scribed helps the group members find and explore nuggets of honesty essential to meaning-making and change. Sometimes it feels like stirring the pot, which is often the first step to helping a group make change. How many times have you been hired to help an organization solve a problem when in fact, the stated problem turned out to be covering up another, more complex issue? Sometimes, as the consultant, our role is to rename or redefine the problem so it can be adequately dealt with. Organizations act a bit like family systems. Often their failures are a result of human relationship challenges within the system.

Graphic facilitators can help organizations adapt to the unpredictable effects of change, not unlike the ways art therapists help families and individuals. Without guiding structures, such as those created by graphic facilitation, discussions may not thrive. If we simply draw the verbal content, we are missing much of what is exciting in the group process.

An organizational event can be viewed as a creative, living entity as it grows and unfolds in front of the participants and in front of the visual practitioner in the meeting room. It holds within it the seeds of change and action, which can lead to a desirable future for the organization. Language alone cannot tap these multiple aspects of an event. How the experience is interpreted and made visible by the facilitator creates a reality, which is permanent over time and manifests group meaning. A visual map can illuminate potential cultural and organizational change.

While training to practice art therapy, the therapist develops skills to help others translate emotional material into imagery, in order to enable in-depth discussion. In an organization, the interchange back and forth between the group's words and the drawings on the wall creates a rich and engrossing dialogical dynamic. The graphic facilitator reflects voices and metaphors back to the group members, validating their experience and preventing them from forgetting the vital nuggets that have now been made manifest on the paper's surface. Group participants are able to see a reflection of their process on the mural, which typically generates confidence and the capacity to go deeper. The created mural affirms and validates a direction that simple conversation may not. It pushes boundaries by encouraging exploration.

When I'm wearing my graphic facilitator's hat, I do not ignore my art therapy training. It enriches my process, and makes my work with clients easier. For example, when a meeting begins, I listen for symbols and metaphors expressed by the group members. As they see me begin to draw, it helps bring them psychologically into the room. It helps the group begin to focus and wonder what lies ahead for the meeting. It becomes a back and forth, between me and the group. I am a witness, facilitator, and guide to the group process. I am quiet and a bit physically distant. I may not talk very much. I want the group to unfold in its own way. I may describe what I have heard when I am drawing, and I often show curiosity for what I'm experiencing. Sometimes I show empathy for what the group is expressing, as it helps them to move into new directions. This usually flows naturally. If I am present and attuned to the needs and interactions of the group, my work resonates with them.

Unlike art therapy where the client drives the process through their own art-making, in this approach I describe, the *graphic facilitator is the artist*. We, as graphic facilitators, create the documenting mural and most importantly choose what to interpret in the mural; the creative process for group participants is not one of personal art-making. Rather, it is the graphic facilitator whose sensitivity and skills are essential, but are not unlike the sensitivity and skills of a good art therapist. Often overlooked by group members as they focus on the business of the meeting, the graphic facilitator can grab the varieties of content in the room and choose to portray them or not. I believe art makes a richer experience.

The created mural can be thrilling to group members; it opens to them a world of aesthetic visual meaning typically not "seen" through words alone. The creative artistry of the mural becomes an additional and exceptional group member who is willing to confront with honesty, to explore with directness, to illustrate what is said and to reveal what is unspoken. As I mature as a graphic facilitator, I get bolder about making interpretations of group dynamics in the murals. I dare to choose metaphors that may be confrontive. I think about how to convey tensions or conflicts. I experiment and check with the group to see if my thoughts or metaphors fit for any of them. If I am wrong, the group will tell me, and I ask them to tell me. If I am right, I push the group to move their conversations into new directions. Sometimes a few group members will resonate with my images and dare to openly discuss previously unnamed conflicts with the rest of the group.

The mural is both documentation and a trigger for forward movement and change at the same time. The graphic facilitator *publicly* enacts a deeply creative and usually private process: On a two-dimensional surface, using colors, metaphors, symbols and words, she or he creates an intriguing world of feelings not usually seen with the "naked eye." Like the art psychotherapist, the graphic facilitator creates an ambience of safety and structure for group participants. We also try to create enthusiasm, curiosity, and a sense of play resonating within the room and invite people to participate.

In my role as a graphic facilitator, I find it important to create a potential space in the meeting room, through the use of myself, and the drawing. To the group, I speak at the beginning of the day about my process and what group members can expect to see. I describe why it will add value to their day, deepen their experience, and promote inclusivity. I welcome jokes about how I choose to draw something. Sometimes the most important work is in the silent spaces. Murals give groups permission to leave the world of petty irritations with managers and co-workers and make space for newness. I create an environment of curiosity.

In addition to my graphic facilitation work with organizations in the public and private sectors, I co-direct an international art therapy training program in Tokyo and Bangkok. Most of our students are Japanese, Thai, and Philippine working professionals coming from human resources, organizational development, teaching, marketing, nursing, and other backgrounds. They want to learn art therapy skills to enrich their work or to develop new careers in non-profit and corporate environments at the organization level. We teach in English with simultaneous translation, which also provides incredible cultural learning for all of us. The high interest we've seen in our training programs indicates the desire for people to cross-train in art therapy, organizational development work, and graphic facilitation. As I described earlier, the overlapping principles of the professions inform each other, which registrants to our training programs find compelling. In our classes, we teach art therapy and graphic facilitation skills.

One of the challenges when teaching students from management-oriented backgrounds is to assist them to reframe and suspend some of the strategic, product-oriented goals they've been taught to work within. We help them learn skills to move toward a more therapeutic, process-oriented approach. As they mature in this process, they notice improvements in the quality of their work. They notice more success with their clients in organizations.

In addition to teaching theory, we teach and model art therapy techniques and graphic facilitation activities with the students. In role plays and enactments, they then practice these new skills with their fellow students. Gradually, they begin to implement their skills at work, modifying them to suit the participants at the employment site.

A student case study

One of our Japanese students, "Sonya," works in the human resources department of a large corporation in Tokyo. After training with us for several months, she approached her managers at work, asking permission to set up a pilot program for employees at her worksite. The program invited anyone to "come and make sketches to relax" after work hours in a confidential environment. She created flyers and specifically advertised the group in departments she did not deal with for her human resources job, to reduce conflict of interest and increase anonymity. In Japan, this anonymity was incredibly important. Acknowledging the need for therapeutic assistance is not culturally accepted.

The first few weeks, she was disappointed but not surprised that very few people attended. However, gradually, more and more employees came, and kept coming week after week. Word spread that something interesting was happening every Tuesday. She noticed themes emerge: middle-aged men were especially attracted to the process, and wanted to explore their fear of pending retirement. What would they do after they left the company? Some of them had trouble naming any interests or hobbies; their work had taken priority, leaving little space for other things. Sonya's training, the art materials she spread out in the room, the strength of the camaraderie, and the potential creative space growth and curiosity for the participants. This curiosity and enthusiasm, and for some an increased sense of self-esteem, trickled down to their daily job performance. Participants reported less depression and suicidal ideation. Ultimately, Sonya was making space for unspoken emotions and meanings for the participants, and within the company.

Sonya does not label her now very popular group a "therapy" group (associations and stereotypes would hinder employees from attending), but she knows the power it holds to affect change in participants and the organization. She receives regular supervision to monitor her own progress. Her success as a manager in the human resources department at this company, however, played a big role in her success working as an art therapist. Her work in this organization could be considered an intersection between the two fields. Her ability to navigate the facets of the organization, including its hierarchy, culture, and staff expectations, along with the art therapeutic techniques, all contributed to the popularity of the group and its positive outcomes.

When working as a graphic facilitator with large or small organizations, participant experience is enhanced with the incorporation of art therapy techniques. As the relatively new field of graphic facilitation advances and becomes more sophisticated, facilitators without these therapeutic skills will have trouble attuning to clients' complex challenges. Let's borrow some of the wisdom from the art therapy field while we navigate forward.

MICHELLE WINKEL co-authored *Graphic Facilitation and Art Therapy: Imagery and Metaphor in Organizational Development* with Dr. Maxine Junge. She is a trained organizational consultant, art therapist, and graphic facilitator with 20 years of experience working with groups, organizations, and individuals. Key clients include the U.S. Secretary of Education Arne Duncan, the City of Los Angeles Housing Authority, Accenture, University of Victoria, RCMP, Public Works and Government Services Canada, The Vancouver Board of Trade, the California Mental Health Director's Association, and the City of Sacramento. Details about visual planning at www.unfoldingsolutions.com and art therapy at www.ciiatglobal.org.

Kinesthetic Modeling
Re-learning how to grope in the dark

John Ward

> *Dear Team,*
>
> *For next week's meeting please gather and bring 25 small ordinary objects in a bag. There should be no words, numbers, letters, or symbols on them, nor any institutional messaging. And do not include anything precious as these items will not be returned to you.*
>
> *Please do this task yourself. Do not delegate it.*
>
> *Your bag will be your boarding pass (required) for our session.*
>
> *I'll see you on Tuesday.*
>
> *John Ward*

What would you expect from a meeting that was preceded by an email like this?

I share six stories about smart people with the best of intentions. Overly conscious approaches have blocked their work. In each case, the usual solutions and incremental thinking had failed—original thinking was required.

In each story, I introduce Kinesthetic Modeling,[1] an intuitive experiential facilitation method I've developed and used for nearly 20 years. Kinesthetic Modeling helps these groups and individuals deal with what every professional hates: being on the spot and in the dark about what to do next. On these occasions, people desperately want to make sense where there appears to be none. More critically, decisions need to be made. Kinesthetic Modeling grows from the need to shift habitual thinking patterns and move away from logical, linear sequential modes, while not blocking or clouding the intellect.

In the primal ignorance of infancy, you naturally groped. When you were a baby you tried things out, enjoying every minute of the process until something clicked. Then you incorporated it into your repertoire and mindsets. Groping at work, however, is not acceptable—yet it is the first skill you need to indulge when you are surrounded by unknowns, chaos, and insanity. It is time to reclaim one of the earliest proficiencies you ever mastered.

Kinesthetic Modeling relies first on the quirky fact that people invest great meaning in ordinary objects when they handle them. Second, because our hands and eyes are so intimately and vigorously connected to our brains, they think in concert. This psycho/physiological fact has lost currency as our media obsesses on the brain and pop-neuroscience. Sensory thinking modes open us up to what is known as *embodied mind*. This allows us to make new meaning out of what is constantly surprising us in our world. Kinesthetic Modeling is a playful approach that coaxes us to show up in our own fashion and releases us to do the original thinking for which we yearn.

I. Twenty-five pieces of junk break the ice

Surprise interrupts habitual thinking patterns, making way for imagination and collaboration.

At the beginning of meetings, I act quickly to prompt some spontaneity. "OK everyone, you've all been wondering about that strange email I sent you last week. Let's find out what's behind it. Dump all your junk out onto the middle of the table."

Hundreds of nondescript, even ugly items tumble out. Nonetheless, a palpable glee emerges. Folks can't help themselves as they reach for something and exclaim about how cool it is. In many groups, this initiates an animated round of comparing and sharing. I listen and watch. The less I direct the proceedings, the more people will open up. Even those participants who hold back and only watch become valuable, if skeptical, observers.

"Pick up three things that catch your eye...

...and place them on the table in front of you."

Next, I ask them what they see in each other's choices. Usually they are already having that excited discussion. Following their momentum, I listen for images, feelings, ideas, stories, explanations, and analysis. I name them for the group's benefit, sometimes charting them on paper at the front of the room. We often return to these distinctions throughout the modeling process.

An ice breaker, with almost no rules, is unfolding. Intact teams come to know each other more intimately; and strangers get valuable impromptu first impressions.

Before we move into the meeting, I point out how many images have surfaced, and how expressive everyone is in their choices and arrangements. I also point out the crucial distinctions between images and ideas.

WHAT'S GOING ON HERE?

- The absurd email **invitation** a week before the session cracks open the wondering mind. What has this got to do with our issue? I'd better be ready for anything. Or more problematically, I'm not going to go along with this kind of nonsense!

- **Habit** cuts two ways. Survival and prosperity require that we form categories and routine responses to the deluge of inputs we face. Normally, in business-as-usual situations, this is smart, effective, and efficient. But those habits blind us when our environment changes in unfamiliar ways or there are hidden forces at work. At times like these, **surprise** opens minds and buys a grace period to do some original thinking.
- Without symbols or messages, we project more of what is going on in our minds onto **ordinary objects**. These benign physical items shift us away from verbal, quantitative conventions. Handling, inspecting, and arranging them introduces valuable kinesthetic, visual, nonverbal thinking modes.
- **Miniatures** charm us—Coaxing imaginative stories out, inviting us to play.
- **Ideas** and explanations tend to lock us into a single notion. They invoke preconceptions and established structures that may be holding us hostage. On the other hand, **images** are sensory, visceral, and emotional. They open us up to exploration and multiple possibilities needed to forge new understandings.
- Graphic facilitation supports Kinesthetic Modeling seamlessly as it routinely integrates words and images.
- As a standalone icebreaker, this activity is followed by the question, "What has happened here that will enable us to have a better meeting?"
- As a prelude to a day of more involved kinesthetic modeling, it shows people that they can express themselves, recognize what others are thinking, and be creative. Later when I ask them to build a model of a complex situation or issue, they sense that it is something they can do.

II. Tower of Babel

In this story, a small group with almost no planning is going to build a single model of their situation… in silence.

A tight-knit team of high-performing executives came to my studio for a year-end recap and planning session. The Northern California leader brought her five regional office directors. The East Coast-based company honored them with its Top Performing Region Award for forging new territory in their industry—four years running! This team did not lack for original thinking; but they had a huge problem. Corporate did not have a clue as to the huge significance of this team's work. While prospering for the past 30 years, the company was smothering my clients with rigid bureaucracy. While they were allowed to do whatever they wanted to innovate and earn their yearly trophy, this team was not allowed to skimp on the stringent systems compliance. The six people in my studio were drained and dispirited.

These folks knew their situation inside and out. They'd fretted and talked it to death. So we plunged right in and built a model of it. It's important to start KM quickly with a minimum of talk. Discussion and planning at this point will reinforce preconceptions; conversely, silence during the modeling activity keeps them at bay. People are incredulous that this could work; but I cheerfully remind them that most meetings would proceed more effectively if people just didn't talk.

Through repeated cycles of silent building and verbal debriefs, the group relived all the trials and triumphs they'd experienced becoming a team. They built a jerry-rigged rickety tower that would have blown over had we left the studio door open. It reached the heights they aspired to, but it was a hairball of epic proportions.

"You see," they moaned, "this is what we told you about when we arrived." They took a long lunch in town, bought some holiday cards and gifts, and returned reluctantly after two hours.

I proposed another round of work, suggesting that they needed to model through their situation. Four of the six people, including the director, would have none of it.

"This is our boondoggle and we're stuck with it. Let's just buckle down to making plans and action items." Pushing back, I asked if the four reluctant participants would be up for watching while their other two colleagues gave it a go.

"Why not?" they said. The two stalwarts silently prowled my big industrial office. The exec from faraway Sacramento toyed with a ball of string. He tied one end to the top of the tower; and the other to a nail on a rafter up near the ceiling. His colleague from San Jose mirrored his moves. In an instant, everyone was on their feet. Strings reached out to every part of the Bay Area. My entire studio had become a map of their territory. The holiday cards and ornaments came out of their bags to be hung on the strings and draped from strong points on their decrepit tower. At nearly four o'clock, our witching hour, the whole group was abuzz and I asked, "What are you so excited about? Talk to me. I'll capture everything on the wall!"

Take note: all of this action, excitement, and understanding came without words, in silence! This develops frequently in Kinesthetic Modeling. The comments came out spontaneously, with no quibbling over wording. The whole group agreed on the meaning of the activity: "We can use the strings (our image for the future of our industry) to hold up the tower for one more year. We will explain and blatantly promote our vision to Corporate this one last time. We can do this; and if they can't see our value we will go out on our own."

After dictating a high-level list of initiatives to me, they were out the door, exuberant, by 4:15. They shared their eureka moment; Corporate got the message. The next year my clients were brought east to re-envision and re-train the entire organization—a move that led to an industry-wide course correction.

WHAT'S GOING ON HERE?
- Group thinking moves more fluidly when people don't talk. **Silence** prevents interruptions from our chatterbox, argumentative minds. When no one talks as a model is built, several people are able to think simultaneously and in concert. Debriefs often reveal that individuals are hyperaware of each others' trains of thought. Because there were no verbal interruptions, they collaborated more, resulting in themes fully played out.
- **Frustration** at the lunch break: It is natural to push up against an impasse. Skilled scientists and artists know to **step back** at times like this to allow the unconscious to process and make new sense.
- **Iterations** that **alternate** silent building with verbal discussion prevent preconceptions and runaway rationalization from taking over. Proficient talkers and writers can bristle at this; it takes a while for them to learn how to

work pre-verbally. Most groups benefit by a mindstate shift like this at least every 30 minutes.
- Much of the model is filler as we grope non-verbally and kinesthetically for images that will lead to **significance** and new meaning. A great many images that do not make the final cut are entertained and dismissed before we settle on any explanations.
- The model is a foil, a non-threatening armature for us to hang our thoughts on as we discuss and vet them using a variety of our cognitive modes.
- A problem that is well seen and described frequently solves itself. This team spent the day reliving every aspect of their painful situation. Their **breakthrough** came in a flash as a result of this hard work.

III. Rearrange the furniture in people's minds

Kinesthetic Modeling is a robust process with few rules. It works as long as it involves kinesthetic activity done in silence. It produces a tangible, three-dimensional framework on which to hang the group's thoughts and discussions.

Brian's group has discussed their interpersonal communications problems openly. In spite of their candor at many meetings, the group has made no progress. He has used Kinesthetic Modeling with them before, but he calls to ask me for advice, telling me they're short on time: "I can't get out all that junk and go through all the usual steps. I want to use Kinesthetic Modeling with them tomorrow, but I can't figure out how."

My suggestion: Kinesthetic Modeling is not just the use of tiny objects. Surprise them, surprise yourself. Briefly bring up the intractable communication problems. Next tell them they have just five minutes to silently rearrange the room and themselves to make communication as difficult as possible. Then have a conversation. I'd never tried this, so I wished him "good luck."

The next day, in session, several people immediately turned their chairs around and faced the walls or corners. One person left the room and sat outside the door. Another rattled furniture and papers whenever anyone talked. Another stood up repeatedly and noisily emptied his pockets on the table.

Once he was able to get past the raucous laughter, all Brian asked was, "How is what is going on here like your team's situation?" He captured all the answers on a wall chart.

The agenda and the time crunch were forgotten because this was the most urgent conversation they needed to have. Finally, they outed the stubborn substance of their communication dysfunction and addressed it directly. Brian, who is normally a very nuts-and-bolts meeting facilitator, described the effect as "magical."

WHAT'S GOING ON HERE?
- The tremendous **scale change**, as well as the disruption of conventional meeting behaviors, is what surprises everyone this time. It prompts them to finally engage effectively with their predicament.
- The **rearrangement** of ordinary chairs and personal belongings embody the elusive issue in much the same way as the miniature objects in other examples.
- **Humor** and role-playing open people up.
- Visceral kinesthetic activities **break through verbal taboos** that block open discussion of their problem.
- A Kinesthetic Modeling facilitator benefits from being willing to go to the same **edge** to which they ask their meeting participants to go. I often recommend to people I'm coaching that they inject something into their process that they know will create some anxiety for themselves.
- After modeling sessions like this one I'm frequently asked if I use Kinesthetic Modeling for my own issues. But because the process relies so heavily on surprise and wiliness, I'm forced to admit that I simply have not yet learned how to tickle myself.

IV. The roof falls in

Having a great track record can make it easier to deceive yourself. Kinesthetic Modeling is quite benign, yet it challenges assumptions and reveals new perspectives.

In a month-long, three-dimensional business plan workshop, a seasoned and successful entrepreneur built an elaborate model of the way he wanted his business to be. The expansive roof of the structure even embraced the boat he loved to sail on the San Francisco Bay. As he showed us his model, the roof began to collapse. We all jumped to help him shore it up so that he could finish sharing his fascinating vision.

The next week he arrived late, apologizing for his agitated state. He had just backed out of a negotiation with a high-potential client. The deal had promised huge growth and profits for him, but he hadn't slept all week. The night before, he awoke knowing his model's collapsed roof was a warning. The growth he had planned would probably have overloaded his small company's infrastructure, not to mention ruin his life. Without his dark appreciation of the model-building and the collapsing roof, he probably would have rushed into a disastrous contract.

WHAT'S GOING ON HERE?

- Visual and kinesthetic thinking are **spatial** and **multi-modal**, a good antidote for runaway rationalization. I'd never claim predictive powers for the act of building models. I do believe the quiet act of working carefully with your hands opens you up to a whole host of imagery and prospects—elements of a bigger picture that you can then ponder.
- Our habitual logical, linear sequential approaches tend to gloss over the flaws of our initial assumptions and intentions. Add to these blind spots the relentless optimism and happy talk of many organizational cultures, that drive **imagination** to the back burner just when it is needed the most.
- The exposure and vetting of images during Kinesthetic Modeling debriefs is a form of **strategic due process**.
- Working with others, even on individual issues, introduces **new perspectives**.

V. A large tree reaching for the sky

Working with and responding to tangible materials makes pulling the wool over your own eyes more difficult.

At the start of a weekend-long career development workshop, each participant was given an egg-sized chunk of clay. I asked them to quickly shape it into something that represented their passion for their work.

Deborah offered hers, saying, "It's a large tree reaching for the sky. It's solidly grounded in the soil giving me the nourishment I need." Another participant noticed that the tree actually seemed withered and broken,

anchored by a huge chain big enough to moor an ocean liner. Deborah was silent for a moment. Then she burst into tears. "It's true, my hopes for my work have not panned out. I thought I'd love it. But I don't and now I don't know what to do." Deborah spent the rest of the workshop re-examining her career vision. She would not have apprehended her own delusion without sharing an unguarded image with others.

WHAT'S GOING ON HERE?
- Hands often **articulate** thoughts and feelings that we conceal behind our game face.
- Others can help us see our images without bias. They offer **fresh perspectives** that often trigger great insight.
- A Kinesthetic Modeling debriefing trolls for images. Many are generated and appreciated until a few resonate. They are described and examined before we try to explain them.
- Images that any participant sees are taken at face value. There's no quarreling about the literalness or significance. As modeling continues, the relevant imagery tends to stand out and constellate around important themes.

The wisdom of kinesthetic modeling

Kinesthetic Modeling shares features with many experiential and creative thinking methods such as: working in a safe setting, physical movement, mind-body state changes, improv, etc. Through these six stories we focus on the unusual qualities unique to Kinesthetic Modeling:

- using ordinary objects and the physical space around you
- kinesthetic and visual activities—embodied mind
- sensoriness—dropping back into your senses
- trusting images before ideas, analysis, and explanations
- silence—blessed relief from the intellect, especially in groups

Kinesthetic Modeling not only confounds the intellect—a good thing to do every so often—it sidelines our need to have a plan prematurely, and be right about it no matter what.

The experience and outcomes of Kinesthetic Modeling are immediate and resonant to those in the room, groping together, with ordinary materials. However, the models and modeling process are vulnerable to outside criticism. Describing the modeling, showing pictures of the models, and gushing about epiphanies to colleagues who were not in the room are almost always counterproductive. Therefore, it is essential that the modeling be translated into terms that people who were not in the room can comprehend, or that outsiders are invited to have their own Kinesthetic Modeling experience.

And one last story:

VI. Twenty-four M&M's® and one Ziploc® bag

"You told us each to bring 25 ordinary objects!"

An intelligence analyst once showed up at a Kinesthetic Modeling training with 24 generic green candies, without the "m" marks. They were in a small resealable plastic bag. I found it curious, but kept quiet through the two and a half days of training. During the closing, he provided his backstory.

Covert character that he was, he assumed that I was profiling everyone. He wanted to foil that possibility with inscrutable candies in the plastic bag. He'd pitched this notion to his colleagues, but they didn't play along. Nonetheless, he proceeded to show up in Kinesthetic Modeling terms with a poker face. He was caught totally off guard during the icebreaker when his friends scarfed up and ate his candies, every last one of them.

For me this work returns as many surprises as it dishes out. And humor like this is a true blessing at work.

JOHN WARD has 50 years experience in design, craft, and business. He helps people make sense of their lives using arts-based meeting methods. Based in the San Francisco Bay Area, he specializes in leadership development and the online coaching of facilitators who want to use Kinesthetic Modeling in their practices.

Reference

1. The term and technique "Kinesthetic Modeling" is intellectual property of John Ward, copyright 1996-2016.

Becoming a Visual Change Practitioner

Nevada Lane

In the early years of my work as a graphic facilitator, many of my work engagements followed a similar flow:

- Receive call from client interested in including graphic recording at their upcoming event
- Speak with client to go over the meeting agenda, logistics, and fees
- Show up at the meeting, work diligently to accurately and beautifully capture the meeting in a visual format
- Hand off charts and digital images to the satisfied client

After several years of working in this way, I began to miss being a part of what happened after the meeting. I found myself wondering what happened with the housing strategy the team had agreed on during the meeting, or how the marketing team fared after the re-organization they'd spoken so passionately about. It became clear to me that to stay energized and connected to this work, I had to become more connected to the longer-term goals of my clients so that I could be a part of what happened after the meeting and see the impact of my work unfold.

I developed the Visual Change Planner described in the following paragraphs for visual practitioners who have a similar desire to work toward longer-term change with clients, but aren't sure where to begin the journey of shifting their relationship with clients to make that vision a reality.

Meetings, the heart of change

As most visual facilitators have seen, meetings can have real power. They can act as the "crucible events" that catalyze a group or an organization to move from one stage to another. The Visual Change Planner is a tool to help you consider whether or not a meeting connects to a larger change effort, and if so, to identify how else you can provide value before or after the meeting to support the change your clients would like to make.

Not every meeting will connect to a larger change effort, of course. Some meetings, as you've surely experienced, are stand-alone events

---

The image at the top of the Planner showing people on icebergs moving through a body of water reflects the fluid nature of change and the fact that the next step ahead isn't always clear at the beginning of the change effort. You might also notice that the figures in the image are facing different directions and convey different emotional states. The figures reflect people at different stages of Transition, the phrase introduced by William Bridges to reflect the internal process people go through in times of change. Some figures are still looking backward, mourning the past (the Letting Go phase of transition). Some figures are facing forward, dipping a toe in the water or questioning, reflecting the ambiguous and challenging Neutral Zone. A few people are looking to the future, ready to move to the new land, reflecting the phase of New Beginnings. The purpose of including the image at the top of the Change Planner is to gently remind design teams to consider the internal, psychological side of change during the design process. It's not meant to be prescriptive, or to have each process step on the template align with a specific phase of transition.

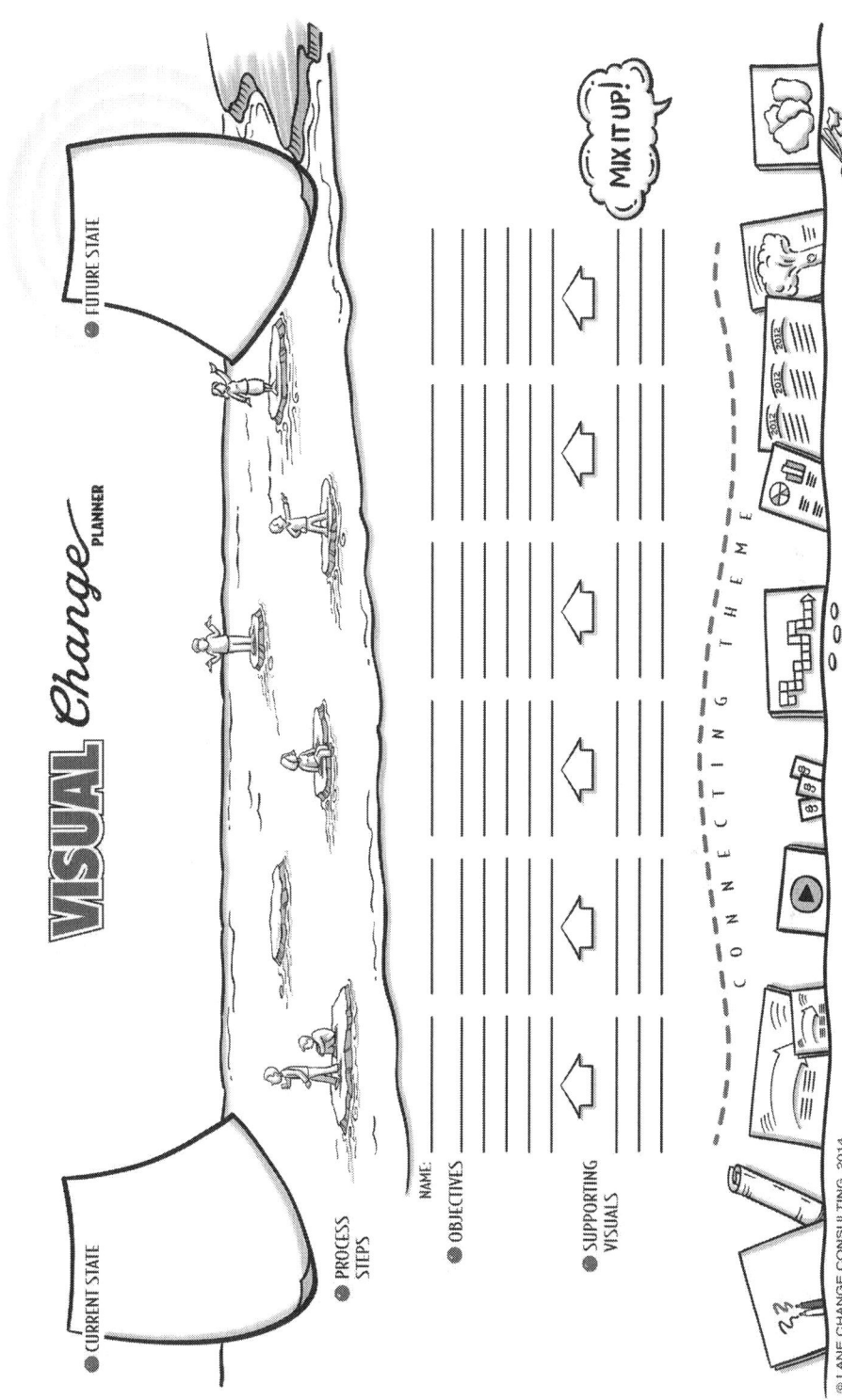

designed to solve a problem, have some fun, or help a group understand something new. Every effort to create change, however, requires people to come together to engage in designing and implementing their future. Keep your eyes open for these kinds of meetings. These are your best opportunities to use the Visual Change Planner and begin to engage more deeply with your client.

There are a multitude of organizational change theories, models and approaches to choose from. The Visual Change Planner is for the most part agnostic about the approach to change you might choose. The Planner is flexible and doesn't outline a specific change process or model, so it works for Kotter 8 Steps[1] converts as well as people who prefer the ADKAR model from Prosci,[2] for example. It does assume, however, that you are aiming for engagement and alignment in your change efforts because organizational and systems change is first and foremost about people.

Using the Visual Change Planner

Below is a step-by-step process for using the Planner with a client, followed by a detailed, real-world case study.

1. **Use the Planner as a conversation guide with your client.**
   I like to have the Planner next to me when I'm speaking with a client about a new graphic facilitation engagement so I can make notes as we talk. It reminds me to have a strategic conversation first, and then move on to logistics and fees.
2. Start at the top of the Planner. **Understand the current state of the client's business and where the client wants to go.** The client will often begin speaking about the details of the meeting they want you to support. Listen, then ask about their broader business objectives. The client's goal may be cultural transformation, or it could be shifting how a team works under a new performance management system. Make sure you understand the broader business context of the meeting.
3. **Identify the process steps that the client has in place to move from the current state to the future state.** One of these process steps is likely the meeting that prompted the client to call you in the first place. Investigate what other

steps the client has already implemented or considered. What, if anything, has already happened to support the business objective before the meeting? What will happen after the meeting? Not every process step will be a meeting, but meetings will often act as anchors or milestones of longer-term change efforts. Clarify the client's objective for each process step.

4. **Identify the visual tools or strategies** that will help support the client's objective for each step. Your options here are limited only by creativity! There are some visual hints at the bottom of the Planner to spur your thinking if you get stuck: graphic recording and visual templates to support bigger-picture thinking and group memory; collage exercises or group drawing to build engagement and tap into creative energy; gameboards to share information or play out future scenarios; and hand-drawn infographics, storymaps, and videos to communicate about change. Keep the solutions varied and always be mindful of tailoring the visual tool or method to the objective of each process step.

5. **Consider the red thread** that connects your visual tools across the process steps. What is the visual metaphor or theme that underlies the visual tools you'll be using? Whether it's a journey across choppy waters to a green and thriving land or a bike race up the Alpe d'Huez to a finish line on top of the mountain, the metaphor must resonate with your client's organization and feel natural in their culture. Beware of imposing a metaphor on the client—what works for you may not work for others. Once you have identified an appropriate visual metaphor, pull it through all of the visual work you do during the change process (like a red thread that ties the work together).

Case study: Making goal setting engaging and transparent

I used the Planner with a 50-person Operations group that needed to transform their annual goal-setting process into one that was more transparent and engaging. The current process elicited groans from most members of the team, and many commented there were a) too many goals and b) too few people who knew what they were. The group had five sub-teams, and none of the sub-teams could articulate the goals of the other sub-teams, despite the fact they were supposed to work together to achieve their goals! In the future state, the group leader wanted:

- A list of prioritized group goals that everyone worked together to develop in a grassroots fashion
- Sub-teams to articulate how they would work with other sub-teams to achieve the group goals
- A transparent and easy way to track and communicate progress against the goals internally and to stakeholders

I used the Planner framework in my discussions with the group leader over a period of a few weeks. We designed an initial change process that evolved as the work progressed. The steps we took, and their corresponding objectives and visual tools, are shown in the table below.

The visual red thread throughout the change effort was the image of a lighthouse, which emerged because the initial meeting location was in a nautical-themed hotel in San Francisco and because it conveyed a message of transparency and progress. The lighthouse image was included on the visual templates, the game board, the dashboard and the storymap. I added other maritime imagery to some of the smaller pieces (the stickers and suggestion cards, for example).

The rewards of making the shift

Being able to develop longer-term working relationships with clients to support their change efforts has been emotionally and intellectually rewarding. My personal relationships with clients who have been open to working together in this way have deepened and I have felt my role shift from being a loose member of the team to being central to the work at hand.

PROCESS STEP	OBJECTIVE	VISUAL SOLUTION
Sub-team meetings	• Draft objectives at a grass-roots level • Sub-teams make recommendations to other sub-teams about possible objectives	• Large visual templates for team leaders to use in guiding sub-team conversations • Pre-printed suggestion cards for sub-teams to fill in and share with other sub-teams called "Our $.02 Cards"
All hands meeting	• Ensure all team members are aware of progress on all current-year Operations objectives • Share draft objectives using templates from sub-team meetings, gather feedback, and identify goals to which multiple sub-teams will contribute	• Custom board game called "Match-a-Goal" where team members match the objective to the sub-team and identify status • Graphic recording during presentations and group discussion • Custom stickers to identify shared goals
Communicate internally	• Make progress against annual objectives transparent	• Large, hand-drawn dashboard with space for sub-teams to post "% complete" stickers
Communicate externally	• Ensure stakeholders are aware of objectives	• Large illustrated storymap showing Operations vision, purpose, annual objectives
Lessons learned session *with extended management team*	• Gather lessons learned to improve next year's process	• Facilitated session with graphic recording • Visual notes documentation

Intellectually, I've found it stimulating to be able to combine my visual thinking skills with my process consulting and organization development skills in a meaningful way. I'm showing up with my whole and most authentic self when I can bring both skillsets to the table, and have noticed that the feeling of dissatisfaction from not seeing the impact of my work has dissipated. I relish the fact that graphic recording has become just one tool (albeit a shiny, fancy tool) in my visual thinking toolbox and I am free to explore and design other tools that really meet the longer-term needs of the client and their work.

Equally rewarding has been to see how some clients, once they truly grasp how visual tools and methods can enhance every step of the change process, begin to overflow with their own ideas for visual tools. In the Operations group example I share above, it was the team leader who came up with the idea for the "Match-a-Goal" game that enabled the sub-teams to learn about the existing goals of all of the other sub-teams in a fun way, for example, and then left it to me to design the actual gameboard and rules of play. The same leader also had the idea for "some kind of sticker" that would be used to indicate which goals were shared by multiple teams on the large, hand-drawn dashboard. Through our work together, this leader has become empowered to work in a visual way. Her visual thinking light switch is now "on."

Final thoughts

For those of you who are curious about organizational change and yearning to work with clients over the longer term to deepen the impact of your work, the Visual Change Planner is a framework for having the conversations with clients that can help you make the shift. For me the shift from working "at the wall" to working "beyond the wall" in deeper relationship with clients has been incredibly satisfying.

NEVADA LANE is a sought-after graphic facilitator and team development consultant based in the San Francisco Bay Area. Her consulting practice, Lane Change Consulting, helps business teams move from ideas to action using the power of visual thinking, expert facilitation, and a deep understanding of the psychology of change. Her clients include many healthcare and high-tech luminaries across the U.S. as well as local and national not-for-profits committed to creating positive change in their organizations and the world. Nevada holds a M.S. in Organization Development and works frequently with the Myers-Briggs Type Indicator (MBTI), the Drexler-Sibbet Team Peformance Indicator and the EQ-i 2.0, the world's leading assessment of Emotional Intelligence. More about her work and upcoming workshops in Visual Facilitation can be found at www.lanechangeconsulting.com.

References

1. www.kotterinternational.com/the-8-step-process-for-leading-change
2. www.change-management.com/tutorial-adkar-overview-mod1.htm

Four Mindsets of a Visual Ecology in the Workplace

Re-visioning language through visual thinking

Misha Mercer

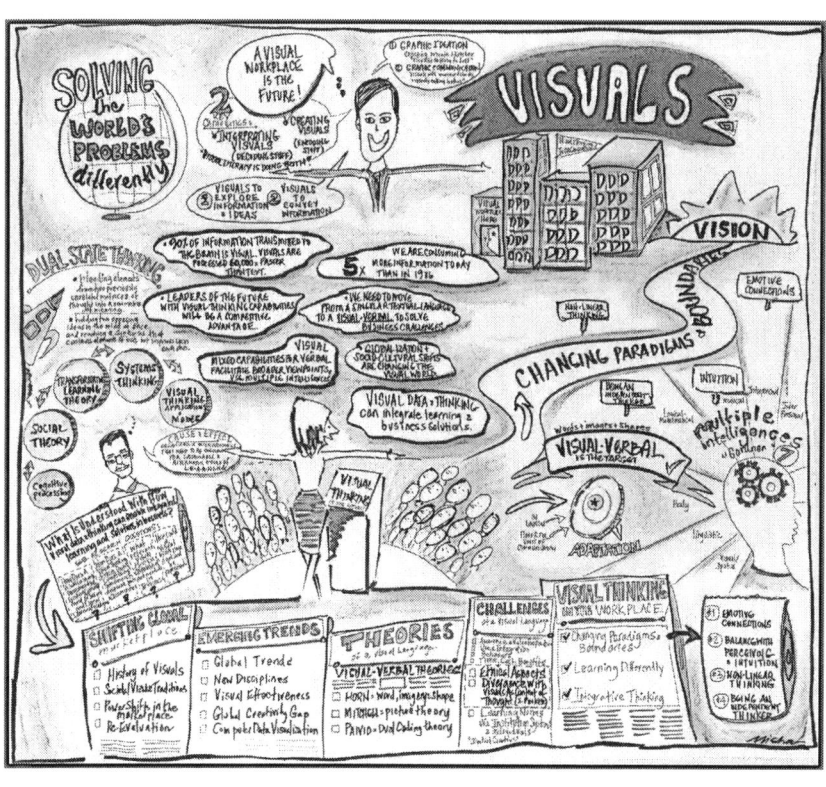

Every time I see Frank, an international software executive I work with, he goes to the whiteboard to draw. Sometimes he writes his summary thoughts into words and places them onto the whiteboard, and at other times he diagrams his ideas. He does this consistently, one-on-one with me and also in groups. On multiple occasions, he has also mapped out his thinking so he could share it with vendors and talent candidates. Sometimes it appears that Frank is sketching ideas to clearly distill complex variables, and working on a whiteboard brings focus. At other times, it seems that he is doing this in order to explain his thought process to his audience. Given the magnitude of moving parts, one might conclude that Frank visually maps on a whiteboard to

1. Bring clarity to his own thinking,
2. Share his ideas with others in a visual way,
3. Enlist others into the complexity once visually mapped,
4. Tell a story, and
5. Reference aspects of his diagrams while gaining buy-in.

Visual language is described as words, shapes, and images integrated tightly together.[1] In this case, Frank would be demonstrating two-thirds visual language, predominantly using words and shapes to convey his meaning and messages. The point is, however, that Frank is using visual thinking methods in real-time in the workplace. The process is messy, abbreviated, quick, and in-the-moment. It allows for deepening of ideas, and also seeing the comprehensive complexity of situations. Consistently this is how Frank learns, teaches, and engages others, as it is patterned behavior. It is natural to him and immediately focuses the conversation with his audience. His techniques are not sophisticated, don't require any additional time, and are always about revealing the components within a system that need solutions, ideas, or further discussion. If this is the premise of visual thinking—distilling complexity, mapping thoughts, quickly bringing attention to the heart of an issue, conversational input, and creating solutions—why aren't all leaders practicing this way? What really is the issue?

As a society and within the workplace, I am not certain we have even tried and failed at instituting visual thinking methods. Rather, it appears that we have never actually made it past debating aspects of visual thinking and literacy, let alone instituting consistent curricula. There seems to be more deliberation of the value, the mechanisms, the applications, and the boundaries of visual thinking by educational scholars and institutions than there is definition of visual thinking and linking the value to the future of our world. As such, the workplace is left to institute creative methods with functional teams to advance innovation, collaboration, and social issues and keep pace with marketplace trends. What would happen if a transformative visual methodology could be an algorithm to explore all ideas, issues, and trends? What if teams put concepts and issues into a visual process at certain points along their incubation cycles and problem-solving journey?

It is not uncommon to hear how quickly individuals say "I do not draw," "I was never an artist," "visuals are not for me," "I don't think that way," and "I am not good with creating things." In the future, these comments could be as outdated as saying today, "I don't use a computer," "I don't have a mobile phone," or "what is Facebook?" As we approach an even more digital and visual future, it would naturally be important to educate the workforce with advanced processing skills. But these emotional- and social- based comments are often filled with deep resistance and bias. The largest problem is that the focus of this resistance is placed on the wrong aspect. Visual thinking is not espoused as a medium for making pretty pictures that everyone likes, but rather a methodology to help what is hidden to be seen. It can be done in a messy or refined way, but the goal is to unpack complex ideas, sketch out thoughts, make connections, and link disparity. So perhaps the key is to debunk the myth that visual thinking is about drawing art and brand it as an incubation formula where art and science coexist.

Some leaders might argue that they don't need to process like Frank does. The question now becomes: What is the risk if we don't start to advance our processing skills beyond the linear, textual, and verbal format?

A shifting marketplace

New marketplace trends in social and digital areas are creating the conditions for an evolving information exchange. With the ever-changing networked world, visual literacy skills of the pre-digital age may no longer be adequate to successfully communicate within a society where the very nature of information is changing.[2] The ability to decode and encode visual content now plays a fundamental role in communication exchanges and questions the proficiency that exists with visual literacy.

Our visual culture, which influences our lifestyle, values, and beliefs, has created new expectations towards learning within the world.[3]

Presently, we are constantly bombarded with messages, consume five times the amount of information that we did in 1986,[4] and absorb 100,500 words outside of work on an average day.[5] Our eyes and brains are the gateway to enormous volumes of data, with 90% of the information being transmitted to the brain visually.[6] Moreover, visuals are processed 60,000 times faster than text.[7] Communicating with images is quicker than with words and this processing speed is why visuals tend to "hit us in the gut."[5] In the context of everyday business, visual-verbal language may offer us a more comprehensive way to navigate the speed and complexity of information and enact new approaches to processing vast amounts of data.

Contemporary culture has become increasingly inundated with visuals. This raises questions about whether organizational leaders are prepared and enabled to demonstrate visual thinking and whether the workplace has kept up with marketplace trends. Consuming, exchanging, and being surrounded by visual data does not equate to being visually literate.[8] Repeated interaction of limited functionality does not mean literacy. Even when exposure to visual content is high, technical proficiency may be low.[8]

A transdisciplinary perspective

Engaging in the idea economy requires a new style of business. Leaders will have to embrace change, harness data, manage risk, enable agility, and empower workplace productivity. This new, transdisciplinary approach may involve looking beyond verbal and textual modes, beyond visual thinking. To get at the root of complex problems, it is necessary to practice comprehensive thinking that links what is disjointed and compartmentalized and encourages a multi-dimensional approach. Additionally, a broader view of thinking helps transcend the silo limitations and disciplinary forms that exist within institutions. The changing landscape will require a breakdown of boundaries and a re-visioning of how leaders get their work accomplished. Language and communication exchange are morphing and transforming from linear to non-linear, from singularity to hybridity, and from simplicity to complexity, suggesting the existence of a new visual ecology.

Possible starting points for transforming the discourse include the following four mindsets. Leaders will need:

1. **Visual Thinking** – Understanding how to engage beyond a singular verbal/textual format at the learning level.
2. **Conscious Analysis** – Evaluating the ability to access multiple frames and how to cognitively process information at the thinking level.
3. **Discontinuous Change** – Examining how to build integrative solutions across complex structures and domains at the system level.
4. **Social Construction** – Reflecting on long-standing beliefs and assumptions related to language at the social level.

Each mindset is part of a complex system within the workplace that ultimately drives engagement, innovation, and improved results.

Mindset One: Visual thinking

Competency begins with understanding. Visual thinking represents a unique view of the world from a different perspective. McLuhan's idiom *the medium is the message* seems prophetic in the high-tech reality in which we now live.[9] It is the notion that the world we shape, in turn, shapes us and creates a circular process of continuous shifts. This constant shift, in reality, helps formulate our beliefs, perspectives, and even our capabilities. The creation of new visual and digital realities poses a world and a

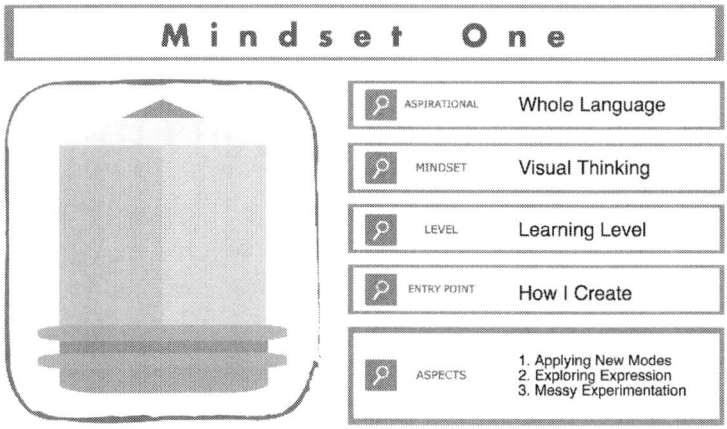

way of knowing, through communication realms never conceived before.[9] If language constantly changes because people and culture evolve, then why wouldn't the visual aspects of language follow accordingly? Our development with these multiple realities—and potentially our survival—will require new thinking. Our abilities to understand what we see, interpret what we experience, analyze what we are exposed to, and create differently will depend on the infrastructure support with a visual language. The exposure to difference will call upon contradictory views that theorists have espoused: a rational, cognitive, and analytical approach and the opposing view of a more intuitive, creative, and holistic viewpoint.[10] Fundamentally, learning visual thinking may require living in uncomfortable space where the answer is not clear.[11] Three areas within mindset one, which explores the range of visual thinking applications, are the following: visual-verbal language, decoding and encoding, and visual communications.

VISUAL-VERBAL LANGUAGE

While a visual language is not new, the re-emergence of how visuals are being used with verbal (textual) language is. Although there are many arguments for one language mode over the other, an integration of visual-verbal language offers a far more powerful unit of communication.

DECODING AND ENCODING

Adjusting to the visual world will require capabilities that enable leaders to decode meaning. Decoding may be done through interpreting society's images and media, which permeate our increasingly complex landscape. Additionally, leaders will need to be able to encode through creating visual materials. In this vein, leaders will need to be trained to create visuals to express and explore ideas.

VISUAL COMMUNICATIONS

Influencing, sharing, and selling ideas happen while communicating with visuals. Using visuals to share ideas with others, whether they are rough thoughts or finished presentations, supports the acquisition of knowledge, retention of information, and faster learning. The graphic communication process assists people with visually talking to others because the visual representation brings increased clarity.[12]

Mindset Two: Conscious analysis

The concept of consciousness has had renewed interest over the years in order to better understand behavior and beliefs. Historically, this led to the importance of what is considered automatic and unconscious with human behavior.[13] Freud introduced the notion of "an unconscious mind motivating our behavior with a combination of innate drives and repressed emotions."[13] Moreover, the conscious mind was prone to rationalization and self-deception. The rise of cognitive science led to the study of the cognitive unconscious, which includes data processing in the brain that happens without being consciously aware.[13] Research shows that unconscious processes may activate a level of control without even knowing it is happening. Conscious reasoning, on the other hand, can often be used for the explanation of unconscious and automatic behaviors.[13]

A reflective ability to think hypothetically about the future and workplace possibilities will require leaders to balance the unconscious, automatic processing (verbal) with the conscious, deliberate processing (visual). Leaders will need to be purposeful with cultivating a visual-verbal language, which may foster new ways of knowing. Three key areas of a conscious analysis mindset related to visual thinking in the workplace include the following: visual mechanics, dual processing, and multiple intelligences.

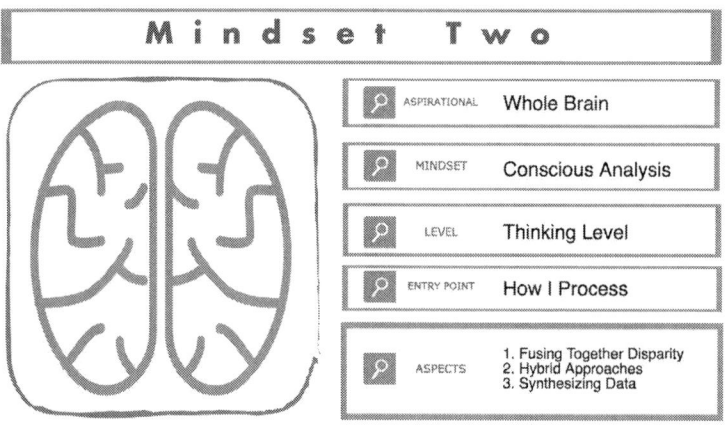

VISUAL MECHANICS

In visual language, meaning is apparent on a basic level but has a complex code that must be learned for true comprehension. Visuals require a new and different way of reading based on percept-concept integration. A visual language encourages more analysis and synthesis that can make the comprehension process complex, involved, and deeper.[1] Learning how words, images, and shapes all distinctively inform meaning will require education and awareness.[1]

DUAL PROCESSING

While our culture has encouraged a strong and enduring left-brain hemisphere, the ability to think in two modes may be as important as it is rare.[14] Research shows that the ability to fuse together incompatible frames and dual thoughts has been identified as a leadership quality that drives the success of exceptional businesses.[15] Dual state thinking is a hybrid view of how two dichotomous ideas of thinking can be integrated.

MULTIPLE INTELLIGENCES

The theoretical framework of multiple intelligences is used for defining, understanding, assessing, and developing people's different intelligence factors. The eight categories of intelligence include the following: linguistic, logical-mathematical, spatial/visual, bodily kinesthetic, musical, interpersonal, intrapersonal, and naturalist.[16] Disputes from leaders who claim they only have a single central intelligence are not valid according to this theory since there are multiple intelligences that work together.[16]

Mindset Three: Discontinuous change

Navigating the landscape to build and maintain a competitive advantage requires a new mindset and a new type of organization that includes visual thinking. The technological revolution and increasing globalization has changed the nature of operating and has presented multiple discontinuities that often occur simultaneously and are not easily predicted.[17] As organizations are faced with exceedingly complicated landscapes and new strategies, flexible ways of organizing will be necessary to stay competitive in an unpredictable marketplace. Visual thinking is one way the workplace can remain agile and relevant. This hyper competition is creating chaotic environments, disorder, disruption, and a substantial amount of uncertainty.

The changes are requiring bold re-visioning, as organizations can no longer survive on incremental changes, but rather need disruptive breakthroughs. Strategic approaches for discontinuities will need to be non-linear and involve approaches that are expansive versus contractive. As such, a massive re-ordering of business practices may be critical for organizations to enable flexibility, speed, and innovation. The following four areas from a systems level examine the importance of breaking down boundaries and assessing impact with visual thinking in alternative ways: non-linear thinking, managing complexity, fostering generative and relational conversations, and evaluating differently.

NON-LINEAR THINKING

Non-linear methods can offer real wisdom and unexpected solutions. Leaders need to make a paradigm shift from mechanistic/linear approaches to recognize this. Believing that problems can be isolated, broken down into parts, repaired, and then restored to wholeness is part of the limiting approach.[18] Rational arguments can bring about the massive suppression of meaning, and when absorbed, we do not know more, but less.[19] The linear mental model that currently exists within organizations represents a form of knowledge, yet it is not sufficient to influence the growth and innovations necessary.[20]

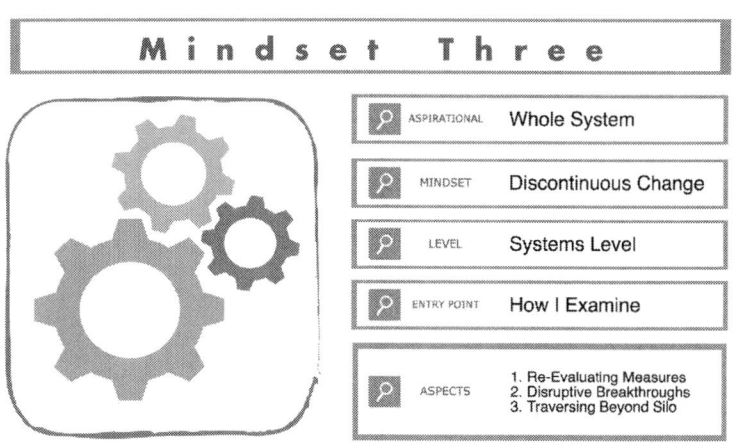

MANAGING COMPLEXITY

There are two aspects of managing complexity for organizations and leaders to consider. The first examines organizational complexity and how a pluralist perspective offers leaders a more diverse way of pushing beyond traditional boundaries. The second area, information complexity, addresses how to assist leaders with processing visual-verbal language and offsetting cognitive overload.

FOSTERING GENERATIVE AND RELATIONAL CONVERSATIONS

A socially constructed perspective offers a profound way of illuminating the interconnected environment and social processing. Incompatible frames and opposing thoughts are perhaps where leaders can discover new insight. Conversations, connections, and a new matrix of meaning can be constructed. The cultural bias with leaders who immediately problem-solve will need tempering to explore deeper solutions through divergent thinking and opposing ideas.

EVALUATING DIFFERENTLY

As organizations and leaders face discontinuous change and increasing complexity, there is reason to re-evaluate how we measure what is impactful. Organizations that aspire to drive new growth will want to examine how things get done and place learning value on failures/challenges in order to foster innovations.

Mindset Four: Social construction

Changing our thinking means uncovering assumptions. Unstated societal assumptions constitute a deep set of beliefs about how the world works.[21] Our propositions about the world are embedded within paradigms—networks of interrelated commitments to a particular view, concept, and language.[19] New paradigms are generated by anomalies where insights that fall outside the range are capable of generating new solutions to a given problem.[19] It will thus be a major challenge for workplace leaders to shift their mindset toward visual thinking if they cling to the long-standing traditional beliefs in existing paradigms. Yet, we are always able to change the construction of our reality and disrupt what we assume to know.

The recent surge of interest in social constructivism has offered a radically new way of understanding, talking, and changing the conversation.[22] In a pluralistic paradigm, dialogical exchanges that embody visual images can bring forth meaning-making and surface contradictory views. Four aspects of social construction that may influence innovation and the adoption of visual thinking in the workplace are the following: social identity, social learning, socio-visual innovation, and finally, unboxed: beyond the boundary.

SOCIAL IDENTITY

Social identity not only has affective consequences with in-group cohesion, but also has a distinct impact on intergroup communication. Communication is a means of creating and reinforcing group boundaries through the use of language and social identity, which can affect how information is transmitted and received. Unconscious bias and tensions can arise in complex ways with group membership.

SOCIAL LEARNING

Individuals are social beings and construct their understanding while learning from social interactions within specific socio-cultural settings.[23] The shift in learning that has taken place is in a social collective rather than in traditional and individual forms of cognitive structures. Context and analysis therefore cannot take place in isolation and without the engagement of social relationships.[23] Key tenets of social learning include identificatory learning, observational learning, reinforcement effects, and attentional processes.

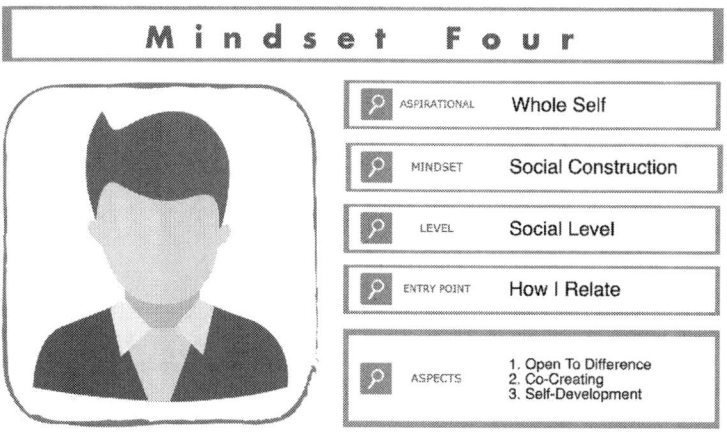

SOCIO-VISUAL INNOVATION

As organizations experience discontinuous change and crisis, innovation is at a premium. Yet many social systems focus on the minimization of behavioral variance and strive for sources of consistency, predictability, and control.[24] Innovative behaviors have a degree of difference and variation, which are often based on a strong motivation toward a vision and independent thinking. Organizations will need to foster unconventional ways of working and seeking originality, which pushes against common norms, but may be necessary to advance.

UNBOXED: BEYOND THE BOUNDARY

Moving beyond the traditional ways of knowing will require that leaders demonstrate a new way of relating and expressing. Making space for creative expression opens up opportunities to explore phenomena holistically and naturally, and thus deepen understanding of the self and the world. Our ability to exchange beyond words and through images easily allows leaders to transcend cultural boundaries.

Visual ecology in the workplace

Current trends demonstrate that the future will be more digital, social, and visual. Marketplace shifts are creating a blur of functional boundaries, where changes are impacting how work gets done and calling into question traditional paradigms of thinking. Learning in the marketplace

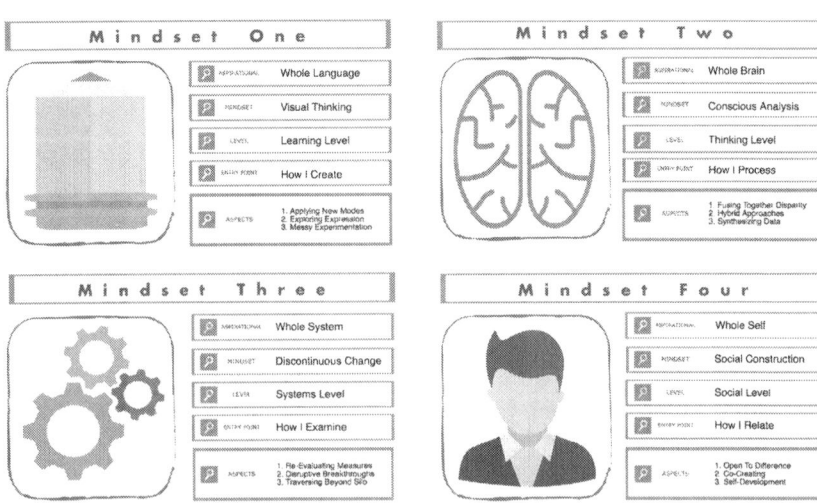

A visual ecology

is shifting from being a recipient of information to being a creator and provider of new experiences, knowledge and services. The intersection of change is encompassing a shift where spectatorship is replaced by authorship and singular perspectives are being challenged by a plea of more holistic approaches.

Re-visioning the future in a rapidly changing world will require disruption. Shifting our thinking must honor the peripheral visions towards a multiplicity of insights that bridge disconnected fragments, beliefs, cultures, and behaviors. The four mindsets illustrate the interdependent nature and broad perspective of gaining visual intelligence to address contemporary complexity in the workplace. Visual thinking is overlapping across and within all the mindsets; therefore, a successful transformation will require a fully integrated and whole approach. This includes whole language, whole brain, whole systems, and whole self. An emerging visual ecology is the convergence of visual learning, which is inclusive of cognitive analysis, social processes, and flexible systems.

Discussion

To thrive in a new, future reality, organizations need to develop a workplace culture that prepares leaders with knowledge and competence to address complex business challenges. This includes fostering a visual ecology and shifting thought patterns: from parts to whole, from adapting to disrupting, from perfect to messy, and from prescriptive to exploratory. All four of these changes require a significant deviation from the norm, which means inner courage and vision will be necessary.

FROM PARTS TO WHOLE

As John Muir famously shared, when we try to pick out anything by itself, we find it hitched to everything else in the universe. An ecosystem is a set of interrelated elements that makes a unified whole, and wholeness encourages us to seek beyond only what is in front of us or next to us. Individual parts cannot be fully understood when separated from the larger ecosystem in which they exist.

FROM ADAPTING TO DISRUPTING

Adapting suggests that only slight coordinate shifts or adjustments are necessary, when in fact, leaders may need to take a more assertive stance.

Disruption is a way to interrupt the normal progress or activity and uproot how we think, behave, and learn.

FROM PERFECT TO MESSY

Our society values perfection. From results, to our brand, and with images, a high value is placed on things being right, perfect, and appealing. Traditionally, we are taught that the endeavour to create an image has worth only related to its visual appeal. The process of seeing new ideas starts with being messy, which may be a paradigm shift for leaders to enact.

FROM PRESCRIPTIVE TO EXPLORATORY

The blueprint of dominant Western culture has traditions and habits of a formulaic society. Immediate action, a measurable plan, and outlined steps with results are highly valued. The prescriptive nature of execution only leaves little space for imagination, independent thinking, and being strategic. To wander, to probe, to diverge and to create may be the critical capabilities of our future.

This multi-decade journey of re-visioning language through visual thinking in the workplace needs to be unleashed. If leaders could begin to integrate visual thinking, like Frank has done, they can completely transform the way ideas are communicated and understood.

MISHA MERCER has spent over 15 years working with senior executives and teams in top Fortune 500 companies as Nike, Microsoft, Starbucks, Schwab, and Hewlett-Packard Enterprise. She leads talent management, organization development, team performance, cultural shifts and senior leadership coaching to drive increased business performance. Misha uses visual methods to foster learning that leverages social groups and collective intelligence to enable breakthrough solutions.

The future will rely on imagining that anything is conceivable, where pre-defined boundaries are replaced with wider edges, allowing infinite variations to be valued. The emergence of creative consciousness begins with a single idea, a pursuit, and a way of being.

Misha holds a PhD in Organizational & Transformative Studies, an M.S. in Organization Development, an M.A. in Psychology and is a certified integral coach. Misha resides in the San Francisco Bay Area. mmercerconsulting@gmail.com

References

1. Horn, R. (1998). *Visual language: Global communication for the 21st Century*. Washington, DC: Macrow Press.
2. Chan, C., Francis, K., Hanson, J., & Kaljana, A. (2008). *Visual literacies*. ETEC. Retrieved from etec.ctlt.ubc.ca/510wiki/Visual_Literacies
3. Bamford, A. (2003). The visual literacy white paper. Uxbridge, England: Adobe Systems Incorporated, Waterview House.
4. Alleyne, R. (2011, February 11). Welcome to the information age – 174 newspapers a day. *The Telegraph*. Telegraph.co.uk. Retrieved from www.telegraph.co.uk/science/science-news/8316534/Welcome-to-the-information-age-174-newspapers-a-day.html
5. Bohn, R., & Short, J.E. (2012). Info capacity, measuring consumer information. *International Journal of Communication*, 6(21).
6. Apkon, S. (2013). *Redefining literacy in a world of screens*. New York, NY: Farrar, Straus and Giroux.
7. Sibley, A. (2012). 19 reasons you should include visual content in your marketing data. Hubspot. Retrieved from blog.hubspot.com/blog/tabid/6307/bid/33423/19-Reasons-You-Should-Include-Visual-Content-in-Your-Marketing-Data.aspx#sm.0001e0xbyxg8yeq3xx11piog60i56
8. Brumberger, E. (2011). Visual literacy and the digital native: An examination of the millennial learner. *Journal of Visual Literacy*, 30(1), 19–46.
9. Jones, B., & Flannigan, S. (2006). Connecting the digital dots: Literacy of the 21st Century. *Educause Quarterly*, 29(2), 8–10.
10. Boyd, R., & Myers, G. (1988). Transformative education. *International Journal of Lifelong Education*, 7(4), 261–284.
11. Quillen, I. (2013, January 29). Why inquiry learning is worth the trouble. *Mind/Shift*. San Jose, CA: KQED. Retrieved from http://ww2.kqed.org/mindshift/2013/01/29/what-does-it-take-to-fully-embrace-inquiry-learning
12. Crilly, N., Blackwell, A., & Clarkson, J. (2006). *Graphic elicitation: Using research diagrams as interview stimuli*. Sage Visual Methods. London, UK: Sage Publications.
13. Evans, J. (2008). Dual-processing accounts of reasoning, judgment and social cognition. *Annual Review of Psychology*, 59, 255–278.
14. West, T. (2009). *In the mind's eye*. New York, NY: Prometheus Books.
15. Martin, R. (2009). *The opposable mind*. Boston, MA: Harvard Business Press.
16. Gardner, H. (1999). *Multiple intelligences: The theory into practice*. New York, NY: Basic Books.

17. Hitt, M., Keats, B., & DeMarie, S. (1998). Navigating in the new competitive landscape: Building strategic flexibility and competitive advantage in the 21st Century. *Academy of Management Executive.* 12(4), 22–42.
18. Barrett, F. (1995). Creating appreciative learning cultures. *Organizational Dynamics,* 24(2), 36–49.
19. Gergen, K. (2009). *An invitation to social construction.* Thousand Oaks, CA: SAGE Publications.
20. Marcy, R., & Mumford, M. (2007). Social innovation: Enhancing creative performance through casual analysis. *Creativity Research Journal,* 19(2-3), 123–140.
21. Meadows, D. H. (1999). *Leverage points: Places to intervene in a system.* (pp.1-19). Hartland, VT: The Sustainability Institute.
22. Shotter, J. (1997). *The social construction of our 'inner' lives.* Department of Communication. University of New Hampshire. Retrieved from http://www.massey.ac.nz/~alock/virtual/inner.htm
23. Gherardi, S., Nicolini, D., & Odella, F. (1998). Toward a social understanding of how people learn in organizations: The notion of situated curriculum. *Management Learning,* 29(3), 273–197.
24. Joy, S. (2004). Innovation motivation: The need to be different. *Creativity Research Journal,* 16(2-3), 313–330.

Rigorous Design of Visual Tools that Deepen Conversations and Spark New Insights

Christine Martell

When we get stuck in ideas, intervention with visuals can help us reach beyond and inspire us to new heights—especially if we remain curious about how others see the world.

When a conversation starts with visuals, different kinds of insights emerge. Ask a question. Invite people to select images in response to the question. See the patterns and unique ideas emerge from the visual cards they choose. The responses to these pictures merge to form a new collective story.

The power of images to create new insights is what led me to design the VisualsSpeak ImageSet in 2005. This curated, 200-image set has been used to facilitate conversations all over the world. In this article I share the rigorous multi-year process my team and I used to develop and test this tool. I include questions for you to answer if you are developing your own visual tools.

Where it started

In art school, I had the opportunity to do my work-study program in the library clipping collection, which is a set of images primarily taken from books and magazines used to serve as inspiration for artists working on projects. Over four years, I learned how to catalog images for other people to use while watching how students, faculty, and alumni interacted and searched for pictures in relationship to their ideas. I then amassed my own personal file cabinet of magazine clippings as I saw how powerful this could be for inspiration.

Fast forward 20 years. I am getting a Masters degree in adult education with a specialization in training and development, with colleagues interested in doing things such as team-building, leadership development, and strategic visioning. My classes were filled with people who had experience in these processes, so school became a perfect incubator for designing tools.

While I had been practicing and getting great results with creative methods in workshops and consulting for years, I didn't know why these tools worked so well. The research and writing skills needed to get my degree also helped me to articulate much of the theoretical basis for why creative processes based on visuals were so effective in reaching people.

Design guidelines

Graduate school inspired me to come up with a standardized visual tool that was effective in the workplace. With hundreds of variables to consider, I needed some parameters to work within.

Drawing from a reservoir of facilitation experience along with conversations with potential customers and business professionals, I started to come up with a blueprint for a successful visually based tool. Below are some of the need-to-haves that were established for the product based on these experiences and conversations.

Audience
- Professionals with some experience with groups in a work setting
- Broader audience than only certified facilitators
- A wide range of participants across multiple variables
  - For both private and nonprofit sectors
  - Audience from multiple cultures
  - Across an organization, from individual employees through board of directors
- Beginners can make effective use of tool without a lot of training
- Advanced users can master tool with in-depth training

Aesthetics
- Professional looking enough for corporate settings
- Not so fancy and expensive that it is unaffordable for other sectors

Use of tool
- Works consistently and quickly
- Deepens conversations
- Helps people reach across differences and communicate more effectively
- Creates shared understanding
- Sparks new insights
- Engages creativity without making people anxious

Testing assumptions

As I learned through testing the tools in various ways, it's impossible to avoid inserting personal bias into the process. While some of the assumptions I made were valid, people often surprised me. Extensive testing with a range of participants taught me what works best for the largest number of people.

To remove as many personal biases as possible and design the most well-rounded product, I designed experiments that tested specific assumptions. By observing people as they worked with the test images and asking questions, I was able to get past some personal blind spots. That wasn't enough, however. These tests had to be conducted by others to rule out any positive or negative influence I might be exerting as the creator. People have a tendency to want to offer supportive answers to the person responsible for coming up with the idea.

The process of testing was a continuous dance of asking whether the changes being made got me closer to the design guidelines. If not, it was necessary to come up with new ways to test, along with the corresponding design changes.

VisualsSpeak Development Team

Bringing together a team

At a certain point I realized I had gone as far as I could by myself. There was a need for a more formalized team that consisted of people with varying degrees of group and individual facilitation experience, as well as with people who had different subject matter expertise.

To help me gain deeper insight, I added a business partner and a team of seven colleagues from a range of disciplines to help inform the development. The group included people with expertise in executive coaching, career coaching, intercultural communication, diversity and inclusion, and drug and alcohol counseling. They worked with me for a year to develop the tool and processes, as well as with their own clients and customers to give feedback.

We developed a number of prototype VisualsSpeak ImageSets and watched how people used them for two years. The development team used them in sessions and reported back to us. As the process narrowed, we asked other professionals to try them in various settings.

Testing, testing, and more testing

By having a group focused on figuring out the best ways to create this new product, the testing took on a new momentum. We tested everything we could think of. We tested the images for how well they elicited information and insights. We also tested the processes we asked participants to go through. If some part failed, we tossed it and moved onto the next.

Everyone I came in contact with became part of the testing. Friends, family, colleagues, classmates, groups. I sought out people who were born in or lived in other countries, as well as people from diverse groups in the US. Because I value inclusion, it was critical that the product be usable by a broad swath of the population.

Testing image categorization

The first product I wanted to produce was designed for use in groups and ended up consisting of 200 images. This was determined to be an ideal number for the average size of groups that people worked with, which is approximately eight to 12 people.

The problem became one of categorization. How could I create a set of images that would contain enough to be a visual communication system without being overwhelming to the participants?

The reason I knew this was going to be a key issue is that when I began experimenting with the concept of facilitating with images, I started out by cutting out and laminating over 10,000 images from magazines and books. That's a lot of pictures to wade through.

When my development team was formed, we came up with a couple of test sets consisting of 4,000 images each, divided into 96 categories. We quickly realized that this was too unwieldy for both the facilitator and participants. The set weighed close to twenty pounds! It wasn't going to be easily replicable, portable, or affordable.

How categories are organized is not universal. If you ask a group of people to sort an identical set of items into piles that are similar, you probably won't get two piles that are the same. Sorting is personal and influenced by the cultural lenses we bring to the task. In testing a category system that worked for the largest number of people, we separated pictures into category-labeled boxes without marking the individual images. When people thought a picture was in the wrong box, we let them move it. If the name we had chosen as a label didn't make sense to someone, we asked them what would work better.

There was a lot of trial and error. We kept charts of information about the frequency of use for the various categories. We used the wisdom of the crowd to finally identify four major categories with three subcategories each for the structure of the first product.

Refining the deck

Throughout the two years of testing, I was carefully watching and listening as people were interacting with the images. As a team, we were tracking the content of the pictures that people were selecting through the category system, and I watched the visual language elements: shapes on the page, whether the images were literal or metaphoric, the textures and patterns.

I started to have a sense of how well an image would evoke the kind of conversation I was looking for. We reduced the number of images as I found the types that worked.

Potential users told us what challenges they needed to solve. If you came within speaking, phone, or email distance, we asked questions and listened to what you said. Every detail of the tool was considered, reconsidered, and tested out. We learned that no matter what we did, it wasn't going to be perfect, so we had to prioritize what was a must-have, as opposed to what was nice to have, and what we might someday have.

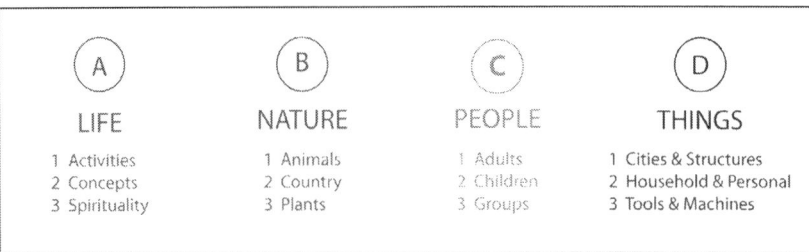

Once we understood what was working in our prototype deck, we started to go out and photograph the types of images we would need for the final product. We spent most of a year taking over 20,000 photographs in order to create the 200 we eventually used for the VisualsSpeak ImageSet. We supplemented the photos my business partner and I shot with some photos our friends took in various locations globally we weren't able to get to, and a colleague worked on a couple of shoots with us to give us a slightly different eye to add more diversity to the images.

Refining the facilitation process

Coming to understand the underlying visual language governing which images were most effective and the categorization of those images was only half of the challenge in creating a finished product. In order to write a user manual and train others in the best ways of using the ImageSet, I had to dive deep into the nuances of the facilitation process. What helped people get deeper insights and what prevented them from doing so? If my team and I could refine the process enough, then it could be used for a wide range of challenges.

For example, there were two basic things that come to mind that would help facilitators to get better results or understand their audiences better. Counterintuitively, we found that giving participants less time than more to select their photographs gave them better results. Also, over time we began to see patterns emerge in how people laid out the photos they selected. Those who had more structured thinking styles laid out their cards in a structured arrangement. Those who were more big-picture oriented tended to be less constrained in their image arrangements.

Through repeated testing and observation we were able to refine the facilitation process to a point that it became the basis or backbone of any exercise for which facilitators would use the product. It also became the underlying process for future products.

What did I learn?

THE IMAGES WE THOUGHT WOULD WORK THE BEST DIDN'T

Images of metaphors and visual clichés did not deepen conversation like we thought they would. Instead, these images became a shorthand that kept the participant from having to dig deeper. An example is the picture of a lightbulb or half-full glass. When people see these, they assume they know what it means and the conversation stops because no one has to go deep into the image to draw new meaning from it.

The spectacular photos from places like National Geographic didn't evoke comment beyond praising the beauty of the photograph. Neither type of imagery reached our desired outcome of rich conversations and ideation.

WHAT WE SEE IS INFLUENCED BY WHO WE ARE

It's not possible to be fully neutral no matter how hard we try. Individual biases slipped into every aspect of designing the product from image selection to facilitation process. It took many eyes to even begin to counter the natural bias each of us carries. And even then, nothing is perfect.

SIZE MATTERS

We knew from talking to people that having different size images was important. A large image says something different from what a small image says, and often would be used to convey relative importance. In order to meet the technical requirements of commercial printing, we had to make some hard choices as to which images would be printed in which size format. The realities of the final cost of the product also played a role in how we structured the ImageSet.

THE PROCESS IS IMPORTANT

At the beginning of all this I was totally focused on discovering which images yielded the best results. By the end of coming up with a product, it became apparent that the facilitation process is vital to how well the tools work.

A successful product launch

After years of research and work, the first tool was successfully launched. Over 10 years later it is being used by thousands of people around the globe in areas like:

- Team-building
- Leadership Development
- Strategic Visioning
- Coaching
- Intercultural Communication
- Therapy
- Education

For me, it was like giving birth to a very special child. One that would help bring people closer together, deepen understanding, and be the spark for new insights long after I'm gone. It's part of my legacy, my gift to the world. Even after all these years, I love talking to people who are getting great results with it. Those conversations continue to inspire me.

Developing visual tools

If you are interested in developing visual tools, here are some things to consider:

IS THE TOOL FOR YOU OR FOR OTHERS?

If you create a tool for yourself, you can rely on your particular skills and experience. If you want others to use your tool, the skills required need to be broader or less specific.

If the tool is for others, will it rely on specialized training? Do you want people to be able to use it quickly by reading a manual or learning through an online course? Will you only share the tool with people who have been through a certification program with you? Can they start getting simple outcomes right away and build mastery over time?

WHO ARE YOU CREATING THE TOOL FOR?

What age group? Do they live or work in a particular area? Do they work in certain industries? Will they use the tool personally or professionally? Will it be used in corporate, non-profit, government, education, or small business? Design consideration change for different audiences.

WHAT DO YOU WANT THE TOOL TO DO?

What might it be used for? What might the user experience? What do you want participants to come away with after using your tool?

WHAT HAVE YOU NOTICED THAT MIGHT BE HELPFUL?

Is there something you have noticed working with visuals that shows promise? Do you have a resource that is being used for something else that could be repurposed?

DO YOU WANT TO CREATE A PRINTED OR MANUFACTURED TOOL?

Do you know how to produce a manufactured product? Do you know how to balance cost per unit with a realistic assessment of how many you can sell? Do you have graphic design skills? Do you know how to prep files for different kinds of printing? Do you own the correct rights to your images for manufacturing?

If you don't have these skills, consider finding people who do or who can help you learn. It's much easier and lower cost to design for what is standard for the printer. If you design without these considerations, cost can be prohibitive. Design for manufacturing is a balancing act between what is possible and what is affordable. All of this will affect the final price you need to charge to be profitable. Can you sell at that price to your target market?

CHRISTINE MARTELL integrates the visual arts to help individuals and organizations learn, grow, and change. She designs and sells visual tools globally through her company VisualsSpeak. She has a BFA from Rhode Island School of Design and MS from Portland State University. She lives and advocates for creative expression in Hillsboro Oregon using her robotic dinosaur, Artosaur. Learn more at visualsspeak.com and artosaur.com.

Imagery That Travels Well

Making yourself understood across cultures with the help of visual language

Peter Stoyko

I'm a nomad. I travel the world working as a social scientist. Much of that work involves studying the subtleties of culture. I'm also an information designer. I translate research findings into explanatory graphics. I collaborate by drawing. I think visually. Over the years, I've discovered that showing is better than just telling regardless of where I am. Visual messages are more compelling and are less likely to get lost in translation. Yet imagery can just as easily cause confusion, unintended humor, and insult. I've had my share of embarrassments. So I decided to use my research skills to better understand how visuals work in different cultures. My goal has been to find better ways to communicate with diverse audiences.

This chapter shares a few of the lessons I've learned. The first lesson is an overriding one. It's about ethics. A traveling researcher holds a privileged position. While I am in the field, the onus is on me to operate with care and respect. Culture runs deep with people: it's the social core around which a person's identity forms. My first duty is to do no harm. My second duty is to approach other cultures with mindfulness, critical self-awareness, and humility. That includes a heightened sensitivity to my own biases and blind spots. Sadly, history is full of blunderers and bigots who blithely trample through unfamiliar places with an ignorant smugness. Yet even well-traveled cosmopolitans with noble intentions regularly experience culture shock. That's the emotional discomfort and rush to judgment that happen when we are outside our comfort zone of familiar norms and settings. Thus, what follows is as much about examining our own cultural assumptions as it is about discovering cultural points of interest.

Speaking of cultural assumptions, we take our own culture's visual language for granted. We forgot that we had to learn the meanings of commonplace images, and so we treat those meanings as self-evident. Often, they aren't. That blind spot can get us into trouble when communicating with others who have had very different upbringings. Let's revisit a few episodes from the learning process.

Episode 1. Visual vernaculars

As children, we learned about imagery from picture books, comics, toys, and cartoons. Those experiences helped us associate ideas and objects with images of varying degrees of abstractness. How else would we know that an enclosed shape with edges made of connected semi-circles is a cloud? Real clouds don't really look like that. Even the fluffy ones don't. How would we know that the cloud shape with a trail of circles is a thought balloon, a (misnamed) metaphor based on the idea that a cloud can represent what a comic character is thinking? If that same cloud shape is attached to a stem, how would we know it represents a tree? We know because cultural products teach us. Now think about people from distant places. Would someone who has spent a lifetime amongst the desert palms recognize that shape as a tree? If there are no fluffy clouds in that desert, would they recognize the cloud? Perhaps. But the question you should be asking yourself is, "Where would they have learned those lessons?"

Our visual vocabularies grow as these arrangements of basic shapes take on meanings. Every time we engage with a new mode of visual expression, such as a comic book or a video game, we add to that vocabulary. Not only that, we also learn new *vernaculars*. When referring to ordinary conversation, a vernacular is a way of speaking. We talk differently depending on the social situation. We may use office jargon when talking formally with colleagues in the workplace. Later on, we may use street slang when bantering with friends at home. That jargon and slang, plus the phrasing that goes with them, are vernaculars. Unless you know the vernacular, you'll struggle to understand what's being said—it won't seem all that coherent nor appropriate. A *visual vernacular* is similar. It's a collection of shared meanings and interpretive conventions that helps us make sense of what we see in a given context. Every genre of video game and movie has a vernacular. Every artistic tradition does too. After enough exposure to each mode of visual expression, the related visual vernacular becomes second nature and interpretation doesn't require conscious effort.

Let's look at a concrete example. The following is the comic vernacular.

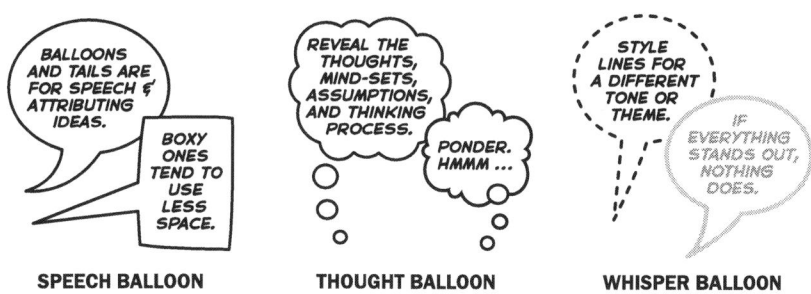

OPEN BALLOON

BURST BALLOON

SYMBOLIC CAPTION

CONNECTED BALLOON

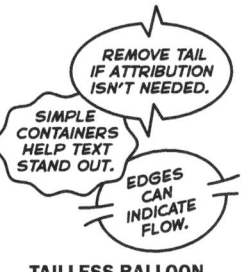
TAILLESS BALLOON

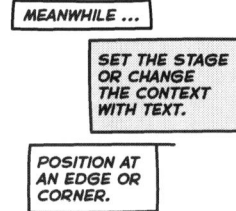
NARRATION BOX

NARRATION BOX

THEMED LETTERING

EFFECTS LETTERING

EFFECTS

MOTION LINE

MOTION LINE (TRAIL)

Comics would be confusing if you didn't know these elements. What are those wavy lines above the cheese? Those lines represent smell, something invisible in real life. The lines are very wavy to symbolize that the smell lingers as it emanates upwards. They are heavy lines to symbolize that the smell is pungent. If that seems obvious to you, it's because you've seen many examples of the form over the years from cartoons, picture books, and comics.

I itemize all the elements of different visual vernaculars for teaching purposes. These inventories or *codexes* can inspire students by showing what communicative options are available. Making the inventories helps me become more self-aware as a communicator by revealing all the meanings and conventions I take for granted. That process also allows me to detect vernacular differences across cultures. Comic traditions are fairly similar around the world. American comics, Japanese *manga*, Franco-Belgian *bande dessinée*, and editorial cartoons share a vernacular. Yet differences exist.

MOTION LINE (FOREGROUND OBJECT BLUR)   **MOTION LINE (BACKGROUND OBJECT BLUR)**

Historically, American comic book artists use motion lines to depict the blur of a foreground object moving across the comic frame. Manga artists, in contrast, use motion lines to depict the blurring of objects in the background, as if the comic frame is a camera that moves with the foreground object. Knowing these vernacular differences can ease communication across cultures. It's like knowing the local words and sayings of your audience.

Episode 2. Visual tropes

As we grow up, we become accustomed to pictograms on signs, symbols on product labels, and icons on screens. Other vernaculars are added to our visual vocabularies. Yet we don't have to learn each image one by one. Commonalities emerge. These commonalities allow us to take some interpretive shortcuts.

Take an example from signage. A circle suspended over a four-pronged shape is a head. Once we learn that, we recognize human figures called "bubbleheads" in different poses without having to relearn each figure from scratch. Bubbleheads are easy to grasp because they are based on the stick figures of kid's drawings, figures which people have been drawing since the days of ancient cave paintings and sand sketches. Even if we change the shape of the bubblehead's body by tapering the limbs, it's still recognizable. Use negative space to differentiate near and far limbs, in the same way that a shadow is cast over receding objects: still recognizable.

That's what it means to learn a *trope*, a non-literal signifier of something. When we learn visual tropes, we learn a set of interpretive rules—rules about how particular shapes can be arranged to form symbolic images. With bubbleheads, the circle suspended above a four-pronged shape is a trope that represents "head" and signals that a human figure is being represented. A detached head can't *literally* float above a living body. A human head isn't *literally* shaped like a ball. A person can't run if an arm and a leg are *literally* severed. Those are stylistic embellishments we learn to interpret. We then apply those interpretive rules to other bubbleheads.

As another example, add a triangular shape to the torso of any bubblehead and we specify its gender as female. We learned that the triangular torso represents a dress and dress-wearing is a norm for females. Does that gendering trope reflect a norm in your society? Would that same interpretation be made in societies where everyone wears a gown-like garment? Or in places where knee-length, A-frame dresses don't exist?

You can see how tropes can be *ethnocentric*. That involves treating your own culture as universal and just assuming that everyone understands you. Tropes can also be anachronistic by locking in outdated norms and fashions into widely used imagery. They become part of the cultural memory, in other words. Yet these norms and fashions may never have caught on in distant places.

How reliant are we on visual tropes to communicate? That depends on how realistic the images are.[1]

BIOHAZARD   **PEACE**   **TURN ON AND OFF**   **CORRECT (OR MAYBE NOT)**   **FORGIVENESS**

Ideograms

Some images are purely symbolic *(ideograms)*. Nothing about their shape suggests a meaning by mimicking something in the real world. We learn those symbols in a way that's similar to learning conceptual words. Different cultures have different symbols but, like words, a few symbols may spread across cultures. Despite the abstractness, some common themes also emerge, such as a circle representing "wholeness," "unity," and "totality" in many folk-art traditions. Yet given the arbitrariness of ideograms, you will sometimes encounter conflicting meanings across cultures, such as the meaning of the check mark in Sweden and Finland ("incorrect" instead of "correct").

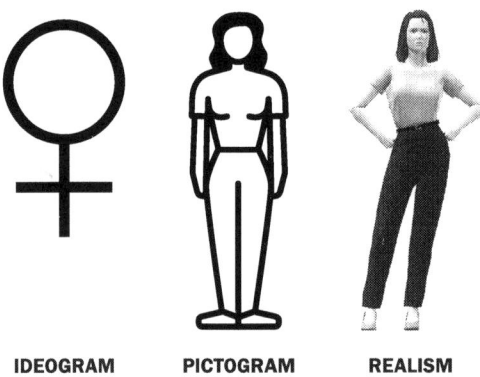

IDEOGRAM   PICTOGRAM   REALISM

Ideograms sit at one end of a continuum. At the other end are *photo-realistic images*. They look like objects in the real world. Not much effort is required for interpretation if you remember seeing a similar object before. That can be a big "if" when communicating across cultures. For example, would showing a photo of a snowman or an igloo to a tropical islander cause bafflement? An item may not exist in another culture, or it may take a radically different form. Either way, photo-realism may be the best way to teach others something new if the image is shown in context (or otherwise explained) and doesn't contain distracting non-essential details ("visual noise"). When we say something "isn't translatable," we aren't just saying the same word and concept don't exist in another language; we are also saying the same exact thing doesn't really exist in both cultures.[2] So show a very typical version of that thing (in context) if possible. Better yet: show two or more versions, so that the person doesn't mistake the specific example for the general concept.

Between pure symbols and photo-realistic images lay stylized illustrations such as pictograms. These are recognizable insofar as 1) we understand the visual tropes used to simplify and stylize them, and 2) they have a close enough resemblance to a known object that we can make a confident guess. That assumes the illustration has an *iconic* relation to its subject, meaning it is supposed to resemble something in the real world. Many pictograms have an *indexical*, or indirect, relation to their subject.[3] For example, the image can be linked to an idea by association or by analogy. That adds interpretive complexity because the viewer has to make that extra link—a link which may be culturally specific.

Take the concept of "travel" for instance. The act of traveling can be shown directly (by example) with an illustration of an airplane circumnavigating the Earth. In terms of tropes, the illustration is made up of a vehicle silhouette (airplane) with a trail-line showing its elliptical path in three-dimensional space (circumnavigation) around a sphere with a map grid imprinted on its surface (globe). The concept can also be illustrated by association as a well-traveled suitcase. The idea of "well traveled" is indicated by the cliché of tourist stickers from various places spread randomly on the surface of the suitcase. Or "travel" could be indicated

"TRAVEL"
(ICONIC)

"TRAVEL"
(ASSOCIATION)

"TRAVEL"
(ANALOGY)

by a selection of travel documents. These objects are associated with travel because we take them on journeys. The concept can be illustrated by analogy too, such as an image of birds flying in a migration pattern. Some concepts can't be represented directly, which is why these indirect methods are useful. The challenge, however, is that associations and analogies are merely suggestive, not obvious, and certainly not obvious to people everywhere. Northern cultures may equate migrating birds with seasonal vacation travel. Indeed, Canadians who travel south in the winter are called "snow birds." But how obvious is the analogy to someone living near the equator? Or for whom seasonal travel is an alien concept? You may have to add additional cues to make the linkages more apparent.

Now think of everything that can go wrong when drawing pictograms that are simultaneously stylized, indexical, combined with symbols, and represent objects that are not recognized outside your culture. My favorite example comes from 1960s America.[4] A human figure is shown overlapping an igloo. The igloo represents "refrigeration." The combined image is intended to mean "refrigerated morgue." What would Inuit people think of their traditional shelter being depicted as dead-body storage? Would they think "refrigeration," given that an igloo is supposed to be a warm shelter? What would someone think if they don't know anything about the Arctic? Would it even occur to them that a building is being depicted? And that the human figure is inside the building? And that the figure is a dead person?

Episode 3. Assigned meanings

We eventually come to understand some stylized illustrations at a glance. That includes pictograms on road signs and warning labels. These tend to be the "controlled" part of our visual vocabularies; controlled in the sense that the look and meanings have been standardized by an authority. Some stylized illustrations are international standards, such as airport wayfinding pictograms. Yet controlling the approximate look of an illustration and affixing an official label does not guarantee the same interpretation everywhere. Take the case of emojis, the standardized icons used in phone text-messages. Emojis can take on unintended meanings in certain places. If enough people reinterpret an image through conversation, then a local meaning can emerge.

TRIUMPH?
STEAMING MAD?
OVER EXERTION?

GRATITUDE?
HIGH FIVE?
PRAYER?

EGG PLANT?
PHALLUS?

SLEEPING?
CRYING?
SNEEZING?

With emojis, it's often the context of the message that offers clues as to the intended meaning of the communicator, not just the officially stipulated label. Xu Bing's Book from the Ground takes that idea to an extreme.[5] The book is written entirely in graphic sentences to communicate with a global audience. Official meanings are often disregarded. The storyline offers contextual clues to aid interpretation.

The "reading" experience is more akin to decoding—the opposite of glanceable interpretation. Some imagery is not as universally recognizable as Bing presumes. Yet these visual sentences are easier to decode than an unfamiliar foreign language. That's why a similar technique is used to make step-by-step instructions for international products. Not everything can be communicated in this way. Expressiveness is limited. Artistic flair would help but at the cost of ambiguity. Complex and abstract concepts could not be added without *logograms*, or images and image combinations that represent words. Chinese writing is made of logograms. Ancient Egyptian *hieroglyphics* are logograms too. Needless to say, these scripts aren't very intuitive.

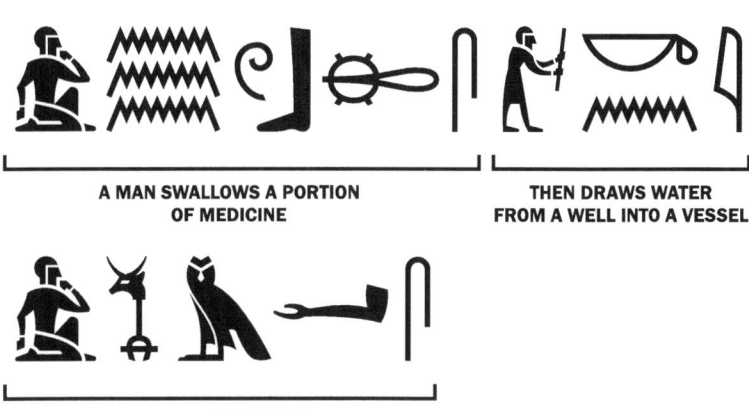

A MAN SWALLOWS A PORTION OF MEDICINE

THEN DRAWS WATER FROM A WELL INTO A VESSEL

THEN WASHES DOWN THE MEDICINE

Note that context can play a bigger role in some cultures. For example, Japanese and Korean are highly contextual languages. A "yes" can mean "no" depending on the context. People are expected to be aware of the underlying norms of the social situation. Likewise with visual communication. Experiments have shown that, when presented a visual scene, Japanese people tend to pay much more attention to the scene's background imagery compared to Americans.[6] That tendency is about detecting contextual appropriateness in a society with relatively conformist social pressures. The earlier example of Japanese manga using motion lines to depict background blur instead of foreground blur is not a coincidence. It's a more fundamental difference in what gets noticed.

Sometimes, visual communicators in those societies rely more heavily on a widely understood social context when using imagery. When I lived in Tokyo, it took me a month to figure out the social context needed to interpret the following pictogram, found on the door of a barber shop in my neighborhood. The barber shop was located next to a commuter train station, a place where overworked and drunk salary-men would disembark during the evening commute to run errands before returning home. I wasn't able to interpret the pictogram ("no drunks allowed") until I saw that social problem play out in several instances. If the context wasn't so obvious to locals, the illustrator might have added some context to the pictogram, such as showing a figure with an alcoholic beverage in hand.

That example brings us to the topic of "uncontrolled" images, those without an officially stipulated, widely recognized meaning. New symbols are invented all the time and are placed on such things as consumer packaging, control panels, and computer applications. That includes the illustrations that visual facilitators and sketchnote artists think up on the spot. Most aren't self-explanatory and so require clarifying labels. Or a subtle distinction isn't obvious. Or an object is recognizable but could be interpreted many ways other than the communicator's intended meaning. For example, a picture of a burger and fries could represent "fast food," "junk food," "American cuisine," or "dinner." Viewers will draw their own conclusion unless the intended meaning is stipulated.

Are word labels a failure of visual communication? No. Each symbol has to be learned somehow. Object resemblance, contextual clues, and familiar tropes only help so much. Labels aren't ideal for communicating across languages. Yet adding a slightly familiar image to a vaguely familiar word might be just enough to get the point across. Even for native speakers of the language, the label has *reference value*; that is, after the label is read once or twice, the viewer becomes familiar enough with the associated illustration that a glance is enough to jog the memory. The viewer can then parse the images on a page, or the icons on a computer interface, or the pictograms on a control dashboard with great efficiency.

Problems occur when the labels are confusing buzzwords or are mismatched with images. Vague and misleading jargon can be used to evade scrutiny, especially in the worlds of business and politics. Visuals can add clarity. Yet some word usages, such as euphemisms, are deliberately designed to suppress imagery in the mind's eye. Pairing a vague word with mildly suggestive imagery doesn't communicate much. Sometimes bad image-label pairings are simply a matter of laziness. Advertisers and website designers are often guilty of using a handful of overused stock icons to represent all sorts of tenuously related concepts.

SEND DIRECT MESSAGE?   **CLIENT SUPPORT?**   **SET UP ACCOUNT?**   **SEND FEEDBACK?**   **ACCESSIBILITY OPTIONS?**

A rule of thumb: if the word-image pairing isn't obvious to someone like yourself, it will probably stump those who are very different. I tell my clients to give up the "zombie" clichés. These are overused words and visuals that have so many potential meanings that they could mean anything. Audiences will ignore an image of two hands shaking or mechanical gears, for instance, instead of pondering the message associated with it. Visualization isn't just scavenging through collections of generic icons and "clip art." Properly brainstorm and research all of the imagery connected to a concept—all of the symbols, associations, and analogies. Select the ones that balance freshness with travel-worthiness.

Shared imagery

These episodes reveal that people perceive images quite differently across cultures. Don't let that intimidate you. Some visuals travel well despite all the cultural variation. There are universals, at least for most intents and purposes. These come in three forms.

First, there are meanings that come from common experience. For example, people throughout the world attribute the same meaning to basic facial expressions: smiles, frowns, looks of surprise, looks of dread, and so forth. It's only when expressions become subtle that culture-specific shades of meaning come into play. Likewise with basic figure poses, such as running or jumping. Once you enter the realm of gestures, however, assuming common meaning can be very dangerous indeed.[7]

| "A-OKAY" BUT RUDE IN BRAZIL | "LIKE" OR "GOOD" BUT RUDE IN THAILAND | "UNITY" OR "DEFIANCE" BUT RUDE IN PAKISTAN | "LUCK" BUT RUDE IN VIETNAM |

The second source of common visual language is the global economy. Like it or not, cultures are converging. Think of all the sources of shared visuals: the advertising industry and consumer packaging; the iconography of web page, computer, and phone interfaces; the charts and graphs of the workplace; video games; blockbuster films; music videos; maps and wayfinding graphics; the art of international youth subcultures, such as street graffiti, sticker-bombs, and T-shirt motifs; the list goes on. Note, however, that this influence depends somewhat on how urban, affluent, and plugged-in your specific audience is. There are generational differences too.

Third, a few images are "in good currency" throughout much of the world. That could be because of ancient cultural influences or modern international standards. For example, a skull and crossbones represents "danger," "poison," and "deadly harm" pretty much everywhere. That doesn't preclude local alternatives, such as an image of a scorpion on warning labels in South Asia. These simply work like synonyms, ones which don't travel as well.

Visual rhetoric

Just as wording can be used for rhetorical effect, so can visuals. Therein lies much danger. I've had experiences using ethnocentric visual analogies in other cultures where the audience didn't get too bothered. Some audiences are intrigued by an exotic foreign analogy. In contrast, sometimes I have chosen a shared image only to have audiences get agitated or uncomfortable. What's going on? Subtle cues and stylistic choices can offer subtle shades of meaning, insinuations, and connotations. Some of these nuances push cultural hot-buttons. Others have a more subtle effect: they are felt but not necessarily noticed. Those impressions have to be managed. Let's explore some specific cases.

Visual hyperbole is extravagant exaggeration that isn't meant to be taken literally. Most visual metaphors are somewhat hyperbolic. Hyperbole is found in all cultures, but formulations differ, as do peoples' attitudes towards them. In some places and social situations, hyperbole is considered a lazy and deceptive form of overstatement. In others, it's an acceptable form of assertion and emphasis that isn't taken at face value.[8] Some illustrators use visual hyperbole to grab attention, add humor, and make sure the point gets across. Depending on the cultural sensibilities of the audience, visual hyperbole can be inspiring or it can insult people's intelligence.

Visualized figures of speech (*idioms*) cause the most miscommunication. Drawing idioms is a *piece of cake* and *it's more fun than a barrel of monkeys*. I think you *catch my drift*: our language is full of these *turns of phrase*, most of which invoke imagery in a way that's *over the top*. That's what makes idioms so tempting to draw: most already offer a visual analogy with rhetorical punch. Unfortunately, such analogies tend to be obscure. As they say in Japan, *don't let your daughter-in-law eat your autumn eggplant*. In other words, as the French say, *don't get rolled in flour*. See what I mean?

Most drawings of people have some element of caricature: certain facial features get exaggerated, even if they are not distorted in grotesque or cartoonish ways. How deftly that is done can mean the difference between authenticity and insult. The way we draw people is full of bias that is hard to see until the tables are turned. That struck me when I went to a faux-European village in the suburbs of Chengdu, China. I came across a sculpture that was supposed to depict a Dutchman, yet I could see how the artist struggled to get rid of certain habits of the conventional style used to sculpt Chinese facial features.

The portraiture style ...   *... Applied to a Dutchman*

That distortion is not just a problem of style but of noticing. I study the work of artists from other places. Then I try to reproduce their work, not to copy, but to see what they see. I incorporate some of those lessons into my style when drawing people with ancestral backgrounds and ethnicities that are noticeably different than my own.

History is full of examples of racist, demeaning caricatures. Know this history in order to understand the caricature prohibitions of various places. Alas, those who take it upon themselves to police these taboos can sometimes be amongst the least knowledgeable about them. Caricatures also don't travel well. A drawing inspired by African folk-art may delight in Nairobi or Lagos but cause anger in Port-au-Prince or Los Angeles. The artistic inspiration may not be evident. If it is, the caricature may be seen as cultural "appropriation" or "trivialization," prohibitions enforced by those who object to cultural blending and any signs of pastiche. What is an "authentic" depiction? What is socially permissible? In some places, the answer depends on the presumed group status of the visualizer, not the qualities of the visual.

Speaking of visual politics, I'm writing this chapter in Cairo, Egypt. It's hard to imagine a place where visual expression is more contested. Democracy protestors express irreverence with street art, or what some activists call "graphic agitation." The state and various political factions compete to align themselves with various ancient symbols that connote national identity. Modes of dress signal various identity claims, such as class, politics, and religious allegiance. Even the absences are revealing. An election is going on but there's no campaign imagery in sight. The dominant religion, Islam, has strict prohibitions against drawing certain things as a way of preventing idol worship and irreverence. Visualizers need to take account of these cultural "framing contests" and "no-go zones."

While on the topic of identity claims, when drawing people, the subtleties of dress and style matter. Take the example of Muslim dress norms. The style of clothing differs in distinctive ways around the world. Grooming norms and the style of headwear can signal whether someone is from Istanbul or Tehran or Abu Dhabi or Jakarta. It's best not to get those details wrong. Having your social identity misrepresented can cause insult. Having it mistaken for the social identity of another group can cause more serious grievance.

It also helps to understand the cultural influences of your own style. I draw in a variety of styles depending on client wants and project constraints. Many of the vector illustrations drawn for this chapter are very crisp, clean, and geometric. That is my default for icon and pictogram work. My style owes a great deal to German modernist iconographers from the early 20th Century, particularly Wilhelm Deffke, Otto Neurath, and Gerd Arntz.[9] I'm also inspired by modern interpreters of that artistic movement, especially Johannes Plass and Heinrich Paravicini, who added street-art techniques.[10] Mixing and matching styles from other cultures can seem incongruent. But then again, it can also be the source of creativity. After all, where would we be without the cross-cultural stylistic blending of Pablo Picasso?

Details have different connotations across cultures. Take color for example. Red signifies danger, alarm, or passion in Western societies. It represents good fortune and health in China. Red can mean "win" in the casino-gaming industry but mean "loss" in the financial sector of the economy. In the Caribbean, I sometimes work on politically sensitive projects where collaborators ask me not to use colors associated with any political party—any political party in twelve countries, that is. That doesn't leave much choice. Images may take on unintended connotations based on the associations attributed to small details.

I make a point of investigating some of those associations. It can be as simple as checking the colors associated with national and religious symbols, political parties, and local sports teams. It's good to keep a record of popular color preferences wherever you go. In some countries, a lack of vibrant colors can make your work seem drab. In other places, vibrant colors are considered brash. Many factors are involved: the intensity of natural light in the place; the color of the natural surroundings; cultural traditions; the restrictiveness of the political regime. Color palettes can be very distinctive culturally. Don't just choose colors based on personal aesthetic preferences. Think about the audience's cultural predisposition too.

Conclusion

This crash-course in cross-cultural communication suggests that visualizers should be more inquisitive about the imagery being used, right down to the fine details. That's partly what "design" means: crafting small details with purpose. It is more than that, however. Become more aware of your own cultural influences so as to not give off unintended signals. It also helps to take an interest in other cultures and the way cultural products teach imagery. That's what it means to become a worldly *flâneur*, or someone who spends time in far-flung places to observe the details of life and interpret larger meanings.

PETER STOYKO is a social science researcher and information designer working for Elanica, an international consultancy devoted to service design, management, and public governance. Details are available at stoyko.net and elanica.com. Peter can be reached at peter.stoyko@elanica.com. Copyright, 2016. Peter would like to thank Jennifer Shepherd, Oliver Caviglioli, and Michael Babwahsingh for comments on an earlier draft.

References

1. This distinction comes from Scott McCloud, *Understanding Comics: The Invisible Art*, New York, William Morrow, 1994.
2. H. Becker, *What About Mozart? What About Murder? Reasoning from Cases*, Chicago, The University of Chicago Press, 2014, p. 16
3. This distinction can be traced back to Charles Sanders Peirce's theory of signs from the 1860s.
4. This example comes from H. Dreyfuss, *Symbol Sourcebook: An Authoritative Guide to International Graphic Symbols*, New York, McGraw-Hill, 1972.
5. X. Bing, *Book from the Ground: From Point to Point*, Cambridge, The MIT Press, 2014.
6. R. E. Nisbett, *The Geography of Thought: How Asians and Westerners Think Differently … and Why*, New York, The Free Press, 2003.
7. A good reference for this is R. Lefevre, *Rude Hand Gestures of the World*, San Francisco, Chronicle Books, 2011.
8. I owe this insight to O. Hafez, "Hyperbolic Expressions in Egyptian Arabic and British English," in N. Kassabgy, Z. Ibrahim, and S. Aydelott (eds.), *Contrastive Rhetoric: Issues, Insights and Pedagogy*, Cairo, The American University of Cairo Press, 2004, pp. 172-173.
9. See Bröhan Design Foundation, *Wilhelm Deffke: Pioneer of the Modern Logo*, Zurich, Verlag Scheidegger & Spiess; Otto Neurath, *From Hieroglyphics to Isotype: A Visual Autobiography*, London, Hyphen Press, 2010 [1946]; E. Annink and M. Bruinsma, *Gerd Arntz: Graphic Designer*, Rotterdam, 010 Publishers, 2010.
10. My favorite showcase of their work is R. Klanten (ed.), *Lingua Grafica*, Berlin, Die Gestalten Verlag, 2001. That inspired two sequels, *Lingua Universalis* (2004) and *Lingua Digitalis* (2012).

The Thermal Lift of Visualization

How to empower people in visual thinking, learning and co-creation

Martin Haussmann
Interviewed by Brandy Agerbeck

Brandy: Your team at bikablo® akademie in Cologne, Germany has taught thousands to adopt visual language to express themselves in their work at meetings. Where did it begin? And tell us about the name.

Martin: About eight years ago, in our "mothership," the organizational consultancy Kommunikationslotsen, I worked in a team of graphic recorders with our facilitators Holger Scholz and Roswitha, mostly within large group conferences. We started a collaboration with Guido Neuland from the learning tool manufacturer Neuland. Guido likes to draw and has been very much into the visual thinking from the beginning. He immediately said, "Let's create a product. Let's do a visual dictionary which covers all the pictures you do in your graphic recording."

I said, "Twenty or thirty pages maybe?" In the end, the first bikablo® turned out to be more than 100 pages.

Guido had already produced a deck of cards for moderation and facilitation called "MoKaBlo." *Mo* for moderation, *ka* for karte, the German word for cards, and *blo* for block. Since our deck was images, the first part of the new name came from Bild, the German word for pictures. bikablo®. We liked the name, it sounded fancy and a bit mystic. That was the beginning.

At that time we didn't think of having our own visual facilitation academy, it was just an exciting name for a book that turned out to be a quick best-seller. A second bikablo® visual dictionary came out with more sophisticated subjects, later bikablo® emotions with visualized people in situations, and now it is a whole range of products.

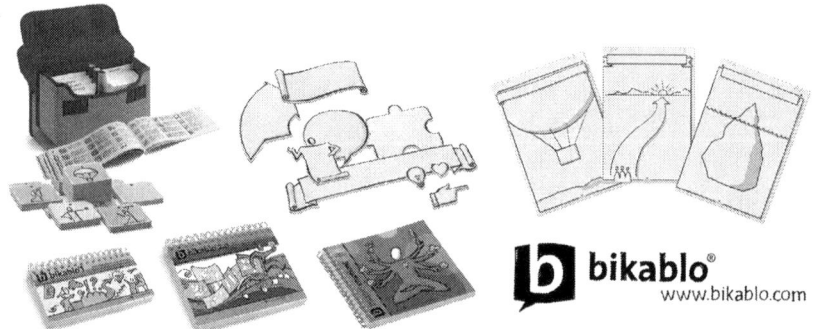

Two years ago, we decided to create our own visual facilitation training company as a spin off from Kommunikationslotsen. Everyone knew it had to be called bikablo® akademie. All our clients knew and loved the brand because it always showed a certain kind of attitude towards visualizing and drawing.

B: *I like that it's a friendly, accessible sound. Also, it's three root words put together—exactly what you are teaching when you are talking about taking simple icons and putting them together to represent more complex ideas. I studied German in high school and when I first saw a bikablo®, I was instantly attracted to the German-ness of all the root words coming together.*

M: Recently I talked to Marcel, our trainer in Australia and New Zealand. He suggested to keep the German spelling, bikablo® akademie, because people down under like the German engineering attitude. I can tell you more about the German craftsmanship behind bikablo® in a minute.

B: *In 2011, you and Holger invited me to do a workshop with your students. The day before, I sat in on the last part of your two-day beginner training. Your participants were sharing their own visualized posters applied what they had learned to a scenario in their work life. Even though I was listening through rusty high school German, watching body language, and watching what people were doing in these drawings—I thought their work was amazingly sophisticated. I think it really reflected how you're talking about first connecting with the joy of drawing, and getting people that sense of mastery even if it's really simple icons. Can you tell me more about how your students develop so quickly?*

M: This is where "German engineering and craftsmanship" fits in. At the bikablo® akademie we have a very strong design-driven approach and that is crucial for our way of empowering people without previous graphic knowledge. We call it the bikablo® technique and we have it copyright[ed] because we want people to learn it "from the source." Today our 20-person bikablo® trainer-team offers basic, advanced, open, and in-house classes for over 2,500 people a year based on this methodology.

To get started, we often ask participants to remember how we drew during childhood. We connect to the success we felt when we were young and we find out the success factors we had when we intuitively drew as children. Not drawing big strokes or filling in with a brush—but take your pen and draw a simple outline. The second success factor is to copy. You see a pictogram or visual in our bikablo® books, or on a road sign or wherever. Children use to copy from classmates' drawings or comic books they like.

For example, we simply ask our participants to write down the letters U, Z, M, and O. Without knowing, they have already drawn a lightbulb, our UZMO lightbulb. The clue is to combine the letters in a specific way:

When they do it again, they remember the shape. They remember the steps. They remember the results, and they also remember that once

they draw this and they look around the room they see 14 different lightbulbs drawn with the same system. Each one is unique. And the next time they draw it, it will be slightly different. You can teach this to everyone in the world in 10 seconds.

This is on the one hand a basic example for our very technical and logic[al], systematic approach—the "German engineering and craftsmanship." And it enables the joy of creativity that is set free by fast learning success in a trustful training community. These are the basic pillars of our training concept.

Let me explain the system behind the bikablo® technique in a visual metaphor:

I come from a very lovely area in Southern Germany, the "Schwäbische Alb." There are lowlands and highlands with cliffs. If you sit up there on a weekend, which I love to do with my wife and little son, you can observe gliders. One day I asked myself: How can they get up there more than 400 meters in the air without an engine? I learned they use the thermal lift—the warm air that rises from the ground to spin up in gentle spirals.

That is the concept of our training. It's always doing small "iterative" circles of learning, moving you up quickly and gently. The thermal lift in our trainings is the group process. At the very beginning, there's a simple invitation:

We ask people to take the first step and learn how to use the materials: hold the pen properly and make bold strokes on the surface.

The second one combines moving lines into basic shapes. We take a lot of time drawing proper circles and squares.

The next iterative loop is to recombine the basic shapes to the visual vocabulary of icons, graphics, containers, and people. The UZMO lightbulb, the doggy-ear-document, or simple people—everything is drawn out of recombined basic shapes. At first, we only drew people with an O and upside-down U, now we have also our system of "emotions"-

people to act as protagonists for visual storytelling. It took us over 10 years to select, refine, and reduce the unique bikablo® iconography, and it's still going on. In this iteration, we also add color. We do our special kind of shading—which is very simple; anyway, we take a lot of time to teach people because they desperately want to know how to do it properly.

Adding text we recombine visual vocabs to senseful key visuals. Text information is very important to us. People frequently forget about it because they think of visualization as just pictures. We also introduce how to improve the handwriting.

Then, with some generative layout templates and imagery, we recombine key visuals and text to complex layouts and pictorial landscapes.

And after learning all this, people recombine these elements with their own work context to create presentation posters or templates for visual facilitation or graphic recording.

It's like verbal language where you first have syllables, then words, then sentences, and then stories. This was the point you saw on your visit, where our participants designed great, sophisticated posters, because they knew how to combine the elements and feel confident in doing so.

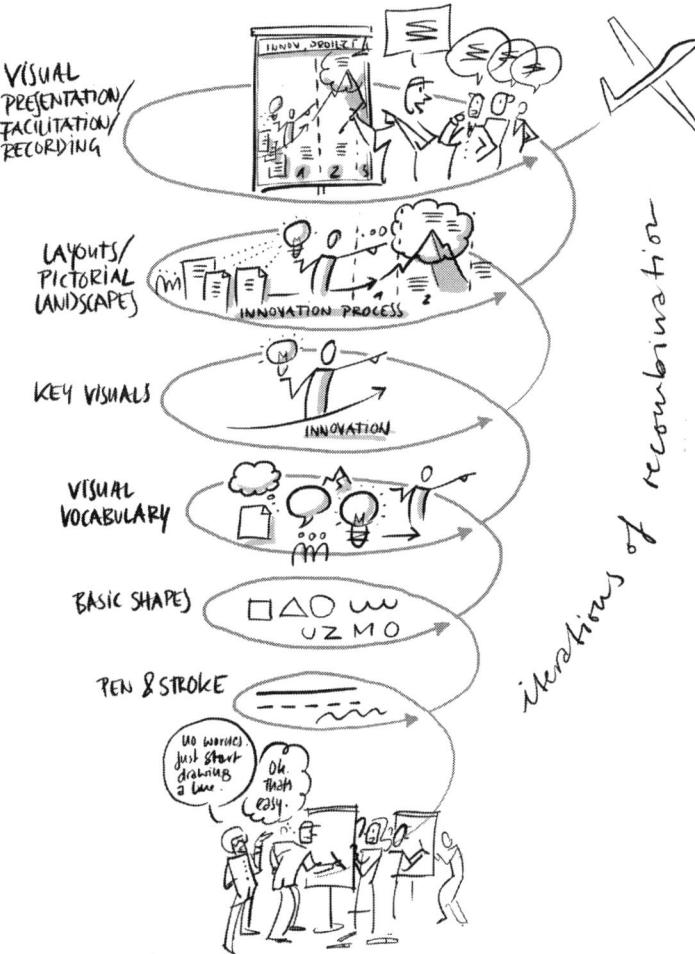

This is what I meant when I said it is German engineering sense because it is very systematic. There are rules for everything. There is a rule for how to hold the pen and how to draw a stroke. Professional illustrators or cartoonists may think this is boring, and some colleagues in the training field (that never visited our trainings) accuse us to limit creativity with our rules, but our participants understand it is completely the other way around, because every rule is an offer and a support to create their own visual storytelling.

Generally spoken the way we empower people is like running a foreign language class. When learning a language, you may like to jot down the foreign words in a vocabulary notebook, and then pronounce them again and again. You learn some basic sentences and expressions you can immediately use, like "How are you?" or "I would like to...". Then you learn grammar and you build sentences. After some time you can possibly add two sentences to one to make a composite sentence, and after some weeks you can express yourself, talk to people, and find your way in a foreign country. It is all about repeating, copying, and combining. In the end it is about putting everything together in an intuitive way to express your own content. That is how to learn a language, and learning visual language is similar to learning "verbal" language, with one difference: Since everyone intuitively recognizes and understands the meaning of common iconography, we start our first iteration with all the "passive vocabulary" we need.

The clue is: you don't need to invent your own words to express yourself. Just learn how to pronounce and use the existing vocabulary and grammar in your personal way and for your individual purpose. Visual language, like Bob Horn suggests, consists of and is about using vocabulary (text, graphics, and pictures), grammar, and rhetoric in a conscious way. Martin Eppler, a Swiss researcher at St. Gallen University, even claims "visual literacy" is crucial for modern management today.

In our classes people learn in two days to design something that looks great, that they can use for their work, they did in a pleasant and sheltered learning atmosphere. Team building in our training is very essential. We get everyone's voices in the room, we ask people to communicate and collaborate. Sometimes we also ask people to draw on one poster together to make it a team experience.

Anyway, I think most of our success is the right choreography to design a training as a learning process that offers an appropriate combination of logic and systematic rules, free flow of trying out, alternations between deductive and inductive learning strategies, appreciative evaluation of participants' results, and free space to visually work on their own topics close to their hearts. At this point I have to praise my colleague Karina Antons who leads the trainer team and develops didactics and methodologies for both basic and advanced formats. She is the one to empower trainers with the ability to find out about their own trainer personality, in order to quickly establish a good resonance with the group and intuitively set the path for both group and individual learning by iterative loops in a sheltered surrounding.

B: *The discipline with drawing proper shapes and working within rules really resonates with me. It's strong because it's systematic. And you cultivate a fun team atmosphere where everyone can celebrate their successes. Where do you find people resisting your process and how do you respond to it?*

M: Usually we don't experience any resistance to our approach. But sometimes people say their results don't look like that way they want it to be. That is why we usually have two trainers in the room, to give people personal guidance and encouragement. The best way to empower people is to encourage them. I have an American friend. He can't draw a proper line. But he loves to draw, because he found out he can express his ideas in his keynotes without being a great craftsman, but he knows that he receives standing ovations when he proudly says: "Even with a poor quality of my line I can deliver my ideas and insights, and I love to do it." Visualization is, like Ben Shneiderman says, not about making pictures, but about creating insight. Communicating good ideas needs inspiration and a little bit of self-confidence, not perfect pen strokes.

In our training, it's a lot about personal care and to help people discover the individual abilities they have. Many participants have a great ability of listening and synthesis, but lack of techniques for creating visual metaphors. There are great artists that can immediately draw graphic novels, but they can't synthesize what they hear. So everyone needs to build upon his individual potential and learn different thing to become a professional visual facilitator. Very important to us is also that our participants join the training because they are fascinated and inspired by the possibilities of visual language, not because their boss likes visualization. So, they take self-responsibility for their learning success.

B: *When you give a custom workshop, you teach 10 to 15 icons for that group. Is that sort of a standard set or do you modify them depending on the industry you're working with?*

M: There are some icons which are universal to us, no matter if we work with an insurance company, or an NGO within social development in Africa, or education or whatever. Usually people are happy if they have easy-to-draw imagery for abstract concepts like analysis, innovation, development, or finance. Everybody also needs to draw people showing interaction and emotions in different situations. This imagery is pretty universal. About three quarters of our basic visual vocabulary is happily used by everyone. Anyway, an insurance company would possibly need more graphs and diagrams and an education center would rather draw team situations with people and emotions.

Whatever industry we are working with—it's always about sharing knowledge, improving processes, enhancing communication and facilitating collaboration.

Something that always struck me: Managers of a caterpillar construction company often don't want to draw caterpillars, because they actually don't work with the product itself, which I think is a sad thing. They are interested in visualizing software, process, optimization, and other abstract management concepts. So the pictograms that we usually use are set at a management level, and management is usually not into the details of their tangible products—they deal with making visual the things that are invisible.

Another important thing I have found out: The people that drive the caterpillar don't need visualization because they can show the caterpillar mechanic, "Look here at the bottom of this engine, there is this screw that needs to be fixed." On the other hand, people that work with intangible things, like optimizing caterpillar production lines in floor shop management—they need a lot of visualization because they find it difficult to express themselves properly.

That is the reason why I think visualization is the 21st-century tool for knowledge-based societies.

B: *Can you share an example of how a group developed their own iconography?*

M: In every training, new icons that can go into our visual vocabulary are invented.

I recently worked with a crisis management group program. If something terrible happens—like a terror attack or a building burning down—they get together to respond. They asked us to train people to be visual facilitators in their meetings.

First, we shared very easy visuals they could draw quickly. Here are some elements that were important to this group:

After refining and practicing those, we began combining these icons in new ways to visualize quick status reports: At 15.10 hours, the headquarter[s] is on fire, nobody knows the number of people inside. Two servers are down because of flooding, one is ok. Forty people are safe, five dead, 10 missed. Police and firemen are on site, ambulance not yet.

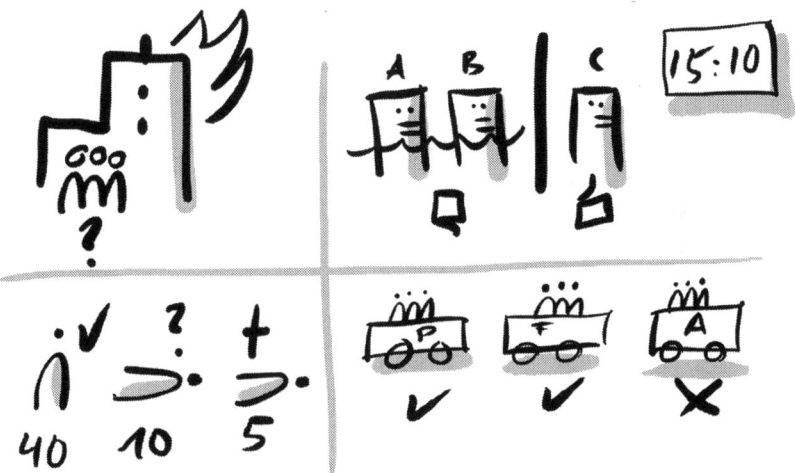

All together we created a huge set of illustrations they can continue using. With this imagery we simulated meeting situations where the visual facilitators would visualize pieces of information quickly on moderation cards and arrange them on a self-designed template.

B: *Where are you taking bikablo® akademie next?*

M: In our current basic training we empower people to develop presentation posters for professional use. Visual presentation in the sense of imparting knowledge for me is one of the three basic applications of visualization.

The second application is documentation. That is usually what graphic recorders do: to simultaneously transform the key insights, messages, or questions of a speech or dialog into a structured, coherent, and attractive design. Sketchnoting, as the "smaller brother" of graphic recording, documents for personal use as a learning technique.

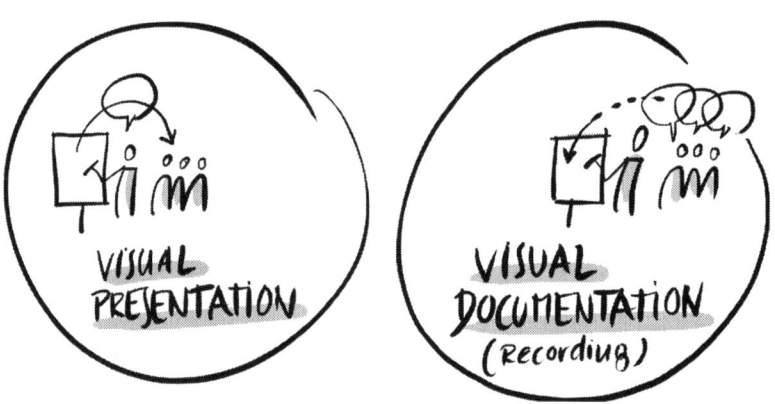

The third circle is exploring: As part of the dialog process, the visual facilitator joins the meeting and maps the dialog "at the speed of sound." For this, we are currently developing new styles, techniques, and methodologies of dialog facilitation and visualization in the cross section with group interventions like storytelling, design thinking, or appreciative inquiry.

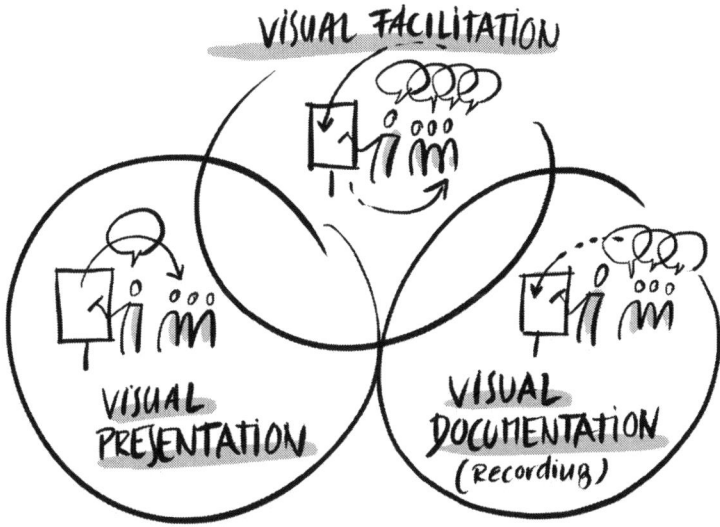

In the end, my vision is to get everyone in a room grabbing a pen and mapping the things they are talking about: visual co-creation. For that, we simplify our existing techniques further, making it even more easy to use the pen as a real dialog and thinking tool, also on the whiteboard or on digital devices. Visualize your ideas immediately, develop together, and reflect and create a iterative common understanding of your project. Beyond that, we're setting up methodologies of self-facilitation—to have every voice in the room and ask the right questions at the right moment in diverging and converging process phases and ensure the conversation and the picture are working fluidly together in a process.

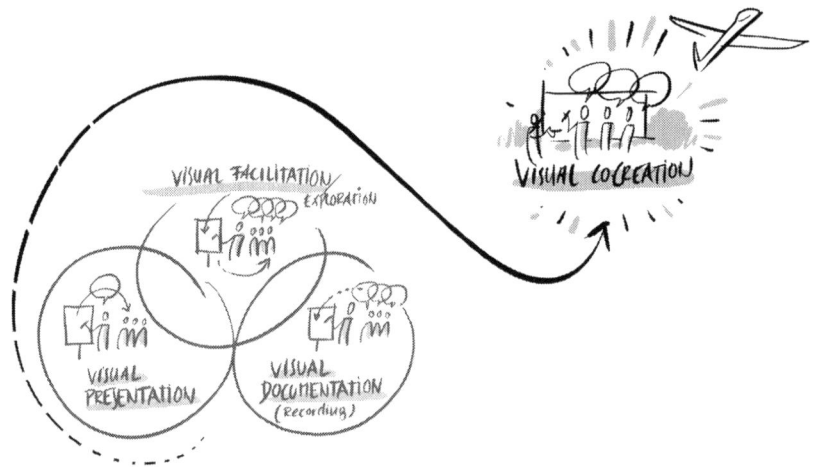

In this understanding, visualization is not a product any more, it is a temporary blueprint for the next iteration, an ongoing process from making the product to being part of the process again. We return to the iterative loops and the dynamics that make the glider soar.

MARTIN HAUSSMANN is a visual facilitator, author, and trainer. He is the executive director of the bikablo® akademie for visual thinking, a 20-person-trainer team that empowers more than 2,500 people per year to think with the pen. As author and inventor of the bikablo® visualization technique he publishes bestselling visual dictionaries and tools under the bikablo® brand, distributed by Neuland.

After being a graphic design and illustration freelancer, Martin started the graphic recorder and visual facilitator team of the German organizational consultancy Kommunikationslotsen in 2006. Today his passion is exploring new techniques, models, and methods for developing and systemizing visual facilitation. Alongside his work in the field of visual thinking, he performs live theater using a self-designed system of hacked overhead projectors. He lives with his wife and son in Cologne, Germany.

Bridging on the Rise

Jayce Pei Yu Lee
Interviewed by Kelvy Bird

What does it mean to be inclusive within a fast-growing field of practice, in the midst of amplified regional change?

A regional view

Kelvy: It seems like you are trying to map out a giant puzzle of inclusion, within an exponentially rapid growth cycle of visual practice in Asia. Can you start us off by explaining, from your vantage point as a multilingual graphic facilitator based in Taiwan, how you see the current state of the field?

Jayce: It's a happening place! It's really happening. There is a strong interest in what's going on internationally, followed by a strong demand to learn locally. People want to see more examples of practice from around the world. The regional demand for graphic recording is increasing. People are interested in anything that is visually related, and people want a more global perspective on how visuals can be used with facilitation.

K: *What do you think is driving the interest in the visual practice, specifically?*

J: A desire to enhance communications—to help with internal training, HR, and cross-department efforts within international companies. Visuals are a very direct way to offer opportunity for quick feedback and review, and for people to see what is actually being discussed during meetings and conversations. **Visuals serve as a bridge for people, right up front.** They are something that can carry across cultures and languages, therefore are especially useful for large global companies. Two years ago, graphic recording added more of a "wow factor" in meetings. But now, combined with general facilitation skills that are being introduced, visuals are very clearly adding another dimension.

K: *How are people in the region coming to know about visual facilitation? What is their background? What is leading people to want to learn more?*

J: People come from many directions. I see two main tracks: one is made of people with no art background, who are generally interested in bringing up their potential to communicate with some basic visual skills. They want to just grab a marker and draw, in any context. The other track is more advanced, people who want to use visual skills in professional ways, existing practitioners who are looking for other types of informational practices.

A sense of origin and where the field is going

K: *So there is an increase in facilitation, overall, and therefore also an increased desire for visual facilitation. What is the evolution of the practice in the region, as you know it?*

J: Well, to understand this better, I reached out to a couple of visionaries in the facilitation field here. Laura Hsu, a reputable facilitator in Taiwan, reflected with me on her earliest memories of graphic recording. She first saw it during several seminars that used the World Café[1] process—that included graphic harvesting techniques—and also during an International Association of Facilitators (IAF) conference back in the 2000s, where the Grove methodology[2] was showing up. Several Asian facilitators brought their learnings back to Taiwan and applied them in the social and public sector. By 2005, graphic recording had also made its way to Taiwan.

Another piece of the puzzle comes from Xiankai Zang, a visual thinking practitioner based in Shengzhen, China. In the early days, he was using mind-mapping for work and internal trainings, then discovered the term "graphic facilitation" by chance in 2007 when searching on the internet and finding Jay Cross's book *Informal Learning*. In Jay's blog, two names were mentioned: Dave Gray and David Sibbet (whose book Zang has since translated). He began to apply these new discoveries within his own organization. This created strong ripple effects among his peers.

Zang attended an IAF conference in 2012 and hosted a workshop themed "Use of visual metaphor to talk, listen and co-create," also applying the concepts within the education sector. According to Zang, the core value of visuals is to provide a tangible and well-grounded co-sharing space for all. Currently he is working on decoding ancient literature such as the Great Learning, Confucian Analects, and I-Ching with visual elements and metaphors.[3]

K: *And where do you now sense the practice is going?*

J: The advance of modern technology, social networks, and social media have made our connection to each other more robust and tenacious than ever. There are two groups with organic growth approaches that demonstrate this.

Visual Thinking Development Center (VTC), established and initiated in Beijing in 2014, is a grassroots, self-organized social network dedicated and devoted to spreading the visibility and accessibility of visual thinking and its application. Cofounded by May Yang and a couple of friends, it's a cross-sector public platform that also focuses on integrating work and life, by offering online-offline networking and learning workshops. It provides an open, fun and knowledge-based environment, with more than 6,000 followers across China. And the numbers keep rising!

ReaDrawing, founded by MuMu in Shanghai, is the first and only self-organized social network in China that digs into the essence of books through drawing. Readers map out the content of a book through their own visual interpretation, making reading an accessible, curious, and fun process. The network's intention and ambition is to revolutionize the way we read by expanding the depth of the reading process.

Certification: To C or not to C

K: We have talked in the past about the enthusiasm in Asia around certification. Can you share a bit about that now?

J: The big C—Certification—of any kind is indeed in popular demand and a current trend in China, as I have experienced. Certification gives someone a sense of approval and qualification. It can be designed into training classes. The paper itself is proof of only one part of a practice, though. It's really a personal choice about how we are part of the bigger Visual Ecosystem.

Ms. Bubble is the founder of Visual-Bubble, a creative company that originated in Holland and now provides visual facilitation trainings and certified workshops in China. She is one of the leaders in the region and advocates setting up industry standards, especially for visual practitioners. Her high-profile exposure in social media and involvement in IFVP (International Forum of Visual Practitioners) has served as one of the strongest currents in the river of change within the visual ecosystem in China.

Another current worth mentioning relates certification to education. Tikka Hun cofounded Tak-Tik.com, a company based in Kuala Lumpur, Malaysia, and has built multi-lingual proficiency and capacity in the region. This has formed up a solid network of Asian graphic recorders scribing in both English and Chinese.

It's easy to fall into the trap of judgment, though, when looking only through a lens of "certified" or "uncertified." As individuals, we need to be mindful about the legitimacy of a "good" or "bad," "professional" or "unprofessional." If we could see this from a wider scope, we could fully embrace the development of all diversities, moving toward a "yes, and" mindset and opening up room for growth, for individuals to learn and to explore at their own pace.

K: Do you think clients would more likely hire those with certification or without?

J: I'm not sure. Trust is an important factor, too. Client's recognition, and their recommendation, *is* a form of certification. There is a network of people, and we refer each other, because we trust each other to add value.

The role of bridging

J: There is a need for our visual community, because of language barriers and because of the firewall in China. Having practitioners with international experience is very helpful to cultivate the soil of learning.

K: *I see. In a way, then, facilitators help close a divide, a gap, between what is happening internationally and in China?*

J: Yes, exactly. China is a huge entity. Even if we were to cultivate visual practice in only one city in China, it's like developing a whole other continent that can be connected to the visual world. The potential to bring diversity into the practice is huge for our community.

K: *You and I met in Tianjin, in 2010, as part of a team working with the Value Web[4]. I still remember how moving it was to watch you from the back of the room, scribing in Mandarin, using a headset that translated English and Chinese inputs. I didn't understand at all what you were drawing, and it didn't matter. In that moment, watching you scribe bilingually, you opened a whole other world of possibility for me.*

Often, we are not aware of a gap in understanding until we see something new and unfamiliar, and then the need arises to bring the newness into our existing picture of reality.

As you speak about the bilingual part, listening to one language and drawing in another, I was reminded of a recent experience in Egypt, watching the scribes work in Arabic, drawing from right to left. And I felt a connection, too, even though I did not know that language.

Visuals bring out the essence of connection, of human-to-human connection. And that is really precious in these times.

Even though we have the language and cultural barriers—the divides—as soon as we grab markers and try to communicate by drawing a picture, that triggers a dialog, a curiosity, a wanting to understand. Something like that is universal. Something I see happening now in China is visuals prompting an eagerness to learn, to find out more. The expansion can be overwhelming. But when we slow down we can ask, "What does that mean? What do I need to do with this? What is next?"

Multi-lingual expression

K: *Your ability to scribe bilingually seems like such a strong advantage in the profession. What is your experience of this?*

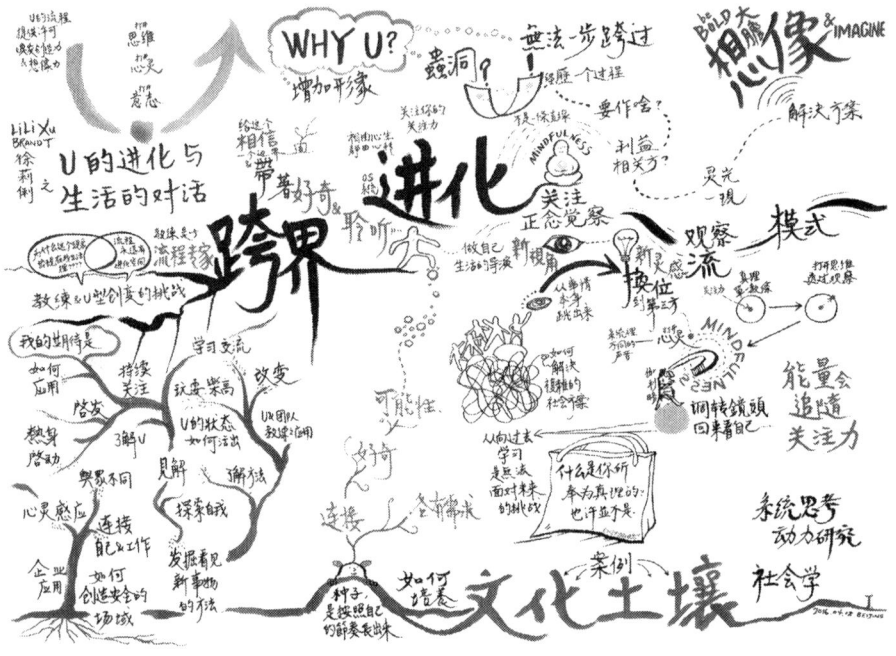

J: In the beginning, I still had a conversion process: English to Chinese. But as I have done more of the work, it has become a faster process. Drawing in Chinese, in Mandarin, with traditional or simplified characters—this is the most comfortable place for me. I have done more and more work recently in local languages, in my mother-tongue.

Writing one word in Mandarin takes time. There is a lot to condense into a recognizable term, or phrase, which is another kind of synthesis in addition to already synthesizing the content.

K: *How is scribing different when you are writing with Mandarin characters?*

There is quite a lot of room for expression. Some words, the form of the words themselves, and the characters themselves, can be very expressive with the thickness of lines, even with just a stroke. For my writing I embed a lot of calligraphy, which is part of the culture.

K: Can you tell me about your background, to better understand the connection between the tradition of calligraphy and your practice of scribing?

J: When I was in primary school, my parents always pushed me to study calligraphy. It was painful at the time, but looking back I realize it set up the foundation of what I do today. My dad was an English teacher, and he could write English letters very beautifully, and my mom too. When I was nine or ten, I would just watch my dad and I would draw alongside him. I still have a vivid memory of that, the freedom of just drawing on the paper in a form that I could not recognize.

Our family moved to New Zealand for educational purposes, and I had an opportunity to take art classes, and then attend art school. My major was typographic design. But when I moved back to Taiwan, there was no such profession. I tried different jobs involving graphics and retail. I experienced an up-and-down and an in-and-out of design fields, and then I met the Value Web in 2010. That was the first time I saw this graphic facilitation practice. It felt like a new frontier.

K: The story of your father is quite touching, and leads me to recognize a parallel of your watching him, in a language you did not know, and my watching you when we first met—and finding a certain curiosity and liberation through observing new language, in new form.

Personal style and vulnerability

K: Again in a specifically Asian context, can you speak to the role of personal style?

J: More diverse influence will help people realize the possibility of finding their niche and their own expression and style. Interpretation matters, and finding what's meaningful for each of us is crucial. We don't need anyone's approval aside from our own. Style is a matter of self-confidence.

K: From where I sit, in Cambridge, Massachusetts, I see the rise of visual practice in Asia occurring with an almost fearless swell of confidence. It does not seem to me that fear is in the way of people learning and experimenting.

Maybe that is a sign of progress and growth. When someone first starts scribing, they feel a great sense of achievement; they are seen alongside their work, and the visibility contributes to their confidence. But with more experience and knowledge, we can also let ourselves be more vulnerable.

In a fast-growing environment like the current China, where being strong and speedy are worshiped by definition, to slow down and be vulnerable can be easily dismissed. But this is where the creativity is born, where rules are for reference and are meant to be iterated.

The Great Learning

K: *I have always admired the drawing of yours that weaves the ancient Confucian philosophy in with Theory U. How is this relevant in visual practice?*

J: In Chinese philosophy, the seven steps of the Great Learning[5]—one of the four books in Confucianism—astonishingly coincide with the path of Scharmer's Theory U. I have had the pleasure to scribe for Peter Senge as he pointed out this homogeneity. In summary "awareness—knowing where to stop—calmness—deep quietness and stillness—grace of being—true thinking—attainment."

There is something about past and emerging future. There is something about slowing down and taking a breath to consider the meaning of information. The thinking informs producing quality work, with reflection, to allow what is being said to happen in its time.

知止而後有定
When you know where to stop, you have stability.

定而後能靜
When you have stability, you can be tranquil.

靜而後能安
When you are tranquil, you can be at ease.

安而後能慮
When you are at ease, you can deliberate.

慮而後能得
When you can deliberate, you can attain your aims.

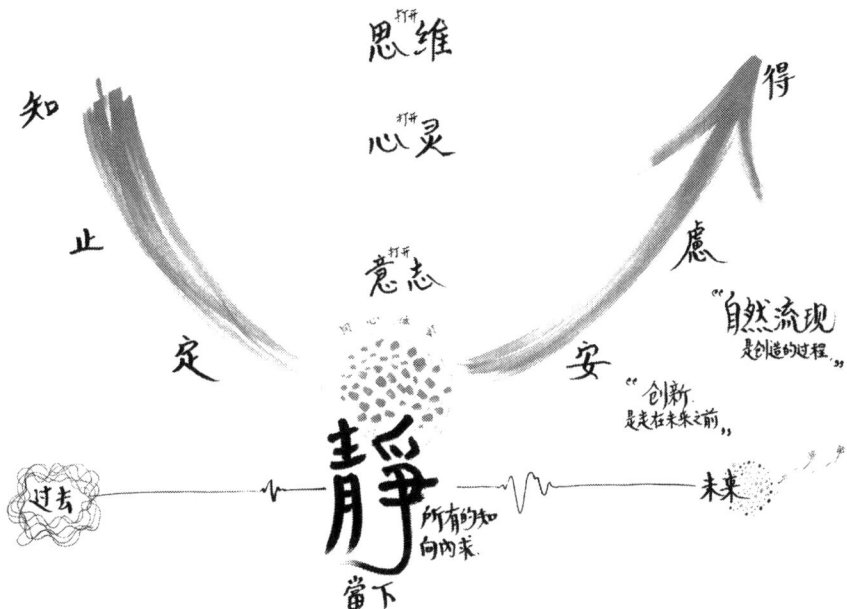

Photo by: IDEAS China 3.0 Program, GITI Group UID Foundation

Visual ecosystems

K: *You mentioned the term "visual ecosystem" earlier. Can you expand on this?*

J: Right now, the groups I mentioned—each circle—are operating at their own pace, and I haven't yet seen much dialog between these circles.

K: *This seems like another example of a call for bridging, like we were talking about earlier, where with more pockets or clusters of people trying to share the practice, the more bridging is required between the groups. We don't know the constellation that exists within the space, until we start to see some points of light.*

J: Hm. Yes. That is a very appropriate metaphor. And each star is already functioning and contributing, like seeds, to help the other seeds. Whatever we each do, we are all contributing to the greater benefit, the greater good.

K: *Anything in conclusion?*

J: Let's have a book tour in Asia! Let's help people have a first-hand experience of the messages shared in these pages. More bridging!

In the West, in Europe or the States, graphic facilitation is a very mature and developed practice. In countries like Japan, Korea, and other Asian countries—this all can be much further explored. Maybe that can be part of the second edition of this book.

K: *As visual practitioners, we are helping people see, and we don't always see what is right in front of us, what the full puzzle looks like. Thank you for helping us to understand more of the pieces.*

J: Yes, yes. You are very welcome!

JAYCE PEI YU LEE is big at heart, small in size, organic in spirit. In between her works and travel, she enjoys the outdoors, cooking, and being at home with her dog Magic Maggie. She is also a member of the Value Web and one of the fellow travelers of Theory U. lee.jayce@gmail.com · jayce.lee@thevalueweb.org

References

1. The World Café process, developed by Juanita Brown and David Isaacs of Mill Valley, California, USA in 1995, is a globally-recognized methodology that brings together groups of stakeholders to engage in generative conversation. More here: www.theworldcafe.com
2. The Grove Consultants International is a consultancy company, founded in 1977 by David Sibbet, based in San Francisco, California, USA. More here: www.grove.com
3. For more information: zangxiankai.blog.sohu.com
4. The Value Web is an international, member-based affiliation that designs and delivers collaborative engagements for leaders and organizations around the world. More at: www.thevalueweb.org
5. The Great Learning was one of the "Four Books" in Confucianism. More here: en.wikipedia.org/wiki/Great_Learning

When We Cannot See the Future, Where Do We Begin?

Bob Stilger

By now, dear readers, you are hopefully wowed, inspired, confused, and invited by this amazing collection of essays. Many of us know that for the new to emerge, we have to get people out of their heads and into their bodies and hearts. For me, this is what visual practice is really all about.

My dancing is rigid, my singing off-key, my drawing blocky. I write here not as a visual practitioner, but as one who needs them as partners in what I do!

I help people listen to each other to find new pathways forward. I'm a conversation host, a facilitator and a thinking partner. My community-based work began in the mid-seventies when I cofounded Northwest Regional Facilitators in Spokane. After 25 years at NRF, as this century began, my focus turned to the global south with The Berkana Institute for 10 years. For the last six years through NewStories, most of my work has been in Japan, especially deep and intense experience with people and communities after the devastating triple disasters of March 11, 2011.

This last arc of work in Japan has made me much more aware of how fragile our lives are, particularly in this age when so much is self-destructing and so much new is being born. In 2015, Eiji Press in Tokyo published my book about my work in Japan (the English edition will follow soon). The title, *When We Cannot See the Future, Where Do We Begin?*, has been a continuing teacher for me and provides the jumping-off point for this essay.

What do we do when the future disappears? In the blink of an eye and the flow of an unbidden tear, the life we thought we knew is just gone. Showing up to work and being told the company is closing and your job is over. Listening as the doctor tells you you have an incurable disease. Returning home and finding a note from your spouse saying he's left—permanently. Hearing on the news that your child's school is under attack. Watching as the ocean's water recedes into quiet and then the roar of a tsunami.

What do we do? How do we proceed? What will inform and guide us as we begin to make sense of our shattered lives? These are times when visual practice is especially important. The future has gone dark. We can't see it. Visual practice opens our eyes to current moment and helps us find our next steps. It helps us remember what's important and to turn to those around us to use what we already have to create what comes after now, today.

My own sensitivity to working with the unknown and the uncertain have been heightened by my work in Japan. A deep, personal relationship with Japan that began when I was a student in 1970 led to an immediate sense of *I must go and help* after the triple disasters of March 11, 2011. At 2:45 in the afternoon an astonishing earthquake with a 9.0 magnitude shook the northeast coast of Japan. Forty-five minutes later, a tsunami traveling at speeds up to 60 miles an hour and at a height of 50 feet inundated the coastal area. The next day the nuclear reactors started to explode at the Fukushima Dai Ichi power plant. Nearly 20,000 people died and more than 500,000 lost their homes or jobs or both. Across all of Japan, lives and dreams were shattered and a door opened towards an invisible future.

Japan has helped me ask: How do we find our way forward when the reality we've lived is suddenly gone? When our lives are likely to be inundated by more and more uncertainty? How do we help ourselves and others even figure out where forward is in this time when so much we have known is dying and so much is being born?

I've done a major dive into this question and have been privileged to work with colleagues to design and host community meetings in the disaster area and across all of Japan. We created spaces where people could begin to make sense. Spaces where they could weep and dream and plan and organize. Sacred spaces. Spaces where it was possible to just be with the enormity of it all. Eventually the capacity to think and reason and analyze would be very important. But in the beginning there are more fundamental questions about where to place our attention. For some, everything—especially life as they knew it—was gone. *What in hell was I supposed to think about? What does reason have to do with it? What should I analyze?*

Thinking and reasoning and analyzing are important but they rarely provide direction. In fact, they need direction. And direction has to come from our other senses. When everything falls apart, we must invite our hands and our heart and our spirit to come out and play, and ask our analytical minds to wait. Where is forward? How do we proceed?

For me, in Japan, surrounded by so much disruption, my normal state was disruption. I was uncertain and unsure and confused. So was everyone I was working with! Mine was not the hero's journey of a knight on a white horse leading people to the promised land. Mine was a journey of learning to trust not-knowing and to stay open to what appears—and to help others find their own next steps. People referred to me as a sacred outsider, because I arrived with listening and with ways that helped them to see themselves and each other.

I began to notice that certain ways of being sustained me and helped me invite others into creative space:

- **Stay connected.** We need each other. Usually we can't find our way forward alone—and we don't need to. After Japan's disasters we just kept doing whatever we could to connect people with each other. Using a variety of dialog approaches which in Japan we referred to as "FutureSessions," we brought people together to be with each other in spaces that promoted respect, curiosity, and generosity. While I was doing my work in the disaster areas, I also had to reach out and connect with others—both with the far-flung tribe I met through my work with the Berkana Institute and New Stories and with my growing community friends and allies in Japan.

- **Be still.** Settle down. We can't do anything new without getting really quiet and opening all our senses. The participants in the FutureSessions we organized were all very busy. When your old life falls away, there's a lot to do. For many, it was a challenge to get still. But we would keep inviting them into silence—sometimes in a circle, sometimes on walks, sometimes exploring in pairs in silence. This silence enlarged the space in which something else could be seen. Personally, I spent more time in prayer and meditation and climbing mountains in silence than I have at any other time of my life. It was just essential. In order to find new ways forward that we can rely on, we must do whatever it takes to find equanimity. We must rid ourselves of the anxieties that either paralyzes us or causes us to spring into hasty action.

- **Listen.** And then listen some more. This isn't the time to make meaning. It's not the time to solve anything. It is time to stay present and to listen to everything that is said as if your life depends on it. Constantly I would invite others to slow down and listen, to open their whole body to listening. And each day I needed to listen deeper and deeper myself. Especially because of my limited Japanese language, I learned how to listen with my whole body—which includes resisting the frequent urges to turn what I was hearing into a nice tidy package of concepts and ideas.

- **Empathize.** Let this listening permeate to the very core. I worked with others and myself to simply open our hearts as wide as we dared. I invited us to just be present for spontaneous outbreaks of grief and joy and hopelessness and possibility. We do not need to seek any of these; we just need to stay present so they each can come to in turn.

- **Stay confused.** Through all of this is the invitation to be willing to stay in a state of confusion. False clarity is dangerous. It provides a convenient and comfortable place—but it is not real. Listen without judgments and conclusions. Listen without seeking answers. Stay confused and stay together for long enough and real clarity will emerge.

The question is, of course, what helps us embrace these ways of being? What helps us make sense? This book has broadened my understanding of the term *visual practitioner*. Reading through the other essays, I now understand it to be just about anything which helps us visualize our lives and our communities in new ways. I love conversation and believe it offers a portal to new possibilities. And conversation can also be very limited, even stifling—trapped in old patterns of thought and confined by bottled up emotions. We need more.

As a conversation host I am constantly looking for what breaks the trace of the past. Looking for what helps us see ourselves and each other in new ways. I need partners to do this. I need Megumi to bring in dance in ways that unlock the blockages in our flows. I need Michael whose music can transport us to other dimensions. Rachel's invitation into spoken word is a crystallizing process. Deborah's drawing reaches people's souls. Tomoko's visual harvesting makes the day unfold on the walls of the room. I can invite people into free drawing or into modeling with clay or into silence, but generally I need practitioners who bring in a variety of media to loosen the constraints of old and tired thinking. The skills of visual practitioners can open a path rarely traveled, the one that takes us deeper and deeper into who we truly are.

Conversation host and leadership coach Bob Silger collaborates with visual practitioner Tomoko Tamari, staying open to what appears

As a designer of spaces where people are invited to co-create new possibilities and new actions, I use anything I can find that invites people's aliveness to step forward in new ways. And whenever I can, I work with visual practitioners like my co-authors here. I realize I rely most on six helpers:

- **Silence.** It always comes back to silence for me. Taking myself to silence. Inviting others into silence. Frequently. Quiet our busy minds. Set aside the relentless chatter. Just be quiet. And then do something. Then get quiet again.
- **Dialog.** Among the silences, we talk. Finding better questions and even an answer from time to time. We speak the truth without blame or judgment and we listen for what has heart and meaning. We seek to build a firm foundation for future action.
- **Nature.** We're not alone. Whenever possible enter into the real world—the one with breezes and trees and ants. Letting go of the concrete and plastic and electronic devices and connecting with the bounty that surrounds us. Conclusions and certainties drift away.
- **Fingers—and toes and shoulders too.** Our bodies know! I'm regularly amazed when someone begins to see what their fingers know when they let Play-Doh tell a story, or when they start to draw pictures of their life. It's delightful to learn to listen to our bodies, discovering what they know about slowing down, being careful, and staying centered.
- **Music.** Notes on winds and cords and voices transport us. We are taken on a journey. Sometimes it is singing together, other times being transported by sound on an inner journey. It quiets our busy minds and lets us relax our tight hold on half truths.
- **Beauty.** Surrounds us. Something different and precious happens when we are embraced by simple beauty. The room that is cleared of clutter. A sparse and expressive flower arrangement in the center. A welcoming entry. A window that opens onto a forest.

I weave these helpers through everything I do. The more all of them are present the more likely it is that magic happens—that confusion switches to enough clarity and grief opens a window towards joy.

In many ways they are simply ways of reminding ourselves that we are part of a living, vibrant universe, and that when we work in concert with that universe we begin to see new possibilities. I've watched Megumi dance people through their grief in workshops in Fukushima. I've been with Michael in Canada and the US when his music has settled the room and invited people into the core of their being.[1] I've worked with Rachel to introduce the form of spoken word using Dekaaz[2] in ways that have made people more and more aware of their experience. I've seen people connect deeply with their own inner voice through Deborah's touch drawings.[3] I've noticed the awe and appreciation people in Kyushu have for Tomoko's visual representations which give them a bird's eye view of what's been going on. These are the gifts of the visual practitioner.

We are constantly surrounded by an ocean of possibilities, but we frequently fail to see them because we're bound up in old ways of thinking. Visual practice is all about making it easier for us to shift our view, broaden our consciousness and make accessible the immense opportunities just beyond our current reach.

Experience. Experiment. Enjoy.

BOB STILGER, the Founder and Co-President of New Stories, uses the power of story to help people create thriving, resilient communities, remember how to listen to and connect with each other, and work together to create a preferred future. After leading a local community development corporation for 25 years, Bob served as Co-President of The Berkana Institute, connecting people using their own resources to build resilient communities in many parts of the world, including Zimbabwe, India, Brazil, and Australia. Since 2010, he has worked extensively in Japan, introducing collaborative spaces called "Future Sessions" and participatory leadership processes. Tokyo's Eiji Press published his book, "When We Can't See the Future, Where Do We Begin," in Japanese in 2015; an English Edition will be published in 2016.

Bob teaches at St. Mary's College of California and Gonzaga University. He has a PhD in Learning and Change in Human Systems from CIIS. www.newstories.org bob@newstories.org

References

1. Michael Jones' fine attunement to music, beauty, and place creates a resonant field in the room where people release constraining boundaries and move into a sense of wholeness. See www.pianoscapes.com
2. Dekaaz is adaptation of Haiku which used the iambic pentameter of the English language with three stanzas with two, then three, then five syllable verses. See www.rachelbagby.com
3. Deborah Koff-Chapin's work with Touch Drawing takes people into a place of deep inner presence where they tune to what is emerging around them. See www.touchdrawing.com

Reflection and Visual Practice

Jennifer Shepherd and Sam Bradd

Reflection is an integral aspect of visual practice. When we make time to reflect, we come to know more about ourselves, see new possibilities for action, and make wiser choices. Along the way, we extend our awareness and care and create openings to expand our competence. This is true, regardless of whether "we" are the ones holding the pen, offering input or bearing witness to the creative process, or interpreting a completed work. We all stand to benefit—personally and professionally—from practicing reflection to make meaning of our work and our experience in it.

We, the authors, have both heard our *clients* reflect out loud when engaging with our drawings. They exclaim: "I hadn't ever thought of my work this way until I saw my ideas presented visibly. It's completely changed how I think of my work!"

Reflection helped a *group* with whom Sam was working to make sense of the conference:

> "It's a busy conference, and I found it valuable to take a break and review the graphic recordings. The images helped me reflect on what was happening and make new connections between sessions."

And, speaking professionally as *practitioners*, we've discovered that the subjects on which we reflect, and the questions we ask, influence what we learn. By expanding our awareness of subjects and the range of questions to ask, we've uncovered blind spots in our thinking and identified more areas to explore in our practice.

For example, reflection helped Jennifer rethink the concept of families:

> "I was preparing for a strategy session with a Canadian non-profit organization. The Executive Director and I were talking about family—a core concept for this organization. As we talked about how family structures have shifted and diversified over decades and how the definition of family has also changed, I realized that my "go-to" drawing of a nuclear family was woefully inadequate. To do justice in my role as graphic facilitator, I would need to explore other ways to capture the essence of the idea of family. Rather than drawing its form—mother, father, kids, and maybe some extended relations—I would need to illustrate ties of mutual consent and the functions of family life."

In our profession, we make dozens of decisions per hour. Reflection on each decision in the moment isn't always possible: sometimes actions are too fast, or possibly routine. How do we know what we show? Architect and educator Donald Schön developed "reflection-in-action," a reflection methodology, because he noticed that professionals are expected to simply know how to do things, demonstrating "actions and judgments spontaneously, unaware of having learned to do these things... and unable to describe the knowing that the action reveals."[1]

Reflection-in-action helped Sam research his own practice for his graduate work.

"I designed a research study about my graphic facilitation. Although it might sound strange to research oneself, I found Schön's methodology a rigorous way to learn about myself. By pausing in reflection, I was able to write about my work, and in this way become more curious about it. The deeper I went, the more questions I had for myself—and the more I enjoyed the process of problem-solving my way out of them."

Your invitation

In this final contribution to the book, as a closing and opening gesture, we invite you—our colleagues, clients, and facilitation partners—to notice areas for reflection in your own practice, whatever that might be.

We have created 65 questions to support your reflection. As we've been diving into our own practice in this area, we've found it helpful to focus our thinking on our relationships with co-facilitators, clients, participants, and the broader field of visual practitioners. We've also benefited from reflecting on our connection with the visual artifacts that we create and how all of these link dynamically when we're working. For simplicity, we've organized the questions into sections. Each section includes questions about one of these connections. The figure below illustrates the recursive nature of reflection.

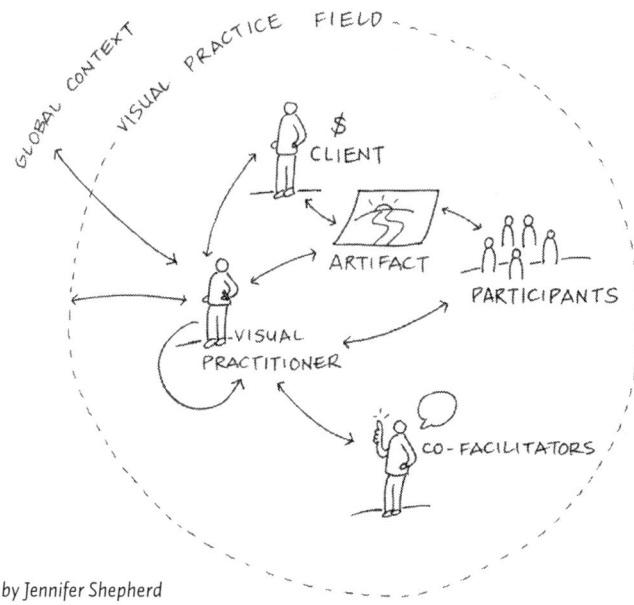

Model and illustration by Jennifer Shepherd

Here are some suggestions for how to use this chapter as a kind of personal workbook:

- Reflect on your own, or gather with peers, clients, and others
- Read the questions aloud, pause, and notice what answers arise
- Phone a colleague and have a conversation
- Write a journal entry and see what emerges
- Bring your thoughts forward to the field of visual practice online or at a conference

We offer these methods as wisdom from our shared experience. We've tried them all, and they work! A few years ago, we were hungry to explore emerging practice themes with colleagues and peers. Having taken the initiative to convene and host a "Deep Conversation Series" with fellow members of the International Forum of Visual Practitioners, we used these approaches to deepen our learning, and started to compile and refine questions that warranted further reflection.

We offer these and many more questions as a gift to the visual practice field. These are only a start. Now, it's your turn. We invite you to share your own questions on the *Drawn Together Through Visual Practice* website so that those of us wishing to deepen our learning may benefit from your insights, and so we may grow the sensemaking practice of reflection together.

Illustrations by Sam Bradd

My relationship with the field of visual practice, our role, and our work to do:
1. What is my wish for the field of visual practice?
2. What do others in the field seem to care about right now, and what about that matters to me?
3. What am I doing to learn with others, if anything? (For example: meet for coffee dates, participate in graphic jams, attend conferences…)
4. What might I share with others to help the field learn and grow?
5. What trends do I notice in the visual practice field right now? What is unfolding?
6. What do I need to pay attention to as the field changes?
7. What helps me distinguish what work is mine to take on and what work might be better suited for another practitioner?
8. If we brought a common message to our clients as visual practitioners, what would we say about who we are, what we do, and how we act?

My self and my visual practice:
9. What is the scope of my visual practice?
10. What ethics guide my visual practice?
11. What are my primary talents?
12. What skills do I need or wish to acquire?
13. When I'm caught by surprise, by something that is said or happens in the room, how do I refocus?
14. When I am working with emotional content, how do I take care of myself?
15. What qualities do I need to have as a competent visual practitioner?
16. What's one value that I bring to my work? What are some of my other core values?
17. What can I learn from accessing vulnerability and humility? How do I bring these into the room and to the group?
18. If I'm working in an unfamiliar context, what resources can I turn to? For example, I might not know the relevant words or images. What do I need to learn or ask before I arrive in the room so I feel prepared?
19. How can I work to support diverse experiences, across difference, to value and hold all voices and perspectives in the room?

My relationship with the client:

20. What do I need to share with my clients about the potential of visual language and practices?
21. What practices can I share to help clients adopt visual thinking?
22. How can I help clients reflect on the impact I can make?
23. What do my clients need to know about me and my unique capacities?
24. What do my clients need to tell me about their projects for me to do my best work?
25. What enables visual thinking practices to flourish in an organization?

My relationship with the artifact I am creating:
26. How do I hold the client's intent and meeting outcomes in mind while I'm working?
27. How do I respond when someone asks me to change a drawing?
28. How do I nourish my creativity?
29. How do I develop my personal visual vocabulary to keep it fresh and relevant?
30. What do my visual icons say about my worldview and my appreciation of context?
31. What technology and platforms do I use for my work, and why?
32. What helps me choose the emotions, words, and unspoken dimensions (or "elephants in the room") to capture?
33. How can the room setup help me do my best work?
34. When does it matter to accurately represent an idea visually?

My relationship with participants:
35. What do I need to know about myself to be in service to the group?
36. What do I need to know—and care—about the group to be in service to myself?
37. What matters about how I am introduced? What do I need to tell someone who is introducing me?
38. What feedback can I ask participants for that can help me reflect, learn, and grow?
39. If I can't just show up, set up, and get to work, then what is needed to connect with participants and the environment?
40. Can I think of a time when a participant came up to me and described how the visuals changed the experience for them? What did we learn in this conversation?
41. How do I tap into group dynamics and choose what belongs on the page?
42. What is my role in orienting participants to the power and potential of visual thinking methods?
43. How can I help participants use the visuals to reflect?
44. What emotional impact could our work have for participants? What could thinking about this bring?

My relationship with the facilitator(s):
45. What conversations do I want to have with the facilitator before a session begins?
46. Knowing sessions vary, what helps me stay nimble and respond in the moment?
47. What do I need to know about facilitation to help me be a good partner?

Participants' relationship with the artifact:

48. How could the room setup influence participants' ability to reflect and make sense of their work?
49. Do participants see the artifact as "something I've done for them," or as "something I've done with them?" Does it change how I do my work?
50. What helps participants feel connected to the artifact and offer input or feedback to the creation? What can happen before, during, and after?
51. What do participants do as they look at the artifacts?
52. What activities could I suggest to use the visual artifacts to help participants reflect?
53. What helps participants make "Big Picture" connections?
54. How can I measure what matters?
55. How can I help participants see things they couldn't see before, and how can they show me things I couldn't see before?
56. What activities could help participants reflect on their own drawings?

The client's relationship with the artifact:

57. What is the specific purpose of the visual artifact to be created? Who is it supposed to help, with what, and how?
58. How will this artifact have use after the meeting?

59. How could the artifacts be used for reflection after the meeting?
60. Have you been in a session where the process of creating the artifact was of greater value than the artifact itself? What is different about these times?

Our work and the future:
61. How might our work be relevant to people outside the room?
62. How do our drawings influence culture?
63. If visual practices were integrated into every profession, what would that look like?
64. How does visual practice shape a future? What becomes possible?

JENNIFER SHEPHERD makes it easy for everyday leaders to clarify what matters, discover new possibilities, and intuitively make their next move. She believes individuals, organizations, and communities can achieve great things when they tap into the latent wisdom within and between them. Jennifer inspires leaders like you to access this wisdom and use it to generate insight and collaborate well. Jennifer is the Principal of Living Tapestries, a consulting practice based in Ottawa, Canada. She holds a Master of Arts in Human Systems Intervention and is an IAF Certified Professional Facilitator. www.livingtapestries.ca

SAM BRADD is a graphic facilitator and specialist in information design. He uses visuals for people that want to engage, solve problems, and lead. Together, we're drawing change. In the last 15 years, Sam has collaborated with the World Health Organization, Google, indigenous organizations and researchers on three continents. In 2016, his side project the Graphic History Collective published a new book of comics because how we tell histories can change the world. He has a Masters in Education (University of British Columbia). Contact: @sambradd and www.drawingchange.com.

Copyright © 2016

Reference

1. D. Schon, *The Reflective Practitioner: How professionals think in action.* London: Temple Smith, 1983, p. 55.

Made in the USA
Charleston, SC
26 July 2016